Hi —

I penn words.

I have great respect for what you have made, and I hope this intention comes across...

FICTIONS AND FACTIONS

Merry Xmas + Happy New Year

Love

AUGY HAYTER

FICTIONS AND FACTIONS

TRACTUS BOOKS

FICTIONS AND FACTIONS

Copyright © 2002 by Augy Hayter & Tractus

All rights reserved. No part of this book may be utilized in any form or by any means, electronic or mechanical, including photocopying, or by any information retrieval or transmission system, without permission in writing from the author or publisher.

La loi du 11 mars 1957 n'autorisant, au termes des alinéas 2 et 3 de l'article 41, d'une part, que les «copies ou reproductions strictement reservées à l'usage privée du copiste et non destinées à une utilisation collective» et, d'autre part, que les analyses et les courtes citations dans un but d'exemple et d'illustration, toute représentation ou reproduction intégrale ou partielle fait sans le consentement de l'auteur ou de ses ayants droits ou ayant cause, est illicite (alinéa 1er de l'article 40). Cette représentation ou reproduction, par quelque procédé que ce soit, constituerait une contrefaçon sanctionnée par les articles 425 et suivants du Code Pénal.

Cover design template by Alain Jacob. Back cover drawing by Maddy Anderson. Front cover painting *Couple* by Stanley William Hayter. The book is dedicated to Judith Eve Edelblute.

Library of Congress Control Number: 2002092207

ISBN 2-909347-14-1

TRACTUS
P.O. Box 6777, Reno (Nevada) NV 89513 U.S.A.
phone/fax (1-775) 345-7585
e-mail: tractusbooks@att.net
website: www.tractusbooks.com
and
TRACTUS BOOKS
43 rue de la Gaîté, 75014 Paris FRANCE
tel. (33 -1) 40 47 63 63
fax (33 -1) 44 07 12 07

CONTENTS

WATCHING THE WOUND'S CUTTING ROOM FLOOR

1. LETTER TO A MAGISTRATE 9
2. VENGEANCE AND UNDERSTANDING 38
3. EYES OF AMBER 39
4. TIME IN TIME OUT 40
5. LETTER TO MARINA 41
6. UNENDING 44
7. NEGLIGIBLE QUANTITY 45
8. THE OPAL 46
9. MY TURNIP 47
10. ANOTHER NIGHTMARE 48
11. DON'T GO 49

WRITING & SHOWBIZ

11. STARTING OFF 51
12. THE LIVING THEATRE 60
13. SHOWBIZ DAYS 62
14. INTERPRETING 83
15. ON BEING CURED 94
16. THE CANVAS 109

STORIES

17. CHRISTMAS LETTER 111
18. SCHNICK-SCHNACK 121
19. THE MONK'S BODY 125

20. SCHWEINEREI	139
21. PSYCHIATRIC DIWAN	143
22. A LOOK	149
23. HOW TO BETRAY YOUR TEACHER	152
24. WYSWYG	167
25. MY WORD	169
26. DIRTY OLD MAN	170
27. THE LEDGER	171

WEAVING ON THE WAY

28. MY TEACHER	173
29. SUFIC LITERATURE AND ACTION	175
30. INTRODUCTION TO *SUFI TRADITION IN THE WEST*	181
31. THIRTY YEARS ON	185
32. STATING THE OBVIOUS	208
33. INTRODUCTION TO *ISLAMIC SUFISM*	212
34. OPEN SECRETS	219
35. THE LAUGHTER OF BABOONS	227
36. INNOCUOUS IKBAL	238
37. SHAH THE WRITER	247
38. MAN INTO GOD	273
39. THE KINGDOM OF GOD	274
40. THE PROCRASTINATOR	277
41. NOTES FOR THE FUTURE	278
ATTRIBUTIONS	283

WATCHING THE WOUND'S CUTTING ROOM FLOOR

LETTER TO A MAGISTRATE

January 10, 2001

to the Attention of Mme. Eva Joly, Examining Magistrate
c/o Editions des Arènes
33 rue Linné   75005 Paris

Dear Mme Joly,

You may remember that I sent you my novel entitled *Watching the Wound* last Oct. 6, 2000. In my accompanying letter to that work I mentioned that the factual basis of the last part of my book was a real investigation concerning AntarFinaPelf which had mysteriously bogged down, and that I suspected that my enquiry was either unduly influenced or completely taken over by this company. In the enclosed letter drafted by Mr Miller himself, you can see for yourself how this enquiry has developed. The original remit for the investigation was to ascertain the whereabouts of Anna Starling, married name Dru, with the idea of tracing her through her husband Marcel Dru, who has been employed in the financial section of Pelf since 1992, when he first met Anna Starling in Damascus, Syria.

After eighteen months of investigation, Mr Sergius Miller, whose company name is Agence Française d'Investigations J.B. KELSON, 3 rue du Départ, 75015 Paris, has unilaterally suspended the service contract he had undertaken on my behalf to trace Mrs Starling through Marcel Dru, on the pretext that I had some unspecified illegal intention in mind.

I spent well over a hundred hours of time in Sergius Miller's office discussing the case with him and he had plenty of time to see whether I had any sort of evil intention towards Mrs Starling and/or her husband. My remit to Mr Miller was quite simple: I wanted to enter into contact with Mrs Starling as unobstrusively as possible and to know where and with whom she was living.

FICTIONS AND FACTIONS

I am now (January 2001) convinced that the detective I engaged was in fact doing exactly the opposite of what he was hired to do: he very carefully prevented me from having any direct contact with Mrs Anna Starling for a year and a half, and he waited until she had gone back to Nigeria with Marcel Dru to cancel our contract.

Only two days before his cancellation of our contract (I was informed of it on Nov. 27, 2000), Mr Miller was still promising that he would be giving me the written file containing all the information he had gleaned on Anna Starling and Marcel Dru, her periods of residence between Damascus, Doha, Paris, London and Lagos, information on her debts in Qatar and Britain, as well as indications regarding her separation from, and renewal of, her domestic relationship with Marcel Dru. The information on Dru was to include his involvement with French security services, his military ranking and his covering of various doubtful money-laundering operations by Pelf Gabon as financial comptroller.

In fact, he cancelled the contract with me without providing me with a single word in writing : all of his weekly or twice-weekly reports were given to me face-to-face. This was probably a deliberate ploy: it means that any legal objection I have to the way he has worked for me will be reduced to his word against mine. The real problem is that it also negates absolutely everything he has ever told me in the context of the investigation, because he now refuses to back up anything he told me face-to-face in writing. This is tantamount to thievery, because who will ever give me back those eighteen months of lost time, during which time the woman I love was separated from the husband she has now gone back to?

Furthermore, throughout this period, Sergius Miller undertook initiatives which were deeply disturbing to the

... LETTER TO A MAGISTRATE

persons under investigation: this was done without my knowledge and without my permission. I was only told about his interventions after the fact, when it was too late for me to prevent such initiatives.

To make the framework of our interaction understandable: I spent many hours in Mr Miller's office discussing both the case and life in general. He ingratiated himself with me and expressed some sympathy for me as a friend. We discussed many different things, including religious convictions—he wanted me to discuss the nature of my Christian & Sufi commitments (I have published a number of books on the subject), and I was interested in what he had to say about his Judaism. In the spring of 99, he proposed to intervene in Marcel Dru's posting through his connections at Pelf, but I specifically forbade him to do so, saying that I did not want to weigh on the lives of Anna Starling or Marcel Dru because I was convinced that any action I undertook to affect their lives would turn against my own interests. The point of my enquiry was not to cheat my way into Marcel Dru's place, it was to protect and enter into peaceful contact with her. I now think it was at that time that Sergius Miller would have begun to take me for an idealistic fool. But what is important is that my intention was clear right from the beginning, and it is also why Miller's claim today (January 2001) that my intentions are in some way illegal hold no water now and did not hold water in May 99 when the investigation began.

I now believe that he sold my enquiry to another party and was possibly acting under instruction in some or all of the actions he undertook. The actions are as follows:

With my agreement, he organised an interview with Marcel Dru at the Pelf building at La Défense, representing himself as a security investigor acting on behalf of Pelf. His story to me is that he told Dru he was investigating his

FICTIONS AND FACTIONS

relationship with Anna Starling, since she appeared to have left behind unpaid debts in Qatar. Dru replied that she had been his girlfriend but that he had broken up with her in late November 1998, when he had found her entertaining another man in the apartment he rented for her in Doha. Dru said that the other man had then paid for the apartment until July 99, but he had then in turn broken off with Mrs Starling. Dru himself had withdrawn the Pelf Visa credit card in her name in November 98: "She took me for a fool" («Elle m'a pris pour un con») he is supposed to have said, and he also implied that he had learnt since their breakup that there had been backdoor relationships with other men as well. "She has something against men, but I don't know why («elle a une dent contre les hommes, je ne sais pas pourquoi»)." *

According to Miller, Marcel Dru also complained that he had her daughter Rebecca and her two daughters on his hands as well because he had to pay the taxes on the apartment while they refused to pay him the rent he was owed. Miller confirmed this with a call to the *Syndic* of the 69 rue Labotte apartment building who told him that Dru had informed him that Rebecca and her daughters were occupying the apartment against his will without paying their rent and that he had initiated expulsion proceedings. (He had, of course, not mentioned to the *Syndic* that the woman in question was his stepdaughter.)

*Sergius Miller says his contact at Pelf was the wife of the present number 2 at AntarFinaPelf, Bertrand Polce de Combine, who was assistant to André Tarantullo, head of Pelf-Gabon throughout the 90s. Miller's idea was to get information on Marcel Dru and Anna Starling by pretending that his enquiry was sponsored by the new number 2, a notorious womanizer whom everyone is scared of in the context of the present restructuring. (Pierre Léthier in *Argent Secret* [p. 129] mentions a nameless Frenchman working for Alfred Servile specialized in the Qatar reigning family who did a great deal of work on behalf of the French *Office général de l'air* and who "made the fortune" of French interests in the region. This could be Dru or someone close to him.)

... LETTER TO A MAGISTRATE

In addition, when asked about Anna Starling's illnesses such as pernicious anaemia and a possible cancer, Marcel Dru is alleged to have answered "She is capable of inventing every illness known to man."

At this first meeting with Marcel Dru, Sergius Miller did not bother to ascertain the identity of the person Anna Starling was alleged to have been with in the studio apartment he rented for her in Doha (he continued to use his Pelf-provided apartment on his own), although he knew perfectly well that this was information I wanted.

Miller also told me that he had received a call from the French DST or DGSE (Direction de la Surveillence du Territoire/ Direction Générale de la Sécurité Extérieure) asking why he had approached Marcel Dru. Miller told me his reply was that his investigation did not concern any security-related issues, and that they accepted this response. I have my doubts on this.

Between June and July 99, at my insistence, Sergius Miller allegedly tried to make another appointment with Marcel Dru and was continually fobbed off, with Marcel Dru always pretending lack of time, etc. Sergius Miller even told me that he made an appointment with Marcel Dru that he did not turn up to. This implies that Dru had had time to check Miller out with the Pelf and security-related hierarchy and had seen that he had no real influence anywhere. If I was to point out my own feeling from the perspective of January 2001 on these events, I would have to say that the pattern of what I would call "irrational occurences" began at this point, i.e. in July 99.

Sergius Miller finally saw Dru again in July/August 99, when I was no longer in Paris, and began to ask him other questions. He had given me a convincing verbatim account of his previous conversation with Marcel Dru, but when reporting to me this time, as soon as I pulled out my pad to take notes he

FICTIONS AND FACTIONS

became totally vague as to what transpired, and told me that when Dru continued to pretend he was not married to Anna Starling, Miller said that he should stop having him on and that he knew they were married and told him when and where. Miller's story is that Dru then turned white and quickly put an end to the interview saying that this was his private life and that he would answer no further questions.

This was a serious initiative: by telling Marcel Dru that he knew he had married Anna Starling at the French Embassy, Doha, on December 22, 1996, Sergius Miller was in fact warning Marcel Dru that he himself was the target of an ongoing investigation.

Of course, this is what Miller told me himself: another possibility is that he was rumbled after the first interview and then forced to work under instructions from Dru or Pelf.

Thus from June/July 99 onward my feeling is that my investigation was basically taken over, either by Pelf or by Marcel Dru himself, because it became more and more difficult to elicit hard information from Sergius Miller. I have no proof, but my feeling now is that he would have been bribed or influenced in some way at about this time. The lack of any written report from Miller, in spite of my repeated requests, confirms this impression. This is not normal behaviour for a legitimate detective agency.

In any case, it was in September 99 that he showed me a Pelf Visa/Carte Bleue credit card made out in his own name. His intention in showing me this was to reassure me by demonstrating how much influence he had at Pelf and how well-introduced he was.

Already at this time I had my doubts, but since I had no other source of information, I decided to play the idiot and

... LETTER TO A MAGISTRATE

spend a great deal of time sitting in his office while he played himself out. The whole thing took over a year. My own situation was that since I had no direct access to Anna Starling, I had no means of forcing him to say what he knew, so I would basically reiterate the same questions week after week and month after month, putting him under pressure to give me more and more information until he was forced to break off. The information on the aunt's death, Anna Starling's debts in England and Clark Topher's employment in Doha (see later) were obtained this way.

Notwithstanding this, my feeling is that he was relatively sincere in telling me what he knew up to the time of the second interview with Marcel Dru in July 99, but not afterwards.

Here is the information I was given up to July 99, and which I consider more or less sincere and dependable. It antedates any corruption by Dru or Pelf, since they had not yet been contacted. Marcel Alain Dru was born in Agen, *département* 47, France, on May 22, 1951. His employment record at Pelf contains a number of anomalies: his job description in May 99 was "ingénieur en logistique" and he has worked for the *Société Pelf-Aquitaine* since 1975. A lot of people are being gotten rid of after the fusion of AntarFinaPelf in 2000, but his position appears to be secure. (When I saw Anna Starling in December 98 she told me he was a low-level accountant and was very amused that I should think him anything else. I thought she was lying to me.)

He was sent out to Qatar as "ingénieur en logistique" and probably draws a salary there in addition to the (modest) salary of FF 16,000 per month he draws from Pelf in Paris. He was married to Marie-Hélène Peaceable by whom he has two children, and the low Paris salary is used as a legal basis for his alimony payments. According to Sergius Miller, his ex-wife

FICTIONS AND FACTIONS

(they divorced in 95) had to take him to court to obtain a court-ordered deduction from his salary. When approached, she referred to Anna Starling as "cette truie" or "that hooker".

An interesting anomaly in Marcel Dru's employment record at Pelf is that his echelon 5 as "cadre supérieure" is at complete odds with his low declared salary. This implies that he has been drawing another salary from Pelf Gabon or Pelf Qatar which is not declared in Paris. Echelon 5 would normally be a basic 50 or 60,000 FF per month, plus benefits (expatriation and education allowances, etc.). The other possibility is that he draws a parallel salary from French intelligence sources.

According to Miller, Dru's comment on Anna Starling's behaviour was "Imaginez-vous qu'une femme d'officier couche avec un soldat" (Just imagine, an officer's wife sleeping with a private) which could infer that he has a military background. Possibly the French Sécurité Militaire? Once again, according to Sergius Miller at this time, his rank as reserve officer in the French army is that of captain, which would mean that he must have been a commissioned officer in the French armed forces at one time in the past. Possibly before 1975? What regiment did he serve in? This is probably on record, but I was never able to get this information from Miller. It was to be part of the report he didn't produce. Another thing that Miller told me was that Marcel Dru was considered to be a "planche pourrie" (rotten plank) at Pelf, and that his own military security clearance had been withdrawn the day after he married Anna Starling.

Anna Starling was born in London on July 31, 1949. She married Marcel Dru in December 1996 and was operated on for cancer of the cervix at the end of February or early March 1997, at which time she was given a "full hysterectomy", which meant the complete removal of her womb.

... LETTER TO A MAGISTRATE

Miller's source for this is supposed to be the doctor who deals with the medical records at the private insurance company used by Pelf. However this information was given in September 1999, and may be inaccurate, particularly since, at different times, Sergius Miller gave me the name of two different clinics (Clinique des Bleuets, rue des Pyrénées and a clinic St. Lambert in the rue Blomet followed by two different hospitals where the operation would have taken place. He then said the operation took place at Villejuif and then said at the end that she had a consultant's appointment with Professor Fourquet at the Hôpital Pierre et Marie Curie on November 13, 2001.

Other information concerning Anna Starling: according to the Police des Frontières (dixit Miller), she spent 6 months in Qatar in 98 and only 3 months in 99. Although she divorced Ricardo Starling in 1995 she continues to use her married name of Starling and not her maiden name of Benthall on her official papers, and she has a French residence card in this name at the address of 6 rue Lavieilleville 75018 Paris.

Among other things Marcel Dru said about Anna Starling (Sergius Miller dixit) was that she owed money to the proprietor's agency for the studio in Doha, that she could no longer set foot in Qatar because of this, and that the financial responsibility for the apartment had been covered by her new boyfriend until July 99, at which time she left Qatar permanently to return to France and live with her daughter.

According to Sergius Miller, Anna Starling and her daughter Emmeline Starling left 6 rue Lavieilleville very suddenly and moved into an apartment around the corner (at 22 rue des Deux Frères, 75018 Paris) in September 99, very soon after Miller had let Marcel Dru know that an investigation was being undertaken concerning her. Miller felt that this sudden change of venue was because of the Pelf investigation on Dru and Anna Starling.

FICTIONS AND FACTIONS

During the first interview Dru asked Miller what "section" he had been in, and not what "régiment"—the word "section" being the terminology normally used in intelligence circles. Miller felt that this was a dead givaway: when he replied what section he had been in before he began private practice, he says it very clearly became a conversation between two colleagues.

Daughter Rebecca Starling Labarre & her two daughters lived in the apartment owned by Marcel Dru and his first wife Marie-Hélène Peaceable at 69 rue Labotte 75018 Paris. She left this apartment in the summer or autumn of 99 and moved into the flat at 22 rue des Deux Frères with her sister Emmeline, born 12.01.71, who works in the public relations department at Disneyland, in a job which, according to Miller, Marcel Dru obtained for her.

My own feeling is that if Marcel Dru really did try to pretend to Sergius Miller (in his rôle as Pelf investigator) that he was not married to Anna Starling, it is a clear sign that he felt himself to be under higher (i.e. possible governmental) protection.

It is also significant that six months after this interview, Sergius Miller was telling me that there was no objective evidence in the dossiers he had found on Marcel Dru and his employment record at Pelf that indicated that he was part of any official or unofficial intelligence setup, i.e. the exact opposite to what he had been telling me from the beginning. When I manifestly did not believe him, he did not pursue the matter.

He also mentioned that there was nothing in Dru's file at Pelf to indicate he had ever been in Syria, which is where Anna Starling met him—I know this to be true from an independent source (my housepainter, whom Anna Starling seduced and joined up with in Damascus). Miller's version was that he had worked for Pelf in Paris and in Gabon in the past, then in Doha

... LETTER TO A MAGISTRATE

for Pelf-Qatar and was now transferred to Lagos, Nigeria for Pelf-Gabon, where he is at the present time (January 2001).

It is now clear that Sergius Miller began to hinder any possible access of mine to Anna Starling from September 99 onwards, even though she was living in Paris. He would tell me things like "you can't see her until we get more information about Marcel Dru" even though he knew I didn't give a shit about Marcel Dru and whatever he was involved in.

According to Miller this could only be done by means of a dumb cloak-and-dagger ploy involving a false *Securité Sociale* investigation, in which a friend of his who worked at the *Caisse de Maladie* for the *Sécurité Sociale* had Emmeline make a call back in order to organise an appointment with Anna Starling for an administrative check.

This whole episode, which took place over September/October/November 1999 rings very fishy indeed: I think I may have been being led on by Sergius Miller who was either telling the truth or else had found a story to keep me bound to the investigation. What he said was that he had had access to an internal Pelf report of a confidential investigation made on Anna Starling at the time she married Marcel Dru, i.e. from December 1996/January 1997.

Although he told me at the time it was an Pelf investigation, if one assumes it existed at all, a Defense-Intelligence oriented investigation would be more likely. The name of her past boy friend, apart from my own, was that of someone called Clark Topher, who, according to Miller, worked on an oil rig. When Miller told me later that he worked at the British Embassy, I told him this made no sense. Miller then told me that he was head of security at the British Embassy, although he also appeared to be listed on the roster of a British data processing company in Doha. Clark Topher was reported to be

FICTIONS AND FACTIONS

married with two children, and, still according to Miller, his wife and children live in London.

Still according to Miller, the relationship between Anna Starling and Clark Topher was long-standing: it had predated her marriage to Marcel Dru and he implied that it had continued on afterwards—assuming of course that Clark Topher was indeed the person wearing Marcel Dru's slippers that he had discovered with Anna Starling in the Doha apartment in October 98. His feeling was that Anna Starling's marriage to Marcel Dru was in part a revenge against Clark Topher's refusal to ditch his family for her. Anna herself told me she married Dru without loving him, she said it was for the medical insurance but this may have been for my benefit.

Although there were anomalies in Miller's story ("she was involved with someone who worked on the offshore oil rigs"), I believed him, basically because it corresponded to my own direct apprehension of her past behaviour with me as well as fitting in with the story Anna herself told me when I saw her in December 98, three weeks after Dru is supposed to have ditched her, and which Miller didn't know about.

Another possibility is that Miller put together enough information from my own acccount of my previous relationship with Anna Starling to invent a likely scenario—the question here would be: why do this? To protect who? I basically feel that he was telling the truth just as I feel Marcel Dru was telling the truth in his first story about Anna—his own comments on the daughter make him look like a shit, not a hero.

At that time she tried to convince me that she had this wonderful simple and trusting relationship with Marcel Dru and she was going to stay with him in Qatar. Having lived off and on with her for four years, I know Anna well and am familiar with the pattern of her lying. She always mixes her

... LETTER TO A MAGISTRATE

lies with something true and verifiable; her specialty is to suppress the main information by embroidering a detail. My feeling was that the relationship she was talking about was true, but it was not with Marcel Dru, who was a convenience: she had never really loved him and probably never would. She mentioned that she was writing a good deal into a computer, and that she had a friend she could call on when there was a problem—I remember tagging that friend as a possible lover.

She recounted a wonderful fairytale version of her life in Qatar to me consisting of magical moments of contact with Bedouin women, with nights spent sleeping (presumably alone) under a tent in the middle of the desert. According to Marcel Dru's first interview with Sergius Miller, she had her own apartment in the centre of Doha and her social life mostly involved people from the British Embassy and other English-speaking expatriates (she has never learned French properly). Marcel Dru's acid comment was that the expatriate women did not like inviting Anna to their parties because she tended to be overly familiar with their husbands—I asked Sergius Miller to try and confirm this information from an independant source, but he never did so.

To return to the account of Sergius Miller's investigation: in December 99, for the first time, I made a real effort to see Anna Starling myself. I had not wanted to intervene in her life if she did not wish to see me and was content to know she was in Paris. At this time Sergius Miller was telling me that he was listening to her phone calls, and that nothing significant seemed to be going on in her life. She stayed with daughter Emmeline and appeared not to be involved with any other man.

I think it was around this time that I told Mr Miller that my intuitive feeling was that her daughters did not know she was actually married to Marcel Dru—(my own basis for this feeling was the fact that she tried so hard to keep me away

FICTIONS AND FACTIONS

from her daughters when I saw her in December 98, coupled with Marcel Dru's apparent confidence when speaking with his apartment building manager that no one could possibly know that Rebecca was his stepdaughter).

In December 98, Anna herself had told me she had no money ("I have learned to make do with nothing") and 3 months later Miller told me she was receiving 6000 FF a month in her bank account from Dru. When I asked for specific information on her bank account from Miller, it was not forthcoming, except for an account in a postbox bank in Leicester, England, which had no money in it.

I am now convinced that Miller deliberately stopped me from seeing Anna Starling in Paris in December 99 and afterwards. When she went to England over Christmas, he told me she was staying at her aunt's house in Kenton/Harrow. She had gone over with Rebecca and her daughters and her husband—when I pointed out that Anna had told me her daughter was separated from her husband, he told me she was back with him again and that they had gone to stay with her father while Anna stayed at her aunt and uncle's.

I was very angry at Miller for letting Anna leave France without giving me a chance to see her, and to placate me he told me that he would put her under surveillance in England and check out if she was with a boyfriend over Christmas and New Year. He told me she wasn't, but would not give me any precise details of where she spent New Year's Eve 2000. He then told me he would keep Anna Starling under surveillance in London in January.

This surveillance was in fact carried out: all the circumstances of her life rang true, she can indeed spend day after day looking at shops without buying anything, and his operatives complained about having to stay in parked cars all

... LETTER TO A MAGISTRATE

the time because there was no one in the street near the house in Kenton. It was like Madonna says in *Desperately Seeking Susan*, "It's got to be a cover, nobody's life could be that boring!"

Miller made a good deal of the fact that she appeared to be seeing a man who accompanied her to restaurants and the Tower of London museum to look at the Crown Jewels. She was seen making sketches with him in a coffee shop, and when he brought her back to Kenton she made sure he left her off some distance away from the house. The relationship appeared to be commercial rather than sexual, although I finally got Miller to tell me that the car with diplomatic plates she was taken home in was registered at the Iranian Embassy. According to Miller, the man was a previous contact from Doha, although he never gave me any more information than this or, more importantly, the source of his information.

He mentioned that she would go and make phone calls, presumably to Marcel Dru in Nigeria, from a public telephone exchange in the West End. He also said that his operatives once went into the booth immediately after she left it and pushed the repeat button: the phone rang at my apartment in Paris.

(This is one of the many confirmations of information I had previously given Sergius Miller: I have in fact been rung up anonymously with silent phone calls time and time again for the past ten years, and I suspect that the only person interested enough to do this would be Anna Starling. Like all the other incidents of this investigation, it can be true and it can not be. The most recent calls have come through an internet computer, which leaves no trace of number).

In January 2000 I phoned the number at 15 Brimstone Gardens, Kenton a couple of times, and a young female voice answered me saying that I had the wrong number. Mr Miller confirmed that the phone number was at the right house, and

FICTIONS AND FACTIONS

that Anna Starling was in the house at this time (Anna's aunt and uncle were not present at that time). The number he had given me turned out to be one digit off.

According to Sergius Miller, he phoned Emmeline Starling a number of times during this period to make an appointment for her mother's Social Security interview. I myself thought that this ploy would not work (since Anna Starling's illness was covered by Pelf's private insurance, she would not consider a convocation by French Social Security insurance as being in any way binding), but since Miller seemed to think it could produce useful information I let him go ahead with it. To my great consternation, he told Emmeline on the phone that he had proof of her mother's marriage at the French Embassy in Doha on December 22, 1996 to Marcel Dru before him. According to Miller, Emmeline was apparently so shocked at this that she asked him to repeat it twice over.

This appears to have caused a breakup between Anna and her daughters, so that she did not come back to Paris but stayed in England until May. She then joined up with Marcel Dru in Nigeria, after having been separated from him since October 98. At the present time she is still with him. They have moved to the south of France and she now has the house she wanted more than me. Thus, thanks to Mr Miller's deliberate action, what was achieved was exactly the opposite of my remit to Miller at the beginning of the investigation, which was to put me into contact with Anna Starling. He kept me away.

Also, Miller happened to mention, just in passing, that her aunt who lived at 15 Brimstone Gardens, Matilda Catherine Hawes, had passed away. This was important information for me and Miller knew it—one of the reasons I took on this investigation in the first place was to deal with possible lawsuits that this person had already threatened against me. She later

... LETTER TO A MAGISTRATE

turned out to be alive. I didn't know whether to laugh or to cry.

All of this has reinforced my feeling that Mr Miller knew a great deal that he was simply not communicating to me. From the vantage point of January 2001, it is now clear that from autumn 99 onwards I was deliberately prevented from having any access to Anna Starling.

In June 2000 Sergius Miller told me that Anna Starling and Marcel Dru had returned to Paris and were staying at some unknown address. He had mentioned that Marcel Dru probably owned other properties in Paris but did not give me any addresses. He also mentioned that Rebecca, Rocky and the two children were living in 69 rue Labotte. When I visited 22 rue des Deux Frères myself, I saw that the name Labarre (Rebecca's married name) was on the letterbox in Anna's writing. When I asked Miller about this, he said Anna and Marcel Dru were now staying at 69 rue Labotte and that he would put their phones on tap and put together all the necessary information. Anna Starling was staying at 69 rue Labotte but since she never came out of the apartment, it was still impossible to organise a meeting between myself and her.

It became clearer and clearer that I was being given half-truths and lies. When I went to see what was going on at 69 rue Labotte myself, there appeared to be work going on in the building and the young movers (possibly Marcel Dru's sons?) were obviously checking me out while I sat on the terrace of the café opposite. My impression was that they knew who I was and what I was there for. When I returned to the rue Labotte the next day, the shutters were closed and Sergius Miller told me that Dru and Anna Starling had gone to Agen on vacation.

At this time I was trying to put more and more pressure on Miller by calling on him every day, and sitting down and spending at least an hour with him when no one else was in

FICTIONS AND FACTIONS

his office. I went over everything with him and cross-examined him on various aspects of what he had said to me.

A number of minor factual points didn't add up. For instance, he told me as if it was the result of a major sleuthing effort on his part, that Anna Starling owed money in England on the sale of the house there. She had guaranteed a loan to her then husband, who spent the money, so that the sale of the house in Buckinghamshire did not cover the money owed and she was liable for the rest. Because of this she had a police record in Britain. Except for the police record, it was all information I had given him myself at the beginning of the enquiry.

There were other strange anomalies: he had told me he had been on a combat mission during the Biafran war in Nigeria, but he seemed to have no idea where Port Harcourt or even Lagos was situated. He confused Niger and Nigeria a number of times, although he appeared to have a good grasp of what life in a French Pelf compound in Lagos might be like, so he was certainly getting some kind of feedback from somewhere. He told me that Anna Starling had been ill during the spring/summer of 2000 in Lagos and had been treated by the Pelf European doctor there, but he would or could not be more specific about the illness.

There was a continual change of Miller's focus about Marcel Dru and his function at Pelf. He would go from being a French spy to being a low-level accountant, and when I would say this is ridiculous, low-level accountants don't call themselves 'ingénieur en logistique' and go on unaccompanied trips to places like Syria, spending half their time on the road, he would then say that Dru was a highly influential financial comptroller whose signature was on a number of documents being investigated by examining magistrates Eva Joly and Laurence Vishnievsky, and he was being put on ice in Qatar

... LETTER TO A MAGISTRATE

and in Nigeria until the legal enquiry into Pelf by the *Brigade Financière* blew over. He mentioned that Dru's name was on the Alfred Servile list of names under investigation, and that he must have a good deal of personal undeclared money salted away in a safe place.

Once again, whenever I asked him for a list of properties owned by Marcel Dru, his first wife and his mother, Sergius Miller would promise to give it all to me when he handed over the final draft of his report, which of course was never forthcoming.

When I was in the United States in August 2000, I faxed Miller asking him to send me the address in Agen, and I was given no answer. When I returned to Paris in September, Miller told me that the apartment at 69 rue Labotte had been sold in July, and when I insisted he find out who the new proprietor was (because I saw for myself it had not been advertised for sale) after much prompting Miller finally told me it had been made over to the sole name of Dru's first wife.

Miller then told me that Marcel Dru was following a Pelf internal training course at Lacq. He would be going back to his post in Nigeria in late autumn and his contract in Nigeria would run until July 2001. He continued to be unable to find any Paris or other address for Marcel Dru, although if he really did benefit from the entrée he boasted of at Pelf, such information would be available. He had to be witholding information from me.

He also said that Rebecca, her two daughters and Anna were staying at 22 rue des Deux Frères. Since by this time I had published a book dedicated to Anna and wished to give her a copy personally, I presented myself at the door, to be told that they were out and would be back later that evening. Early the next morning, I stayed in my car outside the door and was able

FICTIONS AND FACTIONS

to see for myself that no young children had come out of the building to go to school.

Miller was quite infuriated with me, saying that my presence was ruining his own surveillance of the building, that the cleaning woman who saw me would recognize me, and he threatened to pull out if I went on interfering. In spite of my own doubts I decided to let him go ahead with it, even though I didn't really believe Anna and Rebecca were living in an apartment which, according to Miller, they appeared never to walk out of. At this time Miller was telling me that Emmeline was in the United States for her work, (the same job which Marcel Dru is supposed to have found for her)—he supposedly had this information from listening to her portable Mickey Mouse telephone.

When I saw for myself that there were no children going to school, I pointed out to Miller that it made no sense. He then told me that Rebecca was working in a French Ministry (another job that Marcel Dru is supposed to have found her—when last heard of she had been working for a film company) and when I asked Miller to check out her children's school (which he had told me he knew about a year before), he told me he would get hold of the information. He then took nearly a month to say that the two daughters had been taken out of school in midterm (which is almost unheard-of in France—the school system won't let new students in during mid-term). In reaction to my disbelief, he told me that it was a "mutation administrative" which any school in the public system would have to accept. I pointed out to him that whatever her faults, Rebecca was a good mother, she would be unlikely to uproot her children in mid-term and the whole thing didn't make sense. After keeping the suspense going for a few more weeks, he told me in October 2000 that she now lived in Toulouse with her husband, although for unspecified reasons he couldn't find the address. When I

... LETTER TO A MAGISTRATE

asked him to go through the school, he simply resisted and said he couldn't.

We were now in September/October 2000 and I began to insist very strongly that he produce the written report that had been such a long time in coming. He continued to put me off, saying that he was in the middle of drafting it and that I would have it very soon. As I believed less and less of what he was telling me I insisted more and more that he give me his report.

Sergius Miller then produced a final rabbit out of his hat: he told me that he had access to Anna Starling's medical records in Pelf's private insurance scheme, and he had discovered that Anna Starling had a post-operative appointment with her surgeon, Professor Foulquier, at the Hopital Pierre et Marie Curie on November 13. I happen to know the place well, having been treated there myself for cancer. All appointments are centralized at the entrance in order to ensure the proper availability and follow-up of patient's medical records— Professor Fourquet was not in hospital that day and could have received no one. It was clearly a setup.

When I next saw Sergius Miller I pointed out to him that so far all the information he boasted about from his wonderful Pelf sources had turned out to have been a con. He replied that he would start the enquiry all over again.

I decided to wait it out and see what he would do.

Around Christmas 2001, I was told from other sources that Anna Starling was in Nigeria.

On November 27, Sergius Miller gave me a letter (enclosed) in which he says he renounces the investigation because I am asking him to do something illegal and unspecified (with a menacing reference to the Code Civil and

FICTIONS AND FACTIONS

the Code Pénal). I pointed out to him that it had taken him eighteen months to notice I had some kind of evil intent in mind, which meant he must be pretty slow on the uptake. He has a number of faxes and memos that I sent him, and my memory is that there is nothing doubtful about my requests for information. My only requests were for information about Anna Starling and Marcel Dru so that I could see her again.

All telephone traces and personal surveillances were done at his initiative, and at a conservative estimate, can have cost no less than FF 300,000, at a time when we had made a contract for FF 18,000 at the outside. He knew that I would not have more money to pour into this, so his insistence to continue with the investigation at high cost to himself leads me to think that someone or some other entity must have been paying Sergius Miller behind my back in order to ensure my investigation's failure.

The other possibility is that Sergius Miller is an incompetent idiot who messed up his investigation through stupidity and decided to pull out. This is very probably what he will claim when he is forced to justify himself before a court of law. But had this been the case, he would have kept at least some of the money to cover expenses, and he would have written at least some form of report.

The two most significant indications that someone else has been paying for this investigation to fail are the fact that Sergius Miller has refused to commit himself to anything in writing that could be checked against verifiable facts at a later date (for instance, when Anna Starling herself becomes aware of what has happened), and also the fact that my money was returned to me after Sergius Miller had made sure that Anna Starling was no longer in the country.

... LETTER TO A MAGISTRATE

It is because I consider Sergius Miller intelligent that I think he has to have been bribed.

This raises a most important question: who would have any interest in buying out this investigation?

There are three or four possible answers to this question and I will deal with all of them in turn.

First possibility, the French security services. During our long and rambling conversations together, Sergius Miller told me he himself was an ex-military man who was closely involved in various Jewish activities and who has worked both for the French army and probably for Mossad. His network of contacts appears to be mostly pious Jews with a right-wing orientation. He has told me he spreaks Arabic and Hebrew and has an Israeli passport in addition to his French one. According to him he acts as an unpaid security advisor to various French synagogues, and attends regularly on festival days. In return for this service he is given full-page ads for his agency in Jewish organisation yearbooks. He eats strict kosher, which is not easy to do in a normal French social context, and I am convinced that his orthodox religious commitment is not a pose, although in addition to this he has a deep desire to boast about the various covert operations he has been involved in. He suffers from poor health, has high blood pressure and cardiac problems, is only a year older than myself although his baldness makes him look a good deal older.

He is extremely precise about money and quite mean (he tried to sell me a worthless out-of-date office telephone system, telling me to name my own price). He has a card in his own name as a parliamentary secretary, which he uses to get into official buildings.

My conclusion regarding the possibility of French security

FICTIONS AND FACTIONS

services being behind this buyout is that although there is no doubt in my mind that Sergius Miller is connected to the French security services (possibly as an occasional or intermittent low-level collaborator), I don't see why they would involve themselves in personal investigations which don't concern them, unless Marcel Dru, who is also quite clearly an ex-member of an intelligence outfit (the famous 12th floor of the Tour Pelf at La Défense) even if he now only works for AntarFinaPelf, is someone who is much more important to the French State than I have hitherto imagined.

May I make a personal point here: from 86 to 91 I was a member of the NATO secretariat as a translator and précis-writer during which time I had the highest security classification of ATOMAL COSMIC TOP SECRET. In the course of my job, as well as in my previous work for the French Ministry of Defense and the Délégation Générale à l'Armement, I have dealt professionally with a number of confidential matters and have had a thorough security evaluation practised on my person by the British and French authorities together. They were right to trust me: I have never divulged any confidential information to which I was party to anyone, and would not think of doing so.

In 1990 I told my British security case officer that I would be marrying Anna Starling—it was just before she refused to come and live with me in Brussels. When I broke off the relationship and moved back to Paris in 1991, she turned up in Damascus, staying at the home of a New Zealander married to a member of the Australian Embassy—she had met Michael O'Murphy and Clarinda Sadhu when he was painting the walls of my house in Brussels. At that time she would already have been on recent file with the British intelligence services because of the connection to me. When she took up with Marcel Dru in 1992 and travelled with him around Syria, my own security clearance was withdrawn from one day to the next and I was never to work for another military organisation again. This could be a coincidence—but I think not. This injustice rankles: when I went back to being a freelance again, my nomal clientèle was no longer available to me and it made a difference.

Second possibility, and for my money the most likely: the Pelf hierarchy itself introduced the confusion, since they would have a clear interest in keeping Marcel Dru away from any investigation into possible financial irregularities he might be involved in until such time as the Joly-Vishnievsky moneylaundering enquiry is played out and the whole thing has blown over.

This is the most intellectually satisfying reason, but it does depend on a major flaw: one would have to assume that Sergius Miller's claim that Marcel Dru himself is no longer involved with French security but only with covering irregularities as a financial comptroller (the Alfred Servile list) is true, yet this information is dated autumn 99, when the process of disinformation ("you must not see Anna Starling before I have interviewed her about Marcel Dru") had already begun.

I still think it is the most likely of the three possibilities because it involves the most money, hence greed. Bribing Miller would be peanuts to these people, and as I said, Miller himself showed me his Pelf credit card in autumn 99. All he had to do was charge them for all the long hours he spent with me. In fact, I even suggested to him myself that this was what he should do—it did not worry me that he should be paid by Pelf behind my back so long as I was to profit from the investigation as well. It took me a long time to realise I was being systematically lied to, and that these lies had begun earlier than I thought.

If I have indeed stumbled into the middle of a Pelf

FICTIONS AND FACTIONS

financial cover-up, it could mean that Anna Starling herself is in danger.

This is not a paranoid notion: at the moment, Lagos is one of the most dangerous cities in the world for white people and all one has to do to get someone killed there is kick them out of a taxi in the Apapa docks. Ever since they began the "Bar Beach Spectaculars" in which pickpockets are put before the firing squad, the stakes are such that thieves might as well kill you because their punishment is the same whether they do or don't.

Third possibility: that Marcel Dru himself paid Miller to keep me away from his wife. Possible, but unlikely—he would have to spend his own money to do this which I don't think he would be willing to do (e.g. his meaness vis à vis Rebecca and her daughters over the rent and his reported general stinginess which Anna mentioned to me years ago). He would not consider me a particularly dangerous personal rival, although he might be unhappy at me spreading the word about his occult connections.

It is interesting that he should have induced Anna to stay with him a year after he had stopped paying for her rent and credit card and six months after he had so disparaged her to Sergius Miller. What has he got that I haven't?

Fourth possibility: that Anna Starling herself got wind of this investigation and has been hiding from me. In December 98, she left a message on my answering machine which was a complete fabrication, and she knows she would have to answer for that. Her specialty is to transform her own actions into dreamlike narrative, but I don't think that applies here. To run a complicated double-cross like this, she too would have to spend money, and I don't think she has money to spend. If the

... LETTER TO A MAGISTRATE

double-cross was run by Marcel Dru, he would have the money to pay, but since he pretends to his own wives that he has no money (I remind you that his first wife had to take him to court to get her alimony paid directly out of his modest Paris-based salary) he would be unlikely to get involved.

It could be that he engineered a breakup between Anna Starling and her daughters in order to put Anna back under his influence and get her out of the way, but all of this must remain a hypothesis until such time as the protagonists of these events give their own sworn versions before an examining magistrate or a court of law.

In the foregoing document I have tried to state what has been going on over the past eighteen months as simply and clearly as possible, not denying my own interpretation of the facts but stating them objectively enough for them to be interpreted differently from what I think. The fact that I have been led up the garden path is now clear: this does not please me but I had to let it happen to become aware of the overall pattern of what was going on.

I repeat, the letter of cancellation of contract by Sergius Miller is particularly significant, insofar as he refuses (1) to provide any written proof of activity, and (2) to keep anything for the large amount of expenses he incurred (nearly three months of surveillance, enquiries in three different countries, etc.).

Another very significant aspect is the fact that it was without any prompting from me that Sergius Miller himself said that Marcel Dru was involved in the moneylaundering transfers that have emerged through the enquiry into Pelf Aquitaine Internationale and Pelf Gabon. He also said that his name was on a list of contributors and intermediaries that was found in the archives of Alfred Servile, and that this was why

FICTIONS AND FACTIONS

he had been transferred to Qatar and Lagos until the enquiry by yourself and your colleagues was over. This information was entirely volunteered by Miller and not coaxed out of him by me.

For obvious reasons, I am in no position to either confirm or deny the truth of these assertions, because to my knowledge I have never been in direct contact with Marcel Dru. The truthfulness of this can only be confirmed or denied by Sergius Miller and Marcel Dru themselves, and I can only repeat what Sergius Miller told me.

Beyond the fact that he shares the bed of the woman I love and that I envy him this situation, I have no particular grudge against Marcel Dru. If the accusations concerning him are a complete fantasy concocted by Sergius Miller, and his name unknown to the Pelf financial investigation, I suggest that this letter be held in reserve until the end of your work, and then destroyed.

I do think that Sergius Miller should be made to answer for his deliberate falsification, and I will be consulting a lawyer with this in mind.

I undertook this investigation because Anna Starling continues to tell me she still loves me, before doing yet another disappearing act, using her daughters as catspaws. Although she is a person who has serious psychological problems, I do love her and I have felt for a long time that she is in the hands of persons who use her and manipulate her. Nothing that Sergius Miller has said would appear to contradict this idea, and without prompting, he did come up with a lot of material which fits in with her past behaviour to me.

Is this because Miller got me to talk to him about Anna and then served me back everything I wanted to hear? If this is

... LETTER TO A MAGISTRATE

so, it is exactly the technique used by Anna herself when she was with me and after. It drives you mad.

If it is true that she has been involved with two men who are both with the Secret Services, the operation involving her will have to have been planned and carried out at a higher level. These people simply never act independently—it would cost them their entire career. If she has indeed acted as a spy against her own husband, she can be in considerable danger at the present time. This is why I feel she needs protection, even if it be against herself.

If anything were to happen to her, or to myself, I would expect you to hand this letter over to the relevant authorities. Of course my hope is that such action will not turn out to be necessary, but I am a determined man, and I don't intend to let this matter slide. If there really is a great deal of money at stake here, an individual life weighs little in comparison.

Greed is a powerful motive among the people I am describing here, but it need not conquer all.

This letter is not an anonymous denunciation: I authorise you to make whatever use of it you deem fit, and I will bear public and private witness to its contents to the extent of my direct experience. If the accusations are a fantasy, however, I suggest the letter be destroyed, because I wish no harm to Anna Starling and her immediate family.

With my respects,

Sincerely yours,

William Phillips

FICTIONS AND FACTIONS
VENGEANCE AND UNDERSTANDING

What point is there in trying to please you
I've not slept for three days
in the expectation of seeing you again
once again   torn between smothering you in kisses
and tearing you limb from limb

Now that our love has come full circle
with me reduced to an animal of prey
silently tracking its one and only nourishment
is the story really going to end here and now
or will you run off and begin a whole new chapter

Have you not understood there's no ridding youself of me
know you not that polar bears put their every footstep
inside the track they have already made
don't you think the time has finally come
to forgive both lies you tell and those they tell you

We all have our reasons and we all of us are justified
if greed was the reason why it's good enough as well
assuming it's really true that that was why
if it was revenge that's good enough too
but revenge on who   and what for

Generalized revenge is only part of a wider story
if you stay with this you become a Hitler
taking revenge on Jews for his mother's unwanted pregnancy
there will never be forgiveness between us
only understanding   knowledge can free us   nothing else

And when you lay down your arms
and open other arms to me once again
we can return to the understanding we once did have
in those far-off yet familiar days we breathed in unison
before I began to write and you began to lie

EYES OF AMBER

Don't think less   think better
don't think out   think through
don't think about being hypnotized
and don't think about anything else
brown eyes   eyes of amber

A door opens into another life
what then do you do
push your way in and make your presence felt
or sidle in on the sly with a pretext
you don't know me but I'm your neighbour

I know we don't know each other very well
yet we've been living parallel lives for a while
we have similar friends   similar affinities
do you like baked beans on toast   so do I
as the hope builds up so does the dreamworld

I quite like your body is it occupied right now
oh really what a coincidence neither is mine
my heart's been broken a few times
yet I'm ready to start again   one has no choice
from those breaks tomorrow's light will shine

The situation's not ideal of course
but then it never is   one loves one's children
so it's hardly surprising to fall in love
with someone of that age   then again
rubbing the lamp of youth may not work

It only works when the being is the same
brown eyes   eyes of amber   open sesame
my own soul in your eyes
how did it get there so fast

FICTIONS AND FACTIONS

TIME IN TIME OUT

Time in   time out
here today gone tomorrow
simply waiting   waiting out
or just watching   watching in

Right or wrong   but mostly right
watching in and watching out
watch the shift   the heave   the clout
don't explain   they'll all find out

It's not the pudding   it's the proof
you got it right from the year dot
shaky evidence on hearsay based
took one look to be blown up

rehearse your murder in my mind
not to break you but to kill
that or those which separate
to make us lose sight of what we are

LETTER TO MARINA

24.05.01

Dear Marina,

I was looking for your letter because I should have replied to you a long time ago, and it's buried in my papers somewhere so that I can't look at it. I must reply to you from memory.

Your letter caused me pain because I realise now that what I said in the book caused pain to you, and for this I am really sorry, particularly because it was in a section of the book where you're not as present as elsewhere. I though that other parts of the book might give offense to you, not that part.

There's one thing I must insist on: this book, even if it deals with things which were once true, is as much a recreation of reality as your own sculptures. The book was written more than ten years after the events that inspired it took place, and writing as if it was a journal in real time is a stylistic effect. It is part of the created reality, not the reality itself.

It is true that that the loss of Anna was the greatest loss of my life, simply because I still don't understand why it happened. The whole book is written around this enigma, why is it that passion cannot last? The shifting viewpoints on this are very much the content of the book, i.e. both thought and experience.

Since, like you, I am an artist, I had to raise this whole question by plunging the reader into the context, and I frankly think I have been successful in this insofar as everyone thinks it's a realistic psychodrama. It's not. It's a recreated psychodrama which is as much invented as relived. The bathroom in Anna's house was real, the episode that took place

FICTIONS AND FACTIONS

in it invented.

I ask you to understand that the house in Ostend was used just as I used the bathroom of Anna's house in England, as a sort of décor, a backdrop in order to paint the image I wanted to paint. I know that you will feel this differently, but the context of the scene was the way in which Anna reinvented a reality to suit herself by describing my vacation with my wife in such convincing terms, when in fact that vacation never took place. I waited for her to join me in Brussels and she never came.

This episode is important to me, both in terms of why Anna chose other men in preference to me, and also as a phenomenon in itself. My own feeling is that reality is reality: it doesn't change. What changes is our perception of it, and our own interpretation of its varying aspects. When Anna let herself be carried away on the interpretative wave of her own jealousy, she not only recreated a new reality for herself (in which she could exploit my seeming betrayal—because make no mistake, she did indeed have an affair with Michael O'Murphy in Syria, if not before—she also treated reality as a domestic animal, to be tamed or taught to obey at will.

My attitude may seem moralistic, but after watching my mother destroy her life and all her relationships through her increasing inability to distinguish between objective and self-invented reality, I do feel that the issue is important.

I chose to express this by retelling the story you told me about the teapot in the kitchen sink of the house in Ostend. In order to do this and place the emphasis where I wanted it, i.e. on the mental recreation of an objective reality, I had to reduce the importance of the other characters, i.e. Michael and Marina, who become ciphers, bit players in the story. I dismiss Marina's

... LETTER TO MARINA

annoyance by saying she's "Dutch, and stingy" when to my knowledge her model has never been anything less than generous, but I needed to dismiss the individual characterisation of Marina at that point in the story in order to focus on Anna, so I used the cliché of Dutch meanness which pushes Marina into a convenient category and stops the reader thinking about her.

The description of the house was used in the same way, just to paint the décor without entering into the relationship between Marina and her house or teapot because the subject of the episode was the relationship between Anna and reality.

Here, however, I must confess to you that I did indeed find the house depressing, because I felt that you were working out some kind of uncompleted relationship with your parents through the house, that it was always your parents house and that only the garage where you set up your studio really became your own. My feeling was that the house always treated you as a potential enemy, I felt you were always the caretaker, never the owner and, just as I always feel happy and positive in your other spaces in Alba and Paris, I always felt depressed in Ostend. I considered that house hostile to you, and you are my friend, so I felt protective of you and there was nothing I could do or say. I was delighted when I heard you had sold it.

You know, the house in Alba is my mother's house and not mine, and it will stay this way until I make it over completely. I was there last week and called in the mason to make an estimate for new roofs, which need to be installed. The house still carries the weight of Helen's unhappiness, and it will take a lot of work to make the house my own.

All my love,

William

FICTIONS AND FACTIONS

UNENDING

It was little by little that we became ashamed
nothing deteriorates like the disparagement of self
we were perfect together   apart we became weak
mediocre siren-calls began to sound seductive

Yes I know there were children   husbands   wives
there is always something that has to be dealt with first
by putting ourselves last we destroyed each other
and condemned each other to lives of compromise

Who is to say that sex is Godless?   God sexless?
the question is not as idiotic as it seems
every reality exists at its own level
the sacredness of sexual love is obvious to all

The problem only begins when it becomes a game
by lying you played games with me
and undermined the love you felt for me yourself
the infidelities don't matter the lying does

I became a monolith of righteous indignation
a monument to useless dominance
as my rigidity increased with passing time
my roots shrivelled and I toppled with a crash

Now   face down on the floor   I find I cannot die
even though all hope is lost I still cannot give up
your face and breath and hand illuminate my life
crawling in the mud   I love you as never before

NEGLIGIBLE QUANTITY

Please don't sweep me under the carpet
why is it you should want to be rid of me
it's really strange that this is what you wish
wish is want and want is what you fear
why the fear and what is to be done

What is to be done to a negligible quantity
is it something to be forgotten or just ignored
if it is to be ignored does its presence matter
and if it matters why is it ignored
the Coventry conundrum is part of humankind

Money have I none and prestige very little
possibly a thousand people would know who I am
Much Hadham maybe   not even Bishop's Stortford
the trace I leave will be neither wide nor deep
but it will resemble none other

Where does disparagement of others come from
why have you so turned it into an art form
what is it you stand to gain   what joy therein
that roots itself in the destruction of others
whose only choice is to strike back or die

Stay still and watch the organism mutate
nothing holds still a moment   we grow or self-consume
or else the gentle entropy of age takes over
but what still lurks beneath the carpet is passion
when you ignore me you're choking me to death

FICTIONS AND FACTIONS

THE OPAL

Watch and watch over
take and take care of
see and be seen
serve hence serve yourself

There are no magic recipes
to bring beauty into your soul
it had to be there to begin with
cut away the potch   find the opal

The opal was formed so long ago
that you got used to living alongside
without doing anything about it
beauty without revelation has no meaning

You can live a life like a vegetable
or fight your way into humanity
your song can die in your throat
and not even be heard by yourself

I fight and ceaselessly despair
at the lack of love around me
then I look again and I see
that all is manifested in time

For some it will require an earthquake
to bring it to the fore
others will have spent their lives mining
the elusive opal of the heart

MY TURNIP

They tell me your place is very nice
that you have a lovely home in the South of France
that everything is fine for you
money in the bank and a man in the house

But oh my darling what a price you have paid
just to cocoon yourself in derisory comfort
where is the joy what about the passion
that you think you are too old ever to know again

Who are you and what are you for
when a turnip has been yanked from the earth
it can't bury itself again
turnip or woman you will not stay where you are

You try to pretend you now have what you wanted
and reproduce the frustration of the life you left for me
but you cannot ever be happy in such a world
I branded you my lover and you belong to me

FICTIONS AND FACTIONS

ANOTHER NIGHTMARE

This nightmare is worse because my eyes are open throughout
I wake at four doubled up in anger

There was another silent phone call last Monday
one again you play me like a fish on a hook
but the sea bass at least ends up being reeled in
endlessly you pretend not to do what you do

I hire another detective and track you down again
when you first lay eyes on me you are pleased
it is only when I make a grab for your jaw that you're scared
when I force you to stick out your tongue

That is when you begin to understand
you are almost resigned when I pull out my knife
to cut off the tip of your tongue
not to kill you but to put you in my place

So that you too can spend the next ten years in hell
unable to communicate with those whom you love
you too will pick up a call from someone who loves you
and be unable to speak to them

Maybe then the thought will cross your mind
that it might have been possible to behave in another way
that enslaving me as you have done is dangerous to yourself
when you remove all hope   a man does stupid things

DON'T GO

The silence   your silence
how can you   why   why
don't you know
how important we are together
how much more than one plus one

Neurones react upon each other
to multiply into infinity
but they must be set off
they must be associated

How can you kill
don't you understand that breaking off is death
starvation
no one chooses to starve
what happened

what happened
we were together before
and we'll be together after
so why the hell not during

I don't understand   I'll never understand
is it really money
is it reputation
are you serious when you say such things

what happened
why now
don't go
please don't go

WRITING
AND
SHOWBIZ

STARTING OFF

Writing books about real things is dangerous because everybody turns against you. The ones you write about because you are revealing the secrets they don't tell their daughters or husbands, and the ones you don't write about because they feel you should be writing about them.

Those that love you always have a very clear idea about how you should be loving them. Unfortunately, that's not the way it works. How does it work? Actually I don't know. All I know is that it has to do with transparency: it's something that I felt from a very young age and which also belonged to my upbringing, that it's possible to make something come through which actually exists beyond myself, and that this something is real, not fiction. Can you write beyond yourself? Can you live beyond yourself? I think so.

The form of writing I was attracted to right from the beginning was theatre, and it is no accident that all of my work is written for voice in the present tense, like plays or film scripts, and sounds best when spoken aloud.

When I was sixteen I used to come home to Paris from school in England, climb into bed and stay there until it was time to go back to the English public school where I was ragged and despised. I had arrived there two years before with an American accent and a weight problem, and had begun by coming last in the lowest form of the school. My first school report said that I suffered from mental retardation. Although I came top of the form two years later, I was by then in a stream that precluded any possibility of me attending university.

I expected nothing, loved nothing, and despised myself.

FICTIONS AND FACTIONS

I had build up a tremendous resentment against art and artists because I felt rightly or wrongly that I had been shoved into this hell to provide more time for my parents to paint and sculpt. They were having a lot of fun milling around with interesting people and I was in a straightjacket.

Even though my mother wasn't the greatest of child psychologists, she realised that something was seriously amiss. "Why don't you go to the movies?" she said.

I wasn't interested.

"Why don't you go to the theatre?" she said.

"You never do" I replied, and it was true. My parents were both 20th century cultural icons who had fled their families to practise their craft in Paris, and the artists who came to the studio were a veritable Gotha of everything that was most alive in the art of the time. Brassai and Arnold Newman took the family photographs (except that there was all this painting and sculpture cluttering up the frame), but I myself was less than impressed. They worked at home and never went out. Cultural exploration was not something to be shared with children.

But my father had recently done some line drawings for a short-lived literary quarterly called *Merlin* (thank you Alex Trocchi and Corneille) that was lying around the house. On one of my days-in-bed I had chanced to read it and was fascinated by a play called *The New Tenant* in which a man rents an apartment, moves his furniture into it and is buried alive underneath an infinity of furnishings. The play was by a totally unknown writer called Eugene Ionesco.

By chance (assuming there is such a thing as chance), another play by this same writer was opening the same week at the Théâtre de la Huchette, a tiny little theatre with a stage the size of a hankerchief. When I turned up all the seats had been sold, but since I was young and fresh they decided to ignore fire regulations and I was handed a little wooden stool which I could sit on in the aisle. I put my stool right in front of the small stage and proceeded to lick the ice cream cone I had just bought. The midsummer heat in the tiny theatre was oppressive, and when the curtain went up and Mr Smith went on and on about Bobby Watson, "the cousin of the cousin's cousin" and "the freshest cadaver ever seen in Great Britain", I was enraptured. This play was everything I had lived through over the past two years, this totally incomprehensible British public school and society, terminally embroiled in a series of mysterious rituals that were impossible to fathom.

Suddenly a terrifying shriek from the audience cut into the confined space of the theatre. I looked around behind me, saw nothing, then looked back at the actors on stage and saw to my horror that they were all looking at me. Then I looked down and realised that the scream had come from the lady to my left, because the unattended blob of ice cream at the top of my cone had just fallen into her lap.

When I went home after the play my mother was ironing. I sat down in front of her, and even though I was incapable of learning any text by heart for the classroom, I described and recited *The Bald Prima Donna* to her word for word along with *The Lesson* which accompanied it. It was the first play I had ever seen, and its effect was indelible.

From that moment on, the various strands of my life began working themselves together. I would go back to school in England a week early, and stay over in London with Catherine Yarrow in order to go and see plays. In London it was the time of the Royal Court and the so-called Angry Young Men generation of playwrights around George Devine at the Royal

FICTIONS AND FACTIONS

Court. I began to see everything that was coming up at that time in Paris and London, it was where my real life was.

I began to get involved in acting at school, and did some Shakespeare on the steps of one of the fake Greek temples at Stowe. The plays there were produced by the history tutor, William McElwee, who began to make discreet enquiries about why I was stuck in the stream reserved for the academic no-hopers.

Acting was in fact something I already knew how to do. Not that it was a gift or a vocation, I had simply begun doing it in Paris at the age of ten or eleven when American children's voices were needed for film dubbing. By the time I was twelve I was earning my own allowance with dubbing cachets. I became quite good at it, it's just another technique really, genius is not required, but my voice had not yet broken and I found I could play both girls and boys. It was a sort of game: acting came so easily to me that I never took it seriously enough.

The only enthusiastic review I ever got for my acting in a national newspaper was in the *Times* for playing the part of a woman in one of the school plays : nowadays, the *Times* deals with thornier issues, but it didn't go unnoticed at Stowe and it did some good to my self-esteem.

I found out later that McElwee himself wrote the anonymous review but he never said a word and I didn't either. He was the first adult ever to take an interest in me, and he had a wonderful way of treating his schoolboys as intellectual equals. We would be invited to teas which his wife Patience would prepare for us: she was also a novelist (William McElwee had published a couple of novels and had a high reputation as a narrative historian at this time).

I now realise that these teas and socializing were a means

... STARTING OFF

of testing me out and putting me though my paces, and although he and his wife were not insensitive to press articles that had been coming out on my father saying he taught Picasso to engrave (only partially true) I, who had been raised in the art world, had developed a knack for cultural bullshitting (very easy to do, all you do is read the reviews and the backs of record covers) and I had learned to make the right noises in cultured company. To be fair, my parents truly were shakers and movers of their chosen professions, and I was able to hold my own, not just socially but in the sense that through them I developed a feel for the quality of artistic objects, for the products of the human mind. Being a sophisticated man himself with a life that was not limited to the school, Bill McElwee was probably able to see that I was not the drivelling idiot my backwoodsmen teachers had taken me for.

The cultural gap was still considerable, of course. One incident sticks in my mind: I had replied "How much?" to a teacher who had asked me a question in the classroom, and he was so angry at this insolence that he actually wanted to kill me, he was trembling with rage. The truth of the matter was that I was learning British English, and that I had become fascinated with "How much?" as an equivalent to "What did you say?" What I had not understood was that only an oik would speak this way, and in using such language I was showing disrespect for my teacher. There were countless misunderstandings of this type, but I was learning Britishness in the field. What finally reconciled me to Stowe was the sports grounds: I found that I loved games, and this was a great help.

I remember that on the way down the hill to the house in Dadford village, the first time he invited me to tea, McElwee talked to me about what a great pity it was that débutantes were no longer going to to be presented to the Queen at their annual Ball, and what a loss of standards it was for England.

FICTIONS AND FACTIONS

I agreed wholeheartedly. An adult at Stowe was actually talking to me without telling me what a fuckup I was: if he had said that Hitler was a misunderstood genuis, I'd have agreed with him a thousand times over.

Bill McElwee did something for me which changed my whole life : he went to the Headmaster and persuaded him to let me skip forward a year and take my 'O' and 'A' levels at the same time, which had never been done in the school before, thus putting me back in the running for a university place. He became my (unpaid) personal tutor, and I can still remember him going through my essays with his red pencil underlining useless adjectives and checking out my sources to make sure I knew what I was talking about. He was a historian and expected a historian's precision from his students. The difference between fact and opinion was to be clearly delineated. The fact that there is no slack in my language today is something I owe to him; there is no doubt in my mind that he taught me to write.

At the General Paper that year, I was given the highest marks in the whole school. I had chanced to write on a subject I actually knew a lot about, more than most schoolboys, I imagine, because Roland Penrose was a close friend of my father. I had just read his biography of Picasso, and had been discussing it with him, and I used my talks with him to buttress my essay on the importance of *Les Demoiselles d'Avignon* to modern art. It was the first time my family trade had been useful at school: at least it wasn't the humiliation of the first time when, after an article on my father had come out, I had been put in front of a bowl of flowers and told to copy it. As I have no sense of perspective, my failure at this was manifest.

I took my 'O' and 'A' levels at the same time, and it all more or less worked out. I spent all my spare time going to the theatre, and a year later, Bill McElwee had put me down for a

... STARTING OFF

scholarship examination at Oxford. I went up to New College to take the exam, was interviewed by A.J.P. Taylor, and didn't get the scholarship (that would have been too much like the fairy tale he had designed for me) but I was given a place on condition I pass the 'O' level Maths and Latin I had failed before.

All of the schoolboys taking the scholarship exam were lodged in rooms at the college, in exactly the same conditions they would be in when they would later attend the university. This included the ministrations of the "scout", who was the students' personal factotum. Mostly drawn from the pool of ex-service non-coms (it was only thirteen years after World War II), there was one for every staircase who attended to the needs of a dozen young gentlemen.

On the morning of my Oxford exam, the scout gave a perfunctory knock at the door before entering my room to bring me the mug of tea he had prepared at the bottom of his staircase. When I opened my sleepy eyes, I could see that the eyes of this seventy-year-old man were rimmed and red, he had obviously been crying. I sat up in bed and stared at him : "What's wrong?" I said.

"Oxford lost the Boat Race, sir" he sobbed.

All of the major decisions in my life, for better and for worse, have been taken in a split second. I recognized my teacher, thus engaging myself on the Sufi path, in a second. I bought a house and bankrupted myself in a second, fell in love with a woman who was not my wife in a second, fell in love with theatre in a second, and knew in a moment that Catherine would bear my children.

From that particular instant on I knew I would never attend Oxford, even if it was both my father's and my mentor's dream that I should do so. Even if I had a brand-new British

FICTIONS AND FACTIONS

passport, I would not live out my life in England.

Because of my experience in dubbing, which was undergoing a great expansion in Paris at the time, I was able to earn money as an actor right away, and I persuaded my father to pay for acting and mime classes rather than Oxford. My experiences at school had toughened me, and I forged forward into my new career, translating plays into French and English and getting small roles here and there, mostly with impecunious avant-garde theatre companies.

From my English education I learnt a great deal, amongst other things about the overweening power of social conformity. But there was one incident which was really fundamental in turning me into a writer.

It took place during my period as the school dunce, when we were assigned an essay subject : "A Martian visits Stowe". I had my Martian walking about watching exotic things like Cricket matches with the stocky figure of the Cobham house matron, who was famed thoughout the school for clumping about the place with a shooting-stick, stopping one of the boys, fixing him with a gimlet eye, and saying : "And the name is ... ?" So I had her saying this to the Martian, who of course didn't know what she was talking about.

My description of the house matron was not insulting, nor did I have any other feeling than affection for her, which is why I was dumbfounded when I was called into the housemaster's study and informed that I was going to be beaten with a cane for presuming to put a recognisable member of the school staff into a school essay.

I was given six of the best, and it was yet another watershed in my life : because of my low self-esteem at the time, I assumed that I was a coward to have accepted this and

... STARTING OFF

for a long time I felt that I should have made an issue of it even to the extent of being expelled.

But nowadays I have learnt to be kinder to myself : I think now that this incident gave me my first inkling of the tremendous power that some fairly simple written words could wield.

Even if I was fat, ugly and stupid, my words could crack open the monster and make it shoot its venom. My acting would enable me to transcend the body I so hated, and the written word could do the same for my spirit. If I used my words with care and craft, I could get under people's skin.

In truth, I have never looked back

FICTIONS AND FACTIONS

THE LIVING THEATRE

It was Sunday evening   we'd been rehearsing all day long
at the American Center in the Boulevard Raspail
it was the heroic days of radical theatre
and the play I was rehearsing was to end the Vietnam war
    all by itself

There was no food to eat that evening for the 50-odd
members of the troupe   Someone asked what to do
"I know a shop that's still open" I said
so we piled into Ed's black traction-avant and drove
    to a late-night delicatessen
whose proprietors had known me since I was a child

I introduced the actors to the owner as my friends
explained our needs   and they purchased quite a lot of food
both cooked and uncooked   as Ed started up the car
the proprietor's wife came out of the shop and up to my window

"Your friends were taking fruit off the stands outside while
you were buying the cooked food inside" she said
I turned to the guys in the back seat and said "Is this true?"
"No" they said looking very surprised

"What you say is impossible" I told the woman and we
    drove off   on the way back to the Boulevard Raspail
the guys began to pull fruit out from beneath their clothes
"The stores around our theatre in New York would be
disappointed if we didn't steal from them" they said

Ed and I looked at each other and both of us knew
we lived in a different world to these public pacifists
    and private thieves   I went back to the shop next day

... THE LIVING THEATRE

and paid for what had been stolen   the owners looked at me
with eyes of stone   I had brought the devil into their house

and I was indeed responsible   they were right

From that day on I have known I would be judged
     on my conduct   not on my ideas

The next day Judith and Julian called me in   explained
with some hesitation that since Rufus was coming out of jail
he would be taking my place in the cast   not that he was a
better actor   but to improve the racial balance of the troupe
which had too many wasps   I was invited to join their
     European travels and politely declined

The Vietnam war was won or lost by bombs and cold steel
not by actors pretending to be soldiers on a stage
then again theatre is mankind's dreamworld not its reality
our mind-movies the perfume of the spirit
our poetry just another act
to hide our own betrayal of that which we believe in
     or else to reaffirm it

No man is perfect but we must not relinquish our attempt
     to win a battle most men always lose
the struggle of the spirit to change its own constituents
to transform the recycled garbage we consider as our basis
thieves trying to stop a war may not be as stupid as it seems

                                          (for Ed Marcus)

FICTIONS AND FACTIONS

SHOWBIZ DAYS

From the time I saw Ionesco's *La Cantatrice Chauve* and *La Leçon* my vocation as a writer was laid out for me. The whole idea of absurdist theatre was becoming a popular notion at the time, which was the late fifties, and I espoused it with enthusiasm even though I hadn't the faintest idea what they were talking about, because I didn't find life absurd then and I don't find it absurd now. Pointless sometimes; hard, indeed so; disappointing, often; but also joyful and the most wonderful workshop ever invented for learning. The genius of Ionesco was to portray the world as seen by a child, a pre-greed world of pure sensation where all the characters and events are seen through a magnifying glass, impacting on us as if we were still kids. And anyone who doesn't believe that all children tap into a vast body of intuitive knowledge needs their head examined.

I saw just about everything that was playing in London and Paris in the late fifties, and I read everything I could get my hands on, developing my lifelong habit of combing second-hand bookshops. *Look Back in Anger* at the Royal Court was the big deal at the time, I never really saw the point of plays like that, it was what Roger Blin used to call *réalisme serpillière*, the kitchen sink drama the British have always gone for and which never really interested me. I always saw plays like that as a kind of quintessentially British taste, like Marmite or Peptum Peperium. It is no accident that most of the writers of that school moved into television and, like magpies, squatted it and took it over.

It was the time of the great debate about what the theatre was for between the politically active Brechtians and art-for-art's-sake absurdists, with ritual denunciations in the columns of the *The Observer* by Kenneth Tynan who became the

... SHOWBIZ DAYS

spokesman for the political activists, with Ionesco defending the right to poetic licence. I of course was an Ionescian from the word go, he was my hero and in any case I have never believed in the political usefulness of theatre which, with very few exceptions like Brecht (who happens also to be a great poet and storyteller), can only preach to the converted. Agit-prop probably never worked and probably never will. A play can lead you to the water but it can't make you drink. Art is recognition, not discovery. Give the people what they want. If you want more pronouncements, I have a thousand where they came from.

Samuel Beckett was a old friend of my father's, and he had collaborated with him on prints and drawings, so that his books were lying around the house. My brother had already played the boy in the first English-language Paris production of *Godot* and I well remember how envious I was.

Beckett's novels exerted a fascination on me for a number of years, corresponding as they did to my adolescent angst. It was always clear to me that Beckett was not writing fiction at all, but infinite variations on being locked into a dysfunctional family which can only have come from his own childhood. As a writer his imaginative world is entirely closed in on itself without possibility of escape, whereas in his life he was quite outgoing, enjoyed social drinking, and showed great curiosity about and helpfulness to other people. He got Jean-Marie Serreau to hire me as a translator for Adrienne Kennedy's *Funnyhouse of a Negro*, and his patronage carried a lot of weight.

At the time I still didn't know what language to do my own writing in, because being a near-bilingual, I thought I was torn between English and French. One day I told Sam of my predicament and asked him how he himself came to choose what language to write in, and his reply was interesting because

FICTIONS AND FACTIONS

he answered me straight on. "I'm not bilingual" he said, "but writing in French gives me a distance from what I am writing about I wouldn't otherwise have."

My interpretation of this is that Beckett was engaged in an imaginative reconstitution of the real, and this approach turned out to be my lifelong model.

One day I was sitting in a café in Montparnasse with Roger Blin, Beckett, and a few other of Sam's drinking friends when a woman came in and sat down with all of us, not greeting or being introduced by anyone present. She was tall, sort of gaunt and had a presence nearly as forbidding as that of Beckett when he wasn't in the mood to talk. After an hour or so, as if in response to an unspoken signal, both she and Sam rose to their feet and took their leave together, walking away step in step as if joined by an invisible chain. I turned to Roger Blin, surprised, and asked: "Who's that?" "Oh, that's his wife Suzanne" said Roger, adding musingly that the two tramps in *Godot* were in fact a sort of portrait of their long life together.

My father once told me that Sam came in one day to look at his paintings, sat down in front of one painting and scrutinized it carefully without saying a word for about three-quarters of an hour. Then he got up, looked at my father, nodded "Yes", and left. My father was delighted, his work had been looked at and, in fact, properly respected, which, as most artists will tell you, happens less frequently than one might imagine.

My favourite story about Sam Beckett, and there are many circulating around the Left Bank, is still his comment to my father after being congratulated on winning the Nobel prize: "Well, you know old man, if you go on saying the same thing over and over again, somebody's bound to believe you" because among other things, in my own writing it inspired me to mutate my own experience of being ditched by someone I deeply loved into a sort of meditation on the *amour fou* so beloved of the Surrealists. The ancestors of my *Watching the Wound* are André Breton's *Nadja* and *La Femme et le Pantin* by Pierre Louÿs. Strangely enough, one of the cast of real-life characters who inspired *Watching the Wound* is the grand-daughter of the real-life Nadja, who was locked up in a mental ward and whom Breton never saw again.

From the age of eighteen on I was in fact a working actor: I was dubbing children's rôles for movies in English in the early fifties before my voice broke. I became part of the small colony of English-language dubbers that had drifted into the profession, to scratch a living in a difficult country where, for the most part, they didn't know the language. People like Dick Heinz and Joe Weiner were real pioneers, they invented a profession where none existed and did a really fine job of crafting the words of one language into the mouth movements of another.

At this time there was a real market for dubbed films, they were shown on night-time TV throughout the United States. Little by little over the years the quality got worse, because the Italians moved in and began to do without the detecting and writing on the accompanying *bande-rythmo* that characterized the French technique.

Although their work was much more inaccurate, this made their dubbing product cheaper to produce per reel than the French one. When the quality of the product had plummeted enough, the U.S. market powers-that-be decreed that the American public would accept no more dubbed films in America, which effectively destroyed all outlets for European and foreign-language movies in the U.S.A. A whole profession thus shot itself in its own foot, even if "The Industry" also took the opportunity to establish a U.S. monopoly. It is said that in

FICTIONS AND FACTIONS

the twenty-first century the entertainment industry will become the second largest moneymaker in the world, so it's not surprising that the American major players are trying to knife all the other sources of story and film product in the back.

Because of my two languages I had started translating plays just for my own pleasure: the first play I worked on was a television play called *A Night Out* by Harold Pinter, which I loved. It contains one of the most ghastly mother-son relationships ever written, involving a transfer of this relationship onto a horrendously genteel hooker the young hero picks up.

In fact I was a Harold Pinter fan right from the first, having seen *The Caretaker* about six times when it was playing to tiny audiences at the Arts Theatre Club and having read *The Birthday Party* when it was first published by *Encore*. I remember attending a matinée in the company of John Gielgud who was surrounded by a coterie of lissom young men, all sneering at this piece of obscure garbage, and with him laughing along with the others. Ten years later he would be begging Pinter for a part. I was still at school at this time, and the incident helped increase my innate distrust of British and other Establishments.

I took my translation of Pinter's play to his agent, a Mr Wax, who was fairly surprised to see an eighteen year-old schoolboy asking him for the French rights to the play. When I told him that Roger Blin, the creator of *Godot*, had been revising the translation with me, his mouth dropped open. He then told me that he was thinking about doing Pinter's French translations himself, but when I began to speak French with him it was clear he didn't know the language properly. A month later I received a letter from him forbidding me to even show my translation to anyone else and threatening me with a lawsuit if I did so. This made me think a great deal about author's agents

... SHOWBIZ DAYS

and the job they are alleged to perform. More about that later.

Working with Roger Blin was a joy. He was the person who made me realise how much more I needed to learn about the French language, and how my street-learned French was sufficient to act with but not enough to write with. In a way he carried on the process of forcing me to analyse what it was I wanted to say at the point where Bill McElwee at my school had left off.

Roger had been a close friend of Artaud, and knew my father from the good old days of Surrealism. What interested Roger first and foremost was the poetic imagination. His way of working on texts and staging them was to have a lasting influence on me and even today I consider him my model. He was totally flexible in his approach to a play, considering that his production should be quite exactly as flashy as the play itself demanded, and that his job as director was to be invisible in order to give full rein to the author's world. Nowadays, when the director's ego has taken over the role of the playwright, (thus plunging theatre into the category of minor art form) this disciplined approach is more justified than ever.

He had a strong stutter, which hindered him considerably in his daily communication, but onstage it disappeared. To a certain extent it was he that really introduced me to the subtle complexity and elegant perfection of the French language, simply by going over the Pinter translation with me word by word and helping me iron out all approximations and sloppiness of phrasing. I realised then that I was far from being the bilingual I took myself to be: English was to become my real language, the one I was born with, the one my mother spoke to me in when I was a baby, and even if I was to raise my children, dream and make love in French, English would still vehicle the secret garden of my personal imagination.

FICTIONS AND FACTIONS

I had come across a young apprentice writer called Clive Goodwin at the English Bookstore in the rue de Seine who was engaged in writing his first play. It was an episode from his own life involving an upwardly mobile young man who goes to a smart party in the West End, unexpectedly comes across his father serving drinks for the caterer, and pretends not to recognise him. He showed me the play, which was well-written and solid without being a masterpiece—it would have made a good play for television. He too had started out as an actor and had founded *Encore*, the only magazine devoted to new theatre in England, and he was surprised and pleased when I showed him every issue of his magazine on my bookshelf: I had read them all cover to cover since it had begun. In London he already had a certain prestige as a founder of the new counter-culture but in Paris no one knew who he was, so we became friends and I began to write reviews of Paris theatre for *Encore*. By the time I was twenty-one I was Paris correspondant for *Plays and Players* as well, which bought me free tickets to the shows I wanted to see and which I treated as a sort of personal writing exercise in defining what I liked or disliked, and why. In other words I couldn't just say "That was great" or "That was shit" like all the other actors, I had to justify my opinion to myself and to others. In the end, the pressure of trying to be both a participant and a commentator got to me and I gave up my work as a critic because, as I think André Gide put it "The venom of violent denunciation is sourced in the ashes of failed personal work."

When Clive went back to London he set up as an author's agent and, through him, I got a number of commissions to translate and write film scripts. My translation of Ann Jellicoe's *The Knack* was into a long run in Paris and I was commissioned by Michael White to translate Romain Weingarten's *Summer* for the West End. Clive and Michael White were old cronies who had started *Black Dwarf* together with Tariq Ali, so that

... SHOWBIZ DAYS

when White got someone else to do a quick rewrite of my translation, effectively cheating me out of my royalties, my friendship with Clive also went by the wayside. I moved to Rome, produced some more film scripts, and was again cheated by various Italian producers who stole my work. I was thirty years old, none of the ten-odd scripts I had written had found their way onto film, I had a child on the way, and it was time for a career change.

In parallel to the writing and the translating, I had done a lot of work as an actor and assistant, a lot of it unpaid. This didn't worry me any, I was always willing to help out, but it became noticeable that when the people I had worked with began raking it in, I was not being invited to partake in the feast.

At about the same time that I was working with Roger Blin on my Pinter translation, I met Ariane Mnouchkine in the studios of Jacques Lecoq and Monique Godard we both attended. She was just putting together her first production with the *Association Théâtrale des Etudiants de Paris*, an entity she had created to set up her own productions, and since she was the daughter of a film producer, she knew how to organise herself. I felt an immediate affinity with her as a human being: she was a very touching and sweet person who, like myself, had grown up overweight and unhappy in her own body, and like myself she compensated for her shyness with chutzpah. She and I were always the first to get out front and show our scenes and improvs in acting class because if we waited for the others to go first we would never have the courage to through with it.

She was in the process of setting up her first large-scale production, *Ghengis Khan* by Henry Bauchau, to be performed outdoors in the Arènes de Lutèce and she asked me to help out. The logistics of the operation were fairly horrendous, we

FICTIONS AND FACTIONS

had to hire trucks and rent all the lighting equipment and seating, it was like setting up a movie location. I was only an extra waving a spear around in the back, but it was very interesting to see how she worked, and particularly interesting to see how she kept track of the whole operation.

To begin with, Ariane's view of a kind of epic theatre with sound and fury is a vision that she must have had from birth. She can't have been much over twenty when she took on this huge project, but she carried it off without a flaw. She never talked about other theatre directors very much, but a great deal about Orson Welles, whom she must have known as a child because her father produced some of his best work. After that she went on to form her own company, which she invited me to join, but all her people were formed into a workers' co-operative and were holding down outside day gigs to survive, and since I was already earning a precarious living between dubbing and theatre on my own, I didn't want to go and live in a commune where you had to be on tap day and night and which would cut me off from my small income.

It took me a long time to understand what a great theatre director Ariane was, which was surprising since I saw all the elements she put together: the stylization and mask exercises of Jaques Lecoq, the contribution of West Indian friends like the Donzenacs, her own Russianness and the permeability to non-european cultures. She brought in many people from eastern theatrical traditions to help her out, was willing to learn from others, and she had a quite remarkable capacity for maintaining control over a shifting mass of people and intentions without letting it all fall into anarchy. There are always people around to call her a control freak, but right from the beginning she has always run operations the size of an ocean liner, and the buck has to stop somewhere.

... SHOWBIZ DAYS

What is clear was that her sense of stylization and ritual has been a major contribution to the theatre of her time; viz., the slow repetitiveness of her Gorki where you practically felt the mud on the boots of the peasants onstage, the incredible climax of Arnold Wesker's *The Kitchen* where the stage itself seems to be whirling around and around like a top. For reasons already stated I have had less sympathy with her more political work, but I have never seen anything by Ariane that wasn't worth going to look at. Her main problem was always finding an author who was strong enough not to be crushed under the weight of her staging, and it is still her problem today.

What makes a theatre director of genius is as much an organisational capacity as an aesthetic view. A certain amount of opportunism can also be useful. When I was attending the *Université du Théâtre des Nations* in 1960 I came across Jorge Lavelli, a young director who had just come to Paris from Argentina, and I played the part of the Artist when he directed his first play in Paris, Ionesco's *Le Tableau.* The actor playing the part of Le Gros Monsieur was a last-minute replacement and he was so nervous that he blew half his lines. When I finally got to meet my hero Ionesco after the show, his only comment was: "I agree the play needs cutting, but I think you went too far."

I managed to sell enough tickets to friends and pupils of my father at his printmaking workshop to finance the making of the sets and Lavelli and I began to search around for another play to do. I was reading a book called *Pornografia* by Witold Gombrowicz, and our set designer on the Ionesco play, Krystina Zacwatowicz, said: "Oh, that's my cousin, here in my briefcase I've got the designs for the play he wrote and which the authorities in Poland censored before we could put it on." Krystina then pulled a series of extraordinary drawings for costumes and décor out of her bag, and Jorge fell in love with

FICTIONS AND FACTIONS

them immediately. The play, which I also acted in, was put on for the *Concours des Jeunes Compagnies* and won first prize.

This play not only launched the international reputation of Witold Gombrowicz as a writer (he was able to leave Argentina where he had emigrated during the war and move to Europe), but it also launched the reputation of Lavelli who became a major European theatre and opera director.

Gombrowicz's *The Wedding* is probably one of the strangest plays in the modern repertoire. It is a quasi-Shakespearean account of a young man returning from war to be reunited with his lost parents and fiancée, but when they actually meet each other the whole encounter begins to fall apart and turn into a nightmare. His father is a king as well as a tavernkeeper, there is a whiff of homosexuality between the hero (who is also a Prince) and his pal, and his fiancée may well have slept with half the village. In order to stop the rot, our hero imposes a Court wedding on everyone; the ceremony begins with a very Polish fake Mass that is then destroyed by the interruption of the revolting proletariat. It's a very subtle and funny play written in a kind of comic strip romantic style which parodies the great Polish classics like Slowacki and Witkiewicz and which both incarnates and eviscerates Polish religious and secular myth.

In 1959 I had been very impressed with the work the Living Theater was doing in New York and Judith Malina and Julian Beck had been kind enough to read my first juvenile efforts at playwriting. I was commissioned by Françoise Spira in 1960 to translate Paul Goodman's *Medea* into French to be directed by Judith but the project never worked out and the manuscript of my translation got lost. It was the last time I handed my handwriting to anyone.

... SHOWBIZ DAYS

When in New York, *The Connection* had seemed to me to be the most inventive and vital thing going on the theatre at the time. Beck had found a way of integrating the spontaneity of improvisation into daily theatre performances which were a real contribution to the art. The downside was that the mixture of real and fake drug addicts onstage had a disastrous effect on some of the lives involved. Warren Finnerty and Gary Goodrow's performances were unforgettable, but I think they left their lives behind on that stage.

The whole idea of improvisation in public was very much a concern of that time. Happenings (most of them pretty amateurish) were coming into fashion, and through George and Jean Reavey, I hooked up with the beginning of the Open Theater workshop which Joe Chaiken had founded in New York City to counter the excessively psychological and movie-oriented Actor's Studio techniques. What Joe, Peter Feldman and various other people were doing was trying to find physical expression equivalents to emotional states, a sort of Americanization of Artaud and the more expressionistic European theatrical tradition. The warm-up exercises in particular provoked the actors into producing some quite fascinating material which was formed into plays by Jean-Claude van Itallie and other writers in attendance. I don't think I have ever felt such pure joy at being on stage as I did back then. A high like none other.

Lee Worley and Julian Beck used these exercises as a basis for *Mysteries and Smaller Pieces* which was put together in two weeks at the American Center in Paris in 1965, and at about the same time I was using the same exercise material to write my first 'adult' play, a science-fiction piece adapted from a story by Clifford Simak.

The six months I had just spent spent with The Open

FICTIONS AND FACTIONS

Theater was one of the most important experiences of my life. I saw that it was possible to bring the energies of widely differing people together and channel them into a common aim, and of course we were all young and it was a period of discovery and grace. It also provided a lesson in what not to do, because when I came back to work with them again three years later, I found that a lot of competitivity and jealousy had crept in, theses had been written about their work, and numerous articles had come out in specialist magazines like *The Tulane Drama Review*. A pecking order had established itself and my feeling was that the intellectuals who, at the beginning came along to watch the actors, had ended up taking over the whole show. It was no surprise that Joe Chaiken, who was nobody's fool, wound up the workshop shortly after.

In Paris in 1965 I was briefly involved with the Living Theatre, but even though I rehearsed Kenneth Brown's *The Brig* with the idea of joining the Company, I think Judith and Julian realised that I wouldn't fit into the militant/vegetarian anti-Vietnam war commune they were putting together for their stay in Europe. Nevertheless, working in *The Brig* was fascinating, Julian Beck had integrated the Marine training routines into the tissue of the play, in other words if one of the actors looked into the eyes of the MPs shouting in his face he would really get hit in face and body as a punishment. True, the actors playing the parts would pull their punchs as much as possible, but when you got the training rituals wrong onstage you still got hurt. It was quite the most amazing way I had ever seen to keep those daily performances fresh, we were all scared pissless, in other words, as actors, we were in precisely the same situation as the grunts in the Marine prison.

As I said, *Mysteries and Smaller Pieces* was assembled in a couple of weeks to thank the American Center for putting the Living Theater Company up in 1965, and I have rarely seen

... SHOWBIZ DAYS

such a consistently inventive *mise en scène* as was put together by Julian Beck over that short period. It was beautiful to watch a theatrical imagination such as his at work; all the various exercises, bits and pieces (like Jackson MacLow's *Dollar Poem*) were turned into a seamless ensemble and the performance was a triumph.

The play immediately became part of the Living Theater repertory, and just as promptly began to go downhill. When I saw it a year and many ecstatic reviews later, it was exactly the same text and action but it was being performed without the lightness and grace that had characterised it at the beginning and it lasted nearly a full hour longer. Without the element of danger, i.e., the drugs in *The Connection* and the violence in *The Brig*, the Living Theater productions tended to tail off fairly quickly, I think because there was no real working atmosphere in the commune: my impression was that everybody sat around and talked or got high instead of working. Nevertheless, their contribution to the art was considerable, and even though many words have been written about the Living Theater I still feel that nobody has ever really done justice to Julian Beck as an inventor of theatrical form.

At around the same time I was trying to put together a production of my translation of Ann Jellicoe's *The Knack*, and here again I ran into trouble with agents. When I had optioned the play, nobody else was interested in it; I was only twenty-one but because I was still young I had understood that Ann Jellicoe had written a contemporary *commedia del'arte* that beautifully caught the spirit of the youth of the time.

Without being a great work of literature, it really was one of the first works to incarnate the new youth culture : Richard Lester made the play into a successful film, Mike Nichols put the play on Broadway, and since I held the French-language rights, I was suddenly the owner of a hot property. The

FICTIONS AND FACTIONS

legendary agent Peggy Ramsay promptly tried to knife me in the back by contacting the producers I had brought in for the Paris production and offering to cut me out; she could do it because my option was coming to an end before the first night of the show. In the end I was forced into sharing the translating credit with the director I had brought in who hadn't written a word, and the experience left a sour taste, even though the show was successful and the royalties kept me alive for three years.

My strongest memory of that episode is looking at the director who, instead of watching his actors onstage on the first night, was crouched over the keyhole in a door, trying to see if Jean-Jacques Gautier, the critic who put the most bums on seats, was laughing or not. He had gotten rid of the first actress who had played the rôle in Brussels in favour of one that Gautier liked, and the worst thing about all this was that the bet paid off: Gautier's review in *Le Figaro* was enthusiastic and brought in the paying public. It was a far cry indeed from the integrity of people like Beckett, Roger Blin or Jean-Marie Serreau, whom I considered my mentors. Certain things have to be done to learn what not to do. I was in showbiz, not theatre.

Just before this I had been part of a production of Alfred Jarry's *Ubu-Roi* with Victor Garcia, a director who was one of the most imaginative and theatrically creative persons I ever worked with. His inventivity was astounding, he would come up with with twenty ideas a minute which he would sling onto the actors with absolutely no preparation ("Okay darling, you do the next speech hanging by your heels from a fork-lift") and the very cerebral French actors had a lot of trouble following his incessant re-invention, particularly since he never took the trouble to rehearse one idea over and over before coming up with the next.

His habit of casting interesting faces he met in cafés meant

... SHOWBIZ DAYS

that he tended to end up with actors who were all right in rehearsal but who blew up when faced with the pressure of a live audience. Nevertheless, unlike some of the others, I had an instinctive trust in what he was trying to do, which was to bring out the schoolboy humour and surreal anarchy of Jarry's play by making each development of the play totally unexpected. The whole thing was set to music by Jean-Charles François as a modern parody of opera mostly sung in *sprechstimme* and the result was extraordinarily effective: Marcel Duchamp, who was working at my father's workshop at the time, thought it wonderful.

The production won the prize of the *Concours des Jeunes Compagnies* and went on tour, but here again the lack of proper organisation played a part. Actors need to be reassured and Victor provided no backup, just endless technical challenges. I loved it because my own experience in public improvising with the Open and Living Theater made me immune to ridicule, and I also knew that what he was onto, which was finding a sort of fable form for the new theatre, was the right way to go.

I began rehearsing the role of Emanou, the Christ-figure in Arrabal's *Le Cimetière des Voitures,* but here I ran into trouble. My admiration and comprehension of Victor's intention was misunderstood, he was homosexual and alcoholic, I wasn't, but he still fell in love with me. Since he was unable to seduce me directly, he began trying to influence my sexual life by involving me with various members of his entourage. I now regret my own violent reaction to all this, which was to walk away, and I don't think he really meant me harm, but although I had no predetermined moral stance, there were certain exotic erotic mixtures I was scared of. I had just met the woman I was to marry and have my children with: the world of one-night stands in which one becomes a pawn in a game had caused me pain and I wanted to leave it all behind. Growing up as I did in

FICTIONS AND FACTIONS

hatred of my own body, homosexual iconhood was more than I could bear.

Question time: what's the difference between freedom and licence? Do you practise what you preach? Good show, carry on. Was the new sexual freedom of the time actually getting us anywhere?

The two plays I wrote after the science fiction epic deal with these themes. The actress Joyce Aaron, my old friend from the Open Theater in New York, dropped in on me one day, and said "Come on, Augy, it's all very well for you to have become a paterfamilias but there's more to you than that."

She had written a play about two women and their relationships with men called *Acrobatics*, which won an Obie, and she wanted me to collaborate on a one-act play to go with hers about two men talking about their relationships with women. I pointed out to her that men didn't talk to each other about intimate relationships like women did and that I was into conference interpreting which was a tiring job involving continuous travel. I hadn't been writing for ten years since I got cheated by the movie people and I didn't really see myself ever writing again.

But it was nice to have news of old friends and we spent several days talking over our lives, particularly about how all the priorities began to change when you had children. She was doing acting workshops in Amsterdam, I was free-lancing as an interpreter all over Europe and Africa out of Paris, but the friendship between us had held up even though our lives had changed. I just didn't see any possibility of writing the play, but we had a lot of fun catching up on what had gone on over the past ten years. I took her to the Gare du Nord to see her off to Amsterdam and as the train slowly drew away with me waving my hankerchief after her, I suddenly realised I had my story.

... SHOWBIZ DAYS

I transposed the stories we had been telling each other into *The Karma Connection*, but in the play Joyce and I have become two men who both shared the favours of the same girl ten years before. The one who stayed and had a daughter with her has come off less well than the other man, who now lives in Switzerland, because the girl has ditched him and gone off with someone else. The second man, Joe, has married and has two boys, and has very clearly developed some form of religious faith. When asked to explain this he gives an account of his son's stroke, describes how he began to pray in that moment, and how this experience hardened into a form of certainty about the existence of a higher intelligence.

The play was almost performed by a radical women's group in the seventies but when they found out that the name Augy belonged to a man and not to a woman, they decided against the idea. Also, it must be said that a play about finding God was not top fashion at a time when transgression was the thing. Today my feeling is that the play holds up, even if some of the writing is a little obvious. God and shopping may both exist, but it's difficult to write about the two of them in the same breath. The quality of the play is in its atmosphere: you see a real friendship developing between the two men, as opposed to most two-handers which almost always play out some form of conflict situation.

Since the performance with *Acrobatics* never worked out, I decided to write a sort of sequel to *The Karma Connection* which turned out to be a sort of prequel, or whatever one calls it. The next play was called *Middleman* and it charts the relationship between a man, his wife and his lover, with the conflict developing not so much between the three adults, but between the man and his young children, who are never seen on stage. Their voices are prerecorded and the actors mime the scenes with them: the voices of the children are heard but they

FICTIONS AND FACTIONS

themselves are never seen. The man comes to realise that there is no way he can move out without damage to the kids and the same scene of prayer when one of the boys has a cerebral haemorrhage brings the relationship with the mistress to a close.

Roger Blin's reaction to the play was very interesting. Because he had known my father from the time he had helped Balthus on the décor of Artaud's *Cenci* in the thirties, his relationship with me had always been that of a favourite uncle. We discussed the play I had written, and with his usual sensitivity he quite understood why I had not wanted to put live child actors on the stage, that if they were invisible to the audience but not to the actors their presence could become even more forceful, and the idea of the final scene where the adult actors walked off leaving the invisible children in the minds of the audience onstage was something he understood and liked. His technical analysis of the play was perfect, but then he pointed out that there was one thing in the play he could not accept, and that was the prayer in which the hero expresses submission to the will of God.

How was it possible that I, the son of one of the original surrealists who had remained agnostic to the bitter end, how was it possible for me to have gone over to the enemy in this way? It was a moment where there was no cheating possible. "Roger," I said, "it actually happened to me, and it happened in exactly those words. Tom had a stroke when he was seven, and that's exactly what I said. If you had a son in that situation you would say the same: 'If you need a mind, take mine'."

"Never," he said, looking at me sadly, as if I was letting the side down. It was at that point that I realised to what extent the Church had destroyed its own.

Beckett, the lapsed Irish Protestant, or Genet, who dreamt of the Virgin Mary and wrote imaginary mass-like ceremonials

... SHOWBIZ DAYS

that could almost have been drafted in Latin, these were the sons of Surrealism and the Church, not the shopwindow stuff by Dali or Magritte which you see passing for Surrealism in television advertising. It's the pining of good men who have the courage to look from this world into the next and who can find absolutely no consolation or transcendental project.

You could acknowledge the Divine Presence only in the form of blasphemy; submission to God being the absolute and unacceptable transgression. I, who had been raised outside the Church, was in fact free to accept or reject whatever part of it I chose, but they had to reject the idea of God along with the institution.

So Roger Blin, who had an almost paternal love for me, was deeply disappointed, but nevertheless he had read my play with his usual precise attention : "You've got to have two moving spotlights when the children are supposed to be on stage, that way the audience will focus on them better."

He then paid me a tremendous compliment: although there could be no question of him doing the play himself because of its openly religious aspect, he began to talk to me about his own love life, in tacit acknowledgement of the sincerity and depth of the relationships I had described in *Middleman*. It was a subject of some fascination to all of his old friends, like the painter Mayo, who had watched this man who so loved women always enter into relationships which never ever quite seemed to work out.

We were sitting underneath a huge blowup of his beloved Hermine, who was now, as he told me, living with a young man her own age. "She was supposed to drop by last night, but didn't make it." He said that when he first knew Hermine, she was very young, living hand to mouth, ekeing out a living by selling her drawings to clients on the terraces of the cafés

FICTIONS AND FACTIONS

and occasionally exchanging her body for a roof over her head. He took her in and, having seen her in a number of plays, I knew myself that she had developed into a very good and highly serious professional actress.

He then told me about a sort of primal scene, which he told me he had worked back to as a result of psychoanalysis: he was walking with his mother, a good bourgeoise Catholic, in the street in Neuilly when he was nine or ten, and a little gypsy girl came up to them with her hand held out, begging.

In order to please his mother, who disapproved of begging, Roger spat in the face of the little girl, who just stood there and looked at him.

Roger and I then looked up, almost in unison, at the dark Armenian beauty of Hermine in the photo above our heads and neither of us said a word.

After that I took my leave, and it was the last time I was to see Roger Blin; he had a serious heart condition and died shortly after, having gone on working right to the end. But the compliment he had paid me was wonderful: he had reacted to the intimacy of my play by offering me his own intimacy in return.

It was a tremendous encouragement, even if the play has never been staged to this day: it was then that I realised something I had only vaguely felt before: I could do it, but I was not going to be a writer of ideas, attitudes, or anything amazing in the way of technique; the quality I would call on in my future work, whether self-invented or based on experience, was a quality of simplicity and transparency. I could simplify confusion. By this I would succeed or fail.

INTERPRETING

I don't have all that much to say about interpreting. I made many friends in the profession and although it indeed provided me with enough money to raise a family on a part-time job, it turned out to be much more than a meal ticket to me even if it wasn't a vocation to begin with, because I always saw interpreting as a means to an end. I had failed at a show business career and I thought it could provide me with a living for my family while leaving me with enough time left over to write. My calculation turned out to be a good one, although like all things, it didn't turn out to be quite that clear-cut. As happened with the acting, I got bitten by the bug.

After twenty-five years in the profession I now know that it is not an activity which encourages parallel artistic projects that have to be realized over a long period of time, because the type of concentration it induces is short and intense. You live with a packed suitcase ready to travel at the drop of a hat, you put everything else out of your mind, hop onto a plane, see your family and children on the weekend and zip off to another country or continent the week after. This is of course a caricature, but there is some truth to it. It really is a sort of gypsy life with a per diem attached.

Because I wasn't putting anything on paper I thought for a long time that I was lost to writing, then I came to realise that interpreting was a form of dancing with words that was continuously exercising me, even if there was nothing to show for it. When I did start writing again, I found that interpreting had made it much easier to make decisions faster and the process of revising had become much more important. I was increasingly drawn to short forms of literature rather than

FICTIONS AND FACTIONS

longer constructions because poems and short plays could be finished off in a few days whereas more ambitious book-length ideas would simply join their brothers in the never-never drawer of unfinished projects.

When Paul Unwin first gave me a simultaneous interpreting test at the OECD in 1970, even though I made a hash of it, he thought it was something I might learn to do, so he invited me to come into the OECD and work in the silent booth whenever I felt like it. It was a golden opportunity and I made the most of this invitation. Even though I was in a disastrous situation after being laid off after a year at my job, and even after night work to support my two young children made me turn out very fluctuating results at the interpreting school I enrolled in, I always had an absolute certainty that this was going to be the job for me and I was right.

My time at the *Ecole Supérieure d'Interprètes et de Traducteurs* was an invaluable experience but not a happy one. The problem was basically the French higher educational system, which works on the principle of the *concours* or competition, in other words all the students are pitted against each other and the top performers are accepted into the professional fold with the teachers, who begin to *tutoyer* you the day after you've successfully passed your finals.

The only problem with an approach such as this is that the unstated purpose of the teaching becomes the elimination of potential rivals rather than the communication of knowledge. About fifty students began every first year of studies and fifteen would be let into the second year. And at the time of final exams, only about eight or ten would be given a diploma, basically because it was felt that the Paris market couldn't absorb more interpreters. The really gifted students didn't need teachers, they just needed practice, but I saw that the students who had problems

... INTERPRETING

and who really needed tutoring were systematically discouraged.

The quality of the teaching varied enormously. One of the good things was that the teaching was done only by other professional interpreters, which is not always the case in other university interpreting courses throughout the world. This meant that we were given a very good grounding in the reality of the profession, but the drawback was that the teaching interpreters were completely inexperienced as teachers.

As I look at the pattern that emerged, my feeling now is that many colleagues who were truly pioneers in the teaching of interpreting fell into the trap of seeking university respectability by writing theses and developing a lot of useless theory. Interpreting is a craft which is more like carpentry than the accumulation of a static body of knowledge, and academic qualifications are meaningless for the work. You know in five minutes if the colleague is doing the job or not.

As a teacher, Gérard Ilg was dauntingly brilliant, Constantin Andronikof dauntingly elevated—he was deacon of the Russian Orthodox Church in Paris and a theologian as well as being chief interpreter at the *Quai d'Orsay* (French Ministry of Foreign Affairs). He would talk about interpreting as a means of spiritual elevation because the *truchement* or *drogoman* becomes invisible and lets the message pass through him without cluttering it up with his own self, at which point all the fresh-faced twenty-year-olds in the audience would listen to him with their jaws dropping.

I looked as if I was the same age, but I was about ten years older and already had some professional background. Nevertheless it would take me another ten years in the profession to begin to understand what Andronikof was talking about, since the great trap of simultaneous interpreting is that

FICTIONS AND FACTIONS

it appears to be about translating, but it is first and foremost about understanding, and as Rumi points out, saying: "I understand" is like filling your water bottle with sea-water and saying "Here is the sea." It's a fluctuating, difficult and unending process which, thank God, is never over, and which begins with listening. To interpret is to listen. Good interpreters listen harder. One can talk endlessly about this but that is what it boils down to.

Then, as Anne Giannini said to me when I was starting out: «*On reconnaît les bons interprètes à leurs silences.*» You can tell good interpreters by their silences: in other words the good ones have enough confidence to shut up and not begin talking until they understand. At certain times this takes courage.

Because what are you listening to? Words, but not just words. What is the intention? Who is the person? Greedy or knowledgeable? Angry or serene? Seeking sincerely to communicate or producing deliberate obfuscation? And it's all of this one has got to assimilate, not by going through it all on a checklist but by scanning very quickly like a pilot who glances over the fifty dials in the cockpit before takeoff to see if anything is wrong.

You are basically translating the words your speaker is uttering but you are also doing more than that: in order to do your job properly you have to get behind their eyes as well. As Idries Shah points out *"Words are an aspect of the attempted communication of thought. They are not thought."* This is why trying to pour interpreting into the mould of linguistics is doomed to defeat, because linguistics takes the word as the baseline when interpreting uses the word as a point of departure.

Learning interpreting is not so much acquiring

... INTERPRETING

information or, ultimately, even language (the language has to be there to start with), it is making this process become a sort of second nature in yourself, and it demands a tremendous amount of work and effort of the will to do so. The process is a highly delicate one because it involves a kind of self-induced brainwashing, which is why I was so shocked at the deliberate or unconscious sadism of certain teachers, whose basic motivation was to catch people out rather than help them through difficulties.

Halfway though my first year at the school, I was asked to teach the first year students acting and diction, and at the end of this time the offer was withdrawn because various people had made up their minds that I would never be an interpreter. It's true that my results were irregular, basically because I was working at night (writing dubbing scripts for pornographic movies) and my second son was born during the school term. At the time I was so broke that in order to bring Catherine home from the clinic I went around to all my friends telling them that a young lady I knew had got herself into trouble and needed an abortion: I wanted a hundred francs from each of them to pay for it. With the money I paid off the hospital.

The relationship between acting and interpreting isn't what most interpreters think it is. The most obvious relationship concerns diction and self-presentation; in the booth you have to speak clearly, at the right distance and without crumpling your candy wrapping in front of an open mike. But the most interesting similarity is in the basis of the two professions, which both depend on the capacity to develop a sort of psychological mobility.

Actors know that our being is in fact infinitely flexible, that we are multiphrenics rather than schizophrenics. Our

FICTIONS AND FACTIONS

personalities are multiple rather than split in the sense that we are in fact made up of different people and circumstances which can fairly easily be added onto our own fairly narrow experience by combining imagination and observation. To be happy as an interpreter you have to arrive at this kind of imaginative mobility, which is useful for anyone, no matter what their walk in life. Even though you don't incarnate another, you still have to be able to let someone else occupy you entirely without feeling diminished. Here the sexual analogy is inescapable, and it also explains why interpreting is such a feminized profession, thank God. Most men have more of a problem than women about letting their bodies or beings be invaded by another.

Interpreter's frustration is almost invariably linked to the feeling that this process of giving yourself up to serve another is in some way a diminishing of one's own identity. This is of course a figment of the interpreter's imagination, and always has been. Its source is in the grandiosity of the interpreter's imagination about himself or herself, because the social hobnobbing with the shakers and the movers leads us to confuse ourselves with these people.

In fact we're like plumbers just along for the ride, and we have neither the experience nor the motivation of the conference delegates we work for. The most frequent human failing in interpreters is snobbery, but it is the snobbery of servants in the staircase, who are saying "My master is more powerful than yours." And regarding interpreter's worship of the institutions they work for, the less said the better. Nevertheless, when one is interpreting really intelligent or loving people, one is truly lifted up by them and one's own work rises in proportion.

And, to be fair, great interpreting does exist, it is an invisible art form but an art form nonetheless. Andronikof's interpretation of Soljenitsin on French television when he first

... INTERPRETING

arrived in France from the Soviet Union was perhaps the most beautiful piece of interpreting I ever heard, and sharing a booth with a bilingual like Jimmy Poole or men of culture like Stéphane Priacel or Edouard Roditi was an education in itself. Interpreters are quite definitely a breed apart.

Anyway, I wormed my way into the profession without ever finishing off the course at the ESIT. In my second year I was offered a year-long contract in Nigeria, so I went to live there with my wife and two young children and learned my job by doing it. When I came back to face the competitive Paris market, I had already worked enough to join AIIC, the professional open sesame to the world of interpreting, and I never looked back.

I have wonderful memories of interpreting, memories of clients, of colleagues, memories of the joy of taking a plane alone into an unknown country, the tools in my hand being only the knowledge in my mind, seamlessly keying into a new situation with new people and giving satisfaction to those whom I served. Modest triumphs, but real.

My mother died very suddenly at the end of January 1995; and two weeks later on Saint Valentine's Day, I toppled over with a stroke. Face down on the floor and half-paralysed I called out to my wife; she came in and could not make out my words. Thanks to the French medical system I was given blood thinners almost immediately and my hemiplegia withdrew. Surgery had to be performed on my carotid arteries and this resulted in a permanent alteration in the quality of my voice.

Colleagues encouraged me to start interpreting again because my mind hadn't been slowed down even if my speech was a little more slurred. But very quickly I realised that what the colleagues were hearing and what the client was hearing were two different things: I had prided myself on the precision

FICTIONS AND FACTIONS

of my diction but now the labials (p's, b's and m's) were mushy and indistinct, and the voice totally nasal. When you heard my voice in the same room there wasn't too much of a problem, but over earphones or a telephone it was quite difficult to make out. I recorded myself during a Unesco conference and listened carefully to what I had done: the voice was painful to listen to, and I could not expect my clients to be masochists.

I went on working for as long as I could, but when a client at the French *Sénat* complained about my work, I knew the jig was up. Once again back to Andronikof, who had drafted the preamble of the AIIC statutes defining the rights and obligations of the interpreter. In a marvellously untranslatable phrase, it is incumbent on the interpreter to ensure an acceptable quality —"l'interprète se porte garant de la probité de sa prestation"— in other words there is an implicit moral guarantee that the job will be done to the best of the interpreter's ability, and that a true professional will never accept a job he is incapable of doing. No interpreter is perfect, but there is an implicit standard deviation of error one can't go beyond.

One thing I can say is that in all my work as an intepreter, I never threw in the sponge. Sometimes I worked well, sometimes I worked less well, but I always did the best I could within the given circumstances. I was part of the most wonderful profession in the world: my job was to enable others to understand, and most of the time, it worked.

When they stopped understanding, I had to go.

I was back from the dead, without a profession, with no money saved and it was time to do some hard thinking about myself and my life. I had started a small publishing company to publish books connected with the Sufi Tradition, financing most of the printing with money I was earning as an interpreter.

... INTERPRETING

I was editing and compiling books by my teacher and I knew this was a project that had to be continued, but I also knew that I had to face up to my own potential as a writer because I had been avoiding the issue for too long.

Over the years I had accumulated a lot of short poem-like texts which I tended always to think of as my own notes for when I would eventually get around to writing the Great American Novel. As they say, the prospect of imminent death concentrates the mind most wonderfully, and it was clear that the notes were the nearest I would ever get to it. But as I assembled them, I began to realise that they were all in fact telling another story which lay just behind them all, and which formed itself in the mind of the reader, something about searching and finding.

My work was not really poetry and not really storytelling: the movie scripts, plays and acting had not been an accident; the books that were emerging were a kind of theatre of the mind which created its own narrative pattern around recurring themes which mostly had to do with the love of womankind and the love of God. Even though my work was simple and accessible, I knew that no commercial publisher would handle it at the present time because my technique of stringing together short pieces to make an overall narrative means that the reader is forced to stop and start over and over again. Most readers want to be lulled and coddled, and they can't put up with it.

I owe a great debt to all the fellow interpreters who acted as a sort of ongoing market research for my writing efforts. In the booth I would show my little pieces to people who were sometimes sympathetic, sometimes unsympathetic, and the feedback I got was always interesting and valuable. Interpreters are, after all, highly literate people with a keen eye for weakness in thinking, and they all helped me to define for myself what it was I was talking about.

FICTIONS AND FACTIONS

In the seven years since my stroke I have not been inactive: five books compiled and edited on behalf of Omar Ali-Shah in addition to the ones I had done before, three books edited for Ikbal Ali Shah and four books (including this one and a volume of plays) on my own behalf. But even if I am doing exactly what I always wanted to do, writing and editing is still a lonely business and I do miss the sociability and unexpected encounters that are so much part and parcel of the interpreter's life.

A word to the colleagues: I have ceased to attend meetings of the association only because I find it painful to be a voyeur rather than a lover. I am grateful to all those whom I worked with because they all taught me something about myself. Nobody ever talks about this but sharing a booth is an intimate experience, not just because there are usually two interpreters to a booth, but because you are sharing your capacity to understand with a person you may or may not have something in common with; and since you're working as a team and the job has to be done, you suppress what you don't have in common and get on with it. There is a very real personal discipline involved here, and without romanticising our profession I like to think that it is one of the aspects of the job—assuming one can extrapolate it into the rest of our lives—that enable us to become better human beings. Mind you, it works both ways, some colleagues get nastier and nastier.

The intimacy of sharing a booth with a colleague is a weird form of mindreading because you're reading the client/speaker as well as the way the colleague is dealing with him or her. Etiquette between interpreters is pretending you're not really listening to them, particularly when you're working with younger colleagues—they have enough problems with their own self-confidence without you piling any more pressure on them—and if there was one lesson I learned from my own

... INTERPRETING

difficult beginnings in interpreting, it was to be as kind and encouraging as possible to the newcomers.

I still think that sharing a booth with somone may be the nearest thing there is to making love to someone without touching, because they are exposing themselves to you in all their horror and all their glory. The sobering thought is that you're doing the same to them. All right, it's an exaggeration, but male or female, rich or poor, young or old, we are all of us equal in this situation, which is what makes it so interesting. External values no longer count, just the job. Wonderful.

I miss you all.

Augy

FICTIONS AND FACTIONS

CONTRIBUTION TO THT CONFERENCE, GRANADA (TERAPIAS HOLISTICAS TRADICIONALES)

October 1994

ON BEING CURED

If I take the floor here to speak to my friends in the Sufi Tradition about therapy, it is not only because I edited Agha's tapes in order to turn them into a halfway readable book, but also because I am totally unencumbered by any knowledge of the subject, which gives me a freedom of opinion which none of you have.

Nevertheless, my knowledge of illness and therapy is the knowledge which I share with almost every man that walks the earth: I have been ill and I have been cured, although I suppose technically that if one considers that the original illness or wound took place at birth, I am only in a state of temporary remission until the inevitable end.

I do think, however, that the experience of illness was a useful one, at least to myself, and so my contribution is offered here from the point view of the patient, because in a congress of dairymen, whoever listens to the cow?

So here's the story of an illness and the story of a cure, along with a few questions of a more general nature that I will attempt to draw from my own experience, and which congress attenders may or may not wish to use as a basis for discussion.

One day in the late spring of 1985, my wife and I were looking at a television discussion programme of mind-numbing idiocy, in which the star of the show was a French pianist and

... ON BEING CURED

musical promoter called Eddy Barclay, whose chief claim to fame seems to be that he has been married an amazing number of times, knows a lot of movie stars, has a very user-friendly approach to the media, and when they ask him in a more roundabout way: "What's it like, screwing all those beautiful young women?", he will answer with the usual variations on "Great, but the alimony's a killer".

We were in the midst of looking at this mindless pap when Mr Barclay mentioned he had just recovered from cancer. In response to the interviewer's question, Barclay said that he had had a sore throat which didn't get better for a long time, and that he had gone to see a doctor who had diagnosed throat cancer. He had then undergone treatment and was all right at the present time.

My wife and I looked at each other: it was just the symptom I had been complaining about for the past few weeks. The next day, Catherine got the name of a throat specialist from a friend and made an appointment for me. The doctor did the normal thing of prescribing antibiotics, which had no effect. I went back to him two weeks later, he looked down my throat again, asked me to drop by a clinic where he worked, and without saying what it was for, took out an instrument rather like sugar tongs and withdrew a little piece of the grungy phlegm in my throat for further perusal.

When he asked me to come to his office the following week to discuss the results of the lab test with me, I was not entirely surprised to find that a "rampant and invasive carcinoma" had lodged itself on my tonsil. I had just been through a difficult year. Professionally, I had subtitled two feature films, investing in a computer to do it with, and the client, who was a friend of my father and his wife, had simply disappeared with my work without paying me while my father

FICTIONS AND FACTIONS

continued to receive him socially in his home.

I had also had a great disappointment in the Tradition, which I mention here because disappointment, anger and the desire for power can take over the best of us and even affect one's body, and the incident is worth mentioning as a cautionary tale. I had proposed to Agha to try and start up a group in New York City, where a number of people who had previous connections to the Tradition were residing, and I had initiated exercises there in the previous autumn. I was put in charge of the group then relieved of the job about a month later. Nowadays, I would regard such an event as a blessing, but at the time I took it harder.

So if I look at my situation in the summer of 1985, I have a number of parallel personal and professional frustrations in action. My family and interpreting work is going well, but this doesn't really make me happy because I want to be a writer and a big time Sufi Star. I feel unloved and unappreciated by my teacher, have had a disappointing affair with a woman who used me to take over the group in New York (not for long, but that's another story), I am angry and am probably undergoing a classic mid-life crisis.

At the age of forty-five, I look ten years younger, my hair is blond, not white, and I seem to be in the pink. I am an atypical patient insofar as I neither smoke nor drink, and the doctors at the hospital think I have such pretty teeth that I'll go through a whole fluoride bathing process in order to keep them from being yanked out for the radiotherapy. I am being treated in Paris at the Hôpital Pierre et Marie Curie which specialises in radiotherapy whereas the Villejuif cancer hospital, according to medical scuttlebutt, is more specialised in chemo and surgery. My cancer appears to be in a yet fairly undeveloped state, so radiation appears to be the way to go. I put out of my mind the

... ON BEING CURED

fact that the Curies' discovery of radium cost them their lives and try to think positively about my treatment.

I phone Agha to give him the news of my cancer. He has already been told about it and the Paris group has already convened to do the Ya Shifa exercise to give me strength. Agha does not say very much, but there is one thing he says which I will carry to my grave: "It is your enemy and you want to kill it". In other words, no bullshit about "coming to terms" with whatever. It's a fight to the death; the cancer or me.

While I am under treatment, groups throughout Europe, Spain and South America perform exercises on my behalf. There are people in this room today who participated in these exercises, and besides thanking them, there is little I can say beyond the simple fact that I am still with you nine years later. I have absolutely no idea whether or not this effort produced any medical effects, but this I can say. One of the things one drags along behind a difficult and lonely childhood is a feeling of being everlastingly condemned to being unloved and unwanted. When I saw what the possibility of my death meant to the friends all over the world, let alone to my family, this feeling disappeared forever never to return.

Marvellous, not a dry eye in the house.

Of course, if one wants to look at my illness realistically, the cure rate of throat cancers is between eighty and ninety percent. Also, at that time, Aids hadn't yet pushed cancer out of the scarecrow's limelight. But as a poet, it suits me to present myself as a man of indomitable courage, my jaw nobly clenched and staring into the middle distance as I face down my own death.

When they are rolling me into the operating theatre for the endoscopic examination to determine whether the tumour

FICTIONS AND FACTIONS

has not developed elsewhere, somebody puts a card into my hand. I am already fairly heavily drugged with local anesthetic when I look at the card and begin yelling at the top of my voice "Stop, stop, the wrong instructions have been given!"

Doctors and nurses come pounding down the corridor, saying "You musn't get worked up like that, you're going into an operation, you've got to calm down". I hold up the card, and they all look at it, and then look back at me, saying "Yes, so what?"

On the card is written "Remove all teeth".

Just then the dentist who had first examined me comes walking by, whistling, with his hands in his pockets. He bends over me to see what the fuss is all about, takes the card and tears it up, saying "Honestly, the silly buggers" and goes on into theatre.

When they wheel me in, he and the head honcho doctor are immersed in a conversation that has begun some time before. They pursue their dialogue as they delicately ram the instrument down my throat for the recording.

"Here at Curie, we're doing work which is just as good as those guys over in Villejuif."

"You betcha" says my dentist.

"But I tell you what, you know why all the funding goes to Villejuif?"

"Why?" says the dentist.

"Because of the media, that's why" says the head honcho.

"Schwarzenberg?" says the dentist.

... ON BEING CURED

"Exactly" replies Big Doc, "He's President Mitterrand's blue-eyed boy. He's the top talking head on television, ask him about any medical question, he'll come up with a thirty-second opinion that'll fit in nicely before the commercial break."

"They get the coverage and they get the money" says the dentist sadly.

"And all we get is the leftovers here. Our radiation machinery is down half the time and the new stuff is being installed in Villejuif" says the head honcho. "But I tell you, what we're doing here at Curie is as good as anything else in the world, and the guys here do it just as good as Schwarzenberg."

"Gotta get more coverage" says the dentist.

They both look at the endoscope for a moment, and the doctor says to the dentist, "Tell him to keep still a minute, will you?" The dentist leans over me and says "Do you mind holding still a second, so that we can get another reading?"

Terrified, I hold myself as still as a possum.

I hear a whirring and then it stops. The head doctor comes over to me as I lie on the table looking up with the probe stuffed down my throat. He speaks to me for the first time: "It's all right, there aren't any secondaries" he says.

Back upstairs in the hospital room, the anesthetic is wearing off, and Catherine brings me my mail. I open a letter from Brazil: a beautiful and sweet young lady from the friends is shocked to learn of my illness and wants me to get better. In fact, she knows of a ex-priest who specialises in healing cancers, and she will be sending me some herbs from the Amazonian Basin I should take. The only thing is that in order for this cure to work, I must make sure that I don't submit to any modern

FICTIONS AND FACTIONS

technology like chemotherapy or radiation.

When the course of radiation begins at the hospital, I protect myself as much as I can from other patients' emotions by getting there at eight o'clock in the morning and being the first to go under the machine. An added advantage of going in first is that the machinery is still working: breakdowns generally happen later in the day, and the cyclotron or whatever it's called seems to break down at least twice a week.

As I lie on the slab I recite to myself the Fatiha, my zikr and the Ya Shifa. Gazing up at the needle, I think of the ceilings of the room at the side of the Court of the Lions in the Alhambra. I don't know why I do this. Perhaps because those ceilings reflected in the water below are the most beautiful places I know.

The head honcho of the department, the media expert referred to above, generally comes to work at about the time I am laid out on the table beneath the machine. I am there every day on the table at eight-thirty, and every morning he walks in, says hello to the attendant, and ignoring me, casually puts his hand on my neck to feel the tumour. At this time of course, my arms and legs are strapped down and I feel quite humiliated at being handled in this casual way without any kind of acknowledgement of my presence at all. I am a throat and I am a tumour, but I am not a person.

Either I am going to give this prick a piece of my mind, or else I am going to have to do something else: create some kind of relationship. For reasons of obvious self-interest, I don't want to antagonize the doctor that's treating me, so I pursue the latter course. The opportunity presents itself when he speaks English to me; I congratulate him on his good English, and he tells me how he finished off his oncology studies at Harvard Medical

... ON BEING CURED

School. We get into the habit of speaking to each other in English every day, and he gets a kick out of showing his English off to the other members of his department.

After about three weeks of daily treatment during which I get my daily feel-up in passing, he pauses a moment, and then puts his hand back on my neck one more time, keeping it there for a while. He pauses for reflection, and then asks the nurse to call everybody into the radiation chamber immediately, even if they are with other patients. When the whole department of about twenty people is assembled, he informs them that the placement of the rays for my tumour has been carelessly aligned, that the way to the tumour is blocked by the jawbone and thus not entirely bombarded by radiation and that if things were simply left to take their course, about one-fifth of the tumour in my neck would still be there at the end of the treatment cycle. Since radiation is a treatment that cannot normally be practised twice over in the same place, the patient would be forced into other forms of treatment because the department was too careless to do its job properly.

The doctor's cold fury is quite impressive, and it scares me half out of my wits. After all the minions troop out, he smiles at me and goes back to speaking English again. "Don't worry" he says, "with all the hundreds of tumors we deal with in this place, it's very easy for the doctors to fall into their routines, and I've got to wake them up from time to time."

"I'm using you as an excuse. We'll add on three or four extra radiation sessions, change the angle of the machine, and as far as you're concerned, it won't make any difference."

Anyway, as you know, this story has a happy ending, because I am here to tell it. Suffice it to say that I enjoy good health and my tumour never came back.

FICTIONS AND FACTIONS

But I think this story raises a number of therapeutic considerations that may be worth discussing or at least thinking about. Because I am talking about my own case history here, I feel I know some of the answers, but not all. For instance, I have no idea if it was the radiation, my own prayers, your prayers, Agha's prayers or the increase in my own self-confidence and self-trust as a result of one or all of these things that backed me and my immune system up enough to deal with this illness.

The following points can be raised:

1) If I had listened to my sweet and tender friend from Brazil and had foregone high-tech therapy, would I still be alive to tell the tale, or to put it another way, would she have my blood on her hands?

This is a serious matter, because the beginning of wisdom is knowing where your knowledge stops, and the relationship between "soft" and "hard" medicine is obviously important. Also, this knowledge should include a clear awareness of possible distortion. The recent example of the sect leader Dr. Luc Jouret leading his followers of the *Temple Solaire* into what can only be called terminal homeopathy is there to show us how dangerous the prestige of medicine can be when divorced from the Hippocratic Oath and turned towards cultist manipulation. The pyramidal authority structures of medical bodies everywhere in fact encourage cult situations; and an abundant literature shows this to be quite characteristic of psychiatric associations over the last half-century.

Of course, there is no limit to the arrogance of high-tech medicine, as well, because there is so much money involved. How much research money goes into plants or "soft" options? Pharmaceutical companies are heavily committed to new and better molecules, to the exclusion of other options, because the

... ON BEING CURED

former will produce saleable allopathic medicines with a measurable effect. How do you measure a psychiatrist or a homeopath? What is sanity?

On the other hand, every discipline has its craft. If that arrogant old fart of a doctor had not had all that knowledge in his hand, I might not be here to tell the story.

2) What is the difference in therapy between training and craft? At what point does the craft come in, and how is it possible for it to be recognized by those who are not in possession of it?

3) To what extent is it possible to use the "Granada Therapy" as an adjunct to one's training? Examples?

4) What are the limits to a therapy based on inner balance and harmony? What if I want to throw myself out of the window?

5) How and when does one move onto "heavier" techniques, and what criteria does one use to do so?

6) Is there a thesis to be written on the curative properties of the Alhambra?

7) Is there a thesis to be written on the curative properties of television talk shows?

And finally, a few words on the brain and consciousness. Informed opinion in the sixties and seventies seemed to think that the likeliest analogy to the workings of the brain was the computer. This led to a whole raft of articles and books about "cybernetic" awareness, in which the brain was likened to some sort of ultimate calculating machine.

Just as the computer has developed and changed so

FICTIONS AND FACTIONS

immensely since that time, so-called "informed" thinking about the brain and our perception has changed as well. The analogy for the way the brain works is no longer a finite system of calculation like the computer, but an infinitely variable system of reactive adaptation which more than anything else resembles the body's own immune system.

In other words, physiological analysis itself is now saying our intelligence does not come from the amount of information we acquire, but from the flexibility with which we deploy it, and nowadays we are being told this not by philosophical argumentation but by the latest microbiological research.

By now, most of you in this room will have understood the drift of my argument. It is very simply that traditional learning systems, including the Sufi Tradition, have always worked on this basis, i.e. flexibility as opposed to accumulation, adaptation as opposed to construction. We can be pleased or perhaps somewhat bemused that physiological research should at last be catching up with us, but our own problem remains constant, which is the age-old one of integrating this capacity to change into the innermost part of our nature.

Nevertheless, it may be that our way of thinking can make a breach in the fanatical borderline that exists between "hard" and "soft" therapies, and between "hard" and "soft" science. As research heats up in the attempt to find some kind of solution to the HIV virus, most people are still working in terms of some sort of pharmacological barrier, but there are others who are trying to enable the immune system to mutate even faster than the virus. We'll see who wins the race.

Our way of thinking is timeless, but unfortunately, we aren't. Therapist or no therapist, if we can communicate the love in our hearts to the people we come across, we have done something, whether it can be measured or not.

... ON BEING CURED

As far as I am concerned, I am here to learn from you. If there are any young lady therapists who would like to communicate their knowledge of body awareness therapies to me, I will be in the bar downstairs getting drunk. If you feel that this statement is sexist, politically incorrect, and somewhat dumb, you are right.

THE SAGA CONTINUES

Less than six months after the foregoing words were written an unknown hand reached up from within my throat and struck me down again.

At seven in the morning on Saint Valentine's day, I rose up from my chair intending to go to the john, when I suddenly felt that my sphincter had let everything go. I pitched over onto my side and there I was wriggling around on the ground, face-down on the carpet, quite unable to get myself upright again. Once the first moment of absolute panic and horror was over I rolled myself over onto my back, but it didn't help me at all because the left side of my body was entirely paralysed and I couldn't make use of my left hand, arm or leg. Try as I might I couldn't even sit up.

Throughout this incident I never lost consciousness and I realised very quickly that I had had some form of brain stroke with hemiplegia. Our friend Marucha had been walking with a cane since her stroke fifteen years ago, and I remember thinking "Oh shit, it's canes and a wheelchair for me." When I called for help to Catherine, who was still in the bedroom, I realised that I wasn't talking very well either. She came in and immediately called the Samu, which is the French emergency service, explaining the symptoms. "Tell them it's the brain" I

FICTIONS AND FACTIONS

shouted at her, but I don't know if she understood my speech. Both the Samu and the firemen turned up in fifteen minutes with an emergency doctor in attendance who was administering a blood thinner to me about a quarter of an hour after my stroke had declared itself.

My memory of the rest of that day is somewhat patchy because a lot of different people took care of me, but I remember being taken to the neurological ward in the evening, I remember some very courageous orderlies wiping me clean, and most of all I remember recovering the use of my hand, arm and leg by nightfall. "Il a la baraka, celui-là" said one of the doctors to another outside my door (baraka means good luck in French slang, without the mystical connotation it has with the Sufis).

Once again, I had danced towards the edge, and had pulled back before going over.

Then came the period of observation in hospital and all of the tests and scans and arterial checks to see what had happened. A small blood clot had dislodged itself from my right carotid artery; both carotid arteries were highly blocked, which was strange insofar as the rest of my arteries were in good shape; I had no high blood pressure and I neither smoked nor drank. With the help of the cancer specialist that had worked on my radiation ten years before, it was finally decided that it was the external radiation I had received through the neck for my throat that had caused a deterioration. I had been irradiated through both carotid arteries and the buildup of platelets in the artery was situated exactly in the irradiated area. No warning that this might happen had ever been vouchsafed.

When I was taken in for surgery I had still not met the surgeon who was going to wield the scalpel (a situation quite frequent in France where they feel that knowledge is something

... ON BEING CURED

best left to experts). So when they started to administer the anesthetic, I refused to let myself be wheeled into the operating theatre unless I was personally introduced to the surgeon. The message was relayed on with delight by the nurses, and within a few minutes a very angry-looking man was looking down at me from over his surgical mask.

"What's going on here?" he asked me indignantly, "I have studied your file and I know it backwards."

At that point I let them knock me out. I was a file, not a being.

I woke up looking like Robocop or Frankenstein with a very fetching zipper on my throat. The scar took about a month to absorb and doesn't look too bad now. Then I had to go back in and get the right hand artery flushed out and cleaned. The second artery was apparently in a worse state and had to be wrapped up in a Dacron sleeve: when I saw this in my medical file I had a fantasy about having one of those terrible drip-dry shirts from my youth sewn into my neck.

As I write these words I am about three weeks past the second operation: the scar is healing but the nerves in my gullet have been affected and I can't yet feel myself swallow.

I have seen specialists who have told me that my cleft palate should normally heal, that my voice will come back in time and that liquids will stop backing up and pouring out of my nose whenever I try to swallow. Anyway I make my way through each day with the help of painkillers, and I expect things to get better over time.

To my great shame, I have forgotten the name of the young Brazilian lady who offered to send me herbs from the Amazon Basin, and I hope she forgives me. I am not now far from thinking that she was the one who was right all along the line, and that my own patronizing attitude towards her efforts was just another episode in the endless superiority complex of western technological medicine over its native brethren. Then again, an Amazonian leaf may be just as efficient a murder weapon as a surgeon's scalpel.

After all, I must pay homage to the doctors who took care of me. Hi-tech medecine is indeed a most wonderful instrument for dealing with the problems it creates.

May 95

Note from 2002:

I never swallowed properly again and my voice never recovered. Nevertheless I can eat (if I wash it down with vast quantities of water) and I can speak, even if the acting and interpreting is over. I avoid food and socializing at the same time, because it takes longer for me to eat and everybody around the table is forced to watch me chomp away while they wait for dessert.

The good part of it is that I lost about fifty pounds and am more elegant and lissom than before. Having people treat you like you're an imbecile because of your voice handicap is interesting, it makes you realise there are a lot of fools in the world, not even fools, just people who don't look or listen.

Being ill doesn't make you nicer, but it can make you grateful for not being worse off than you are. In hospital you see a lot of souls who have had it far worse than you.

I don't consider myself as cured any more, it's just that the remission is holding so far.

THE CANVAS

Small time   medium time   big time
simple problems   complicated solutions
complicated problems   simple solutions
stop and listen   watch and ward
care for yourself and care for others

Care for others then care for yourself
treat as you would wish yourself to be treated
if you have no money you can still pay a bribe
the bribe you can pay is called consideration
people are bought with consideration for others

You have been bought without even knowing it
you are owned and you find it normal
not to know who the proprietor is
what are you for   what's it all about
there's got to be an explanation for all this

The explanation's simple   you're here and I'm there
you're there and I'm here   we just changed places
no magic   love sometimes   life, quoi
movement   shifting   sliding   slippery sloping
you think you're going backwards but in fact you're moving on

Nothing is big   nothing small   all is happy medium
somewhere in the middle trying not to draw the fire
my failure becomes more manifest as I begin to grow up
from medium   to large   to outsize   to gigantic
a painting must always be larger than the canvas it's painted on

STORIES

A CHRISTMAS LETTER

31.12.98

Hi everybody!

Of all the possible hellish forms of literature known to mankind, the collective letter must be the worst. The problem is not so much in the writer as in the audience, because the news being discussed has got to be watered down to accommodate everyone one knows, which pretty much means that most contentious issues and the more exciting gossip is necessarily swept under the carpet. Still, I'll try. But I warn you, I may not succeed.

To begin with, the family is well and healthy. This has not been such an obvious matter because some of this letter's readers will not have been aware of Catherine's recent health hassles, I tend to hog the limelight on this. Suffice it to say that she carefully waited until her vacation had started before having her routine mammography test done, and the test turned up a tumour in July, three days after I had arrived in New York with the firm intention of spending a month in the country of my birth visiting friends, getting some orgiastic shopping done in NYC and seeing my cousins and their families in the Bay Area. When Catherine spoke to me on the phone, she indicated that she'd like to have her vacation before dealing with the cancer, which didn't sound too good an idea to me, so I hopped on the next flight back to Paris and walked in on her. She was gratifyingly pleased to see me, so we worked out a plan that she would have her endoscopic exam immediately, which she did: the tumour turned out to be undeveloped enough not to have to sacrifice the breast or require chemotherapy after the operation, but only radiation. We therefore went through with the two weeks in Turkey that we

FICTIONS AND FACTIONS

had planned, and Catherine underwent radiation from mid-August to mid-October. As of now the prognosis is excellent, and she will resume her teaching work on a part-time basis halfway through January.

The next six months should be okay, and she will be taking retirement next July, which means that we will be more available to infest our nearest and dearest thoughout the world, and we have every intention of doing so. Be warned.

The kids: Max is still happily enjoying a life of conjugal bliss with his beloved Julie. They haven't spent more than a day or so apart since they first saw each other at a party five years ago, which must be incredibly boring but I guess it suits them. I spent twenty-five years of professional life on the road, so I'm not best qualified to judge this kind of situation. Max was going to come to Turkey with us, but then he was hired for a cabaret-theatre show and had to pig it in a three-star hotel in St. Tropez for three months. Ghastly work, but someone has to do it.

Thomas finished off his final teacher training year in Tours and so I went down there with a rented truck and we moved his stuff back to Paris, where our old friends John and Alice (who also happen to be his godparents) proposed that he occupy their Paris apartment at cost. So he is now rather nicely set up in a very pleasant flat and is teaching his first year of full-time *professorat* at a Lycée in the Paris outskirt of Evry-Courcouronnes. Traditionally, young teachers are always put into the toughest establishments with juvenile delinquency-cum-race/immigration situations, but his school is better run than most and he is able to do his job in OK conditions. I find it a little strange to think that he is now a fully-fledged civil servant, with a job that he can keep until retirement in thirty-five years time.

... CHRISTMAS LETTER

In parallel to these events I received an unexpected subsidy for printing the new Tractus books which had been hanging fire for two years, so I went ahead with their printing, indulging myself to the extent that I included a book of my own pieces among them. *The Rules or Secrets of the Naqshbandi Order* by Omar Ali-Shah and *Lights of Asia* by his father, the Sirdar Ikbal Ali Shah are two books that any publisher would be proud to have on his list, the first being an updating of a set of sixteenth-century meditation/action themes which Ali-Shah shows to be totally relevant to people's situations and thinking today, and the other book being a general introduction to the four main world religions (Islam, Christianity, Judaism & Buddhism), told from their own texts, and without the slightest trace of politically-based manipulation or ideological axe to grind. These are both books that will be as relevant twenty years from now as they are today. RSNQ of course deals specifically with the Sufi Tradition, even if the rules themselves are universally applicable, but LOA should really be in the curriculum of any school or university, because the simple fundamentals of the main religions are no longer part of school syllabuses, and this generalized ignorance is having dire consequences.

About my own book, *The Woman I Love,* I would hope the same long-term relevance applies but it could just be wishful thinking. The title was one on my mind for a long time, but I thought it would better apply to a book about a single relationship. When I realised that I was putting together poems about all sorts of different situations with my own age varying between eleven and fifty-eight, I saw that the title was still valid, because throughout a lifetime a man (or conversely, a woman) loves many men/women in many different kinds of ways. This is why I subtitled the book 'poems on womankind' which I now think is wrong: the book deals with individuals, there is no womanly abstraction there, one loves only one woman at a

FICTIONS AND FACTIONS

time even if the focus changes. I then did something which has caused some comment and which, to my knowledge, nobody has ever done before, I simply made a list of all the women who had affected me enough to induce me to write something, and I found myself with quite a long list, including some who really wouldn't know me from Adam. I then reduced the list to include only ladies whom I could identify with a specific poem. Some were colleagues like Nadine whom I did not write about, but who was the first person who ever asked to keep a copy of a poem I wrote, i.e., the first person who ever valued me as a poet, others were friends of a more intimate nature, as well as my mother and my noble Catherine, who span my lifetime. Flatteringly, some ladies were annoyed not to be on the list: to them I can say that a new cast is being assembled for the reprint, which hopefully will be done soon. If you're really nice (or really nasty—it works both ways) I'll put your name in lights! Casting calls begin in January.

To complete the scandalous overview of this wholesome family newsletter, I should also mention that one of the dedicatees of the book asked Catherine this summer what she felt like having all those names publicly cited alongside hers: "I know who he sleeps with at night" she replied.

But as the actor once said: "Enough talk about myself, tell me honestly what <u>you</u> think of me."

Back to this supremely banal chronicle: in October word came through after years of suspense that the family house in New York City had finally found a buyer, so Catherine and I went there to help clear the house, which turned out to be no sinecure. The weather was unbelievable, a perfect Indian summer, and we managed to do some creative spending in places like Filene's Basement, as well as steal a wonderful weekend in Greenport with Philip Price, but for the most part we had to organise the removal of my late mother's sculpture and effects. In the end we decided that the only way to do it would be to pack a container and ship it all to the country place in Alba, Ardèche. Getting quotes from movers and everything took two weeks and we finally got everything packed away. The place was then so devastated that I couldn't bear the thought of even sleeping there one night and we both cleared out back to Paris without staying on, thus missing many of our friends.

This situation brought out some quite irrational reactions in me, which are not shared by Catherine, Max and Thomas because they have no particular affinity with New York City, where I spent the first ten years of my life. It's true to say that the sale of this house will provide me with the only financial security I'm ever likely to have, but it's also true to say that losing the family house was horrible. I cried all the way to the bank. For good measure I also wrote a couple of very touching poems about being cut off from one's roots. This is in fact a fairly good example of my approach to writing: always based on something real (I have absolutely no imagination at all) but the final product does tend to be a little distorted and has been known to give offence.

The packing of my mother's belongings was an event which was to have interesting reverberations: the moving company tried to make me sign a document, presenting it to me in the half-lit entrance as an "insurance receipt", which was in fact a contract of agreement to an overrun on the orginal estimate of more than two thousand dollars because of "extra packing materials". I refused to sign this and gave them a certified check for the amount agreed on in the original estimate. Then started a wonderful cat-and-mouse game on the part of the moving company, who first threatened to impound the container in New York, and then later in Marseille, unless I

FICTIONS AND FACTIONS

sent them the extra money. My lawyer in New York advised me to pay, saying it wasn't worth taking them to court for two thousand bucks because court and lawyer's fees would cost much more than this. At this point I realised that this was probably a sort of Standard Operating Procedure for movers: if they ransom your household effects for two thousand, most people will pay because they need the stuff immediately (this happened to our friends the Swingles). Since we had no immediate need for my mother's furniture and sculpture, we decided to wait it out. I sent a conciliatory fax to the movers, asking them to itemize their extra expense, and received an Alice-in-Wonderland justification of expenses in which the two blister packs of a dozen rolls of brown tape I saw them using were billed at six hundred dollars. Gold-plated Scotch tape. Since I knew that the container was now in Marseille and hence came under French law, I decided to wait the whole thing out. I told the boss of the moving company that I was sympathetic to his predicament but that he had to deliver the container before I would consider paying him. Finally, three weeks ago, the mover's customs agent contacted me for the documents they needed, asking why wasn't my name and address on the papers the movers had given them. The container was delivered to Alba as planned with two months delay, I paid off extra storage charges to the agent of $250 and the movers never dared send another bill.

I tell this story in awesome detail because I have since heard that this little trick is something U.S. moving companies are in the habit of pulling, so a word to the wise... It's interesting to note that the French legal system provides much better protection to the consumer in cases like this, both because an estimate is a legally binding document here and also because in the U.S.A. misdemeanors are never really prosecuted below $3500. If you cheat someone out of two grand, you're basically in the clear.

... CHRISTMAS LETTER

Catherine, myself and Tom (who had spent his mid-term break with us in New York) got back to Paris and we then left immediately for London for my *soeur de lait* Johanna's wedding party, a very joyous affair indeed, with traditional English folk dancing. There's something very touching about an older couple getting married, and Martin and she seem to fit into the appropriate category of realistic romance. When you get to our age about half of one's friends who were married have become single again, so that getting hitched requires a special act of faith. The betting in the grandstands was that this one would work out.

Of course, staying with Johanna and Martin in their house meant that I wasn't going to escape Johanna's cross-examination about my book. To put this in context it should be remembered that Johanna and I have built a lifelong friendship on the capacity we have to ask each other uncomfortable questions which have to be answered honestly, because Johanna is one of the few people I know besides myself who has elevated truth to the status of a cult. It is rare to find someone who both loves and accepts you and who is willing to drag you over the coals just for the exercise, and she and I have performed this function for each other since we were children.

"You have dedicated your book to thirty different women. Did you ask their permission before putting them on that list?"

"No," I replied, "they are all real, all are either friends or persons who have inspired me to write something, either for myself, for them, or to work out something in my own mind. The list I started with was even longer, but I weeded out all persons to whom I could not assign a specific poem. For the most part, it is difficult to attach a poem to a particular dedicatee, and I have done it this way on purpose. In this way their anonymity is, in fact, guaranteed."

FICTIONS AND FACTIONS

Johanna didn't look too convinced but declined to pursue the matter. I didn't dare tell her that her name had been on the original list but that I took it off because I have not yet written the poem. In spite of my love for her, I don't know if I would dare do so. In fact, there is no justifying a writer. In my life I have sincerely tried to respect my religion, my sense of justice and what I quaintly call my code of honour, and I have paid a greater price for doing this than most of my friends realise. But it is also for this reason that I refuse to water down or censor what I write, it is the one area where I am beholden to no man but myself.

After Jo and Martin's wedding party, Catherine had to get back for her final physical, so I thought I'd kill a few days in London. I didn't feel like selling books so I decided to try and look up one of the dedicatees of the book, who had given me a postal address years ago c/o her aunt and uncle in Harrow, Middlesex. This person had sworn undying love to me in early 1992, telling me that she was moving to Paris to live near me, had moved in with a younger man a month later and had married him without saying a word to me.

I walked up to her aunt and uncle's place in Harrow, and was about to turn away from the door after ringing when, to my surprise, the lady in question came down from upstairs—apparently she now lived in England and was temporarily separated from the man her daughters called her toyboy. We left the house and caught up with each others' news as we walked the streets of the neighbourhood. It was just like old times, really, we managed to recreate both the unquenchable desire and the endless anger in our relationship within about ten minutes of beginning to speak to each other. As we crossed a small footbridge leading to the local suburban railway station, over a yawning chasm far above the main line railway tracks a few hundred yards below, an unfortunate incident occurred; a

... CHRISTMAS LETTER

prime example of being in the wrong place at the wrong time.

She was explaining how she had never been able to trust me because I kept on going back to see Catherine and the kids on weekends when I was living in Brussels: I pointed out that the fact I had left them, had taken a permanent job in Brussels and had bought a house there so that she and I could live there together indicated a certain seriousness of intention. She then cited toyboy as an example saying "He's not the least interested in his kids and wife and doesn't even see them: there's a man who knows how to treat his woman!"— whereupon I picked my friend up and threw her bodily over the railing.

She sailed down almost motionless, without a cry, and landed with a dull thud on the railway tracks way below. I looked at her motionless form, so far away that I couldn't even see her features, and I realised that no one could have survived such a fall. I looked around me and there was nobody on the walkway or on the road above: there had been no witnesses.

Then a couple of young boys in school uniform came casually walking past, whistling. I turned away, walked straight up into Kenton railway station and took the next train back into Central London, where I joined Martin and Johanna for dinner. I left the next day and have been in Paris ever since. I read in the papers that the Coroners' Verdict was Death by Misadventure.

Of course I really do blame myself and I am very aware of the upset it has caused to her daughters, but there has been an unexpected fringe benefit. She always told me in the days of our romance that if she died first she would haunt me, and I feel her presence every day now, ever more powerfully in myself, even more than during that blessed time when we were lovers. For the first and last time, my lady has kept a promise.

FICTIONS AND FACTIONS

In view of our mutual circumstances, I guess there was no other way. Or was there? Maybe there are questions it is better not to answer.

So I hope you've all enjoyed the Hayter family chronicle for 1998, I don't know if 1999 will turn out to be more or less eventful. Maybe a few rapes and a bankruptcy might make it a bit more interesting, I'll see what I can do.

Episodes for the coming year will be, *inter alia*: how will Catherine deal with retirement? How does Augy the blowhard deal with the fact that people won't pay to listen to his voice any more? Will Tom survive the Blackboard Jungle? Will Max finally get discovered and achieve the stardom he has been groomed for?

Tune in next year for the sequel…

The Author

SCHNICK-SCHNACK

The two women lay side by side on two chaise-longues made of white painted planks with mattresses on top. The mattresses were wet from the dip in the pool they had just taken, and they both lay on their backs letting the water dry off their bodies little by little. After a while the blonde woman looked down to check if her nipples weren't getting sunburned, reached down to the bag on the ground next to her, pulled out a tube, unscrewed the cap, and began to rub some skin protection cream into her breasts. The dark-haired girl by her side adjusted the sunglasses on her nose and sighed.

"It's nice to be back on the island again" she said.

The blonde woman carefully screwed the top of the tube back on, stowed it in her bag below, and settled back to concentrate on absorbing the sun.

"Ja" she said, "You can't imagine how the winter was this year in Berlin. The snow it started in October and it ended in April. Ve live like eskimos."

"In England, it was just damp all the time" said the dark-haired girl.

After a moment the blonde woman said: "Did I tell you that Brian came to see me in Berlin this winter?"

"No, did he really?"

"Yes. He needed to have his teeth fixed, and last summer I had mentioned that I had a good dentist in Berlin. So he just phoned me one day and just said "Get me an appointment with your dentist, I'm coming to Berlin tomorrow." It was a terrible situation, I had to find him somewhere to stay at a girl-friend's apartment."

"Summer lovers ought really to hibernate through the winter" said the dark girl sagely.

"But wait" said the blonde, "it was much worse than that even. I made him his appointment and he went and got three fillings and a bridge over three molars at the dentist's, then he went back to England. Two weeks later Raffi and I are sitting having breakfast when the maid comes in with the morning post and I see that there is a bill from the dentist addressed to Mr and Mrs. I was getting the coffee from the kitchen, so that it was Raffi that went through the morning letters, and he put them all beside the plate while he read the Algemeiner Zeitung. I could see the back of the letter next to his plate but I was completely paralysed. Then he put down the paper, opened all the envelopes of the bills and looked at the one from the dentist. Then he looked up at me, put his hand into his wallet pocket, pulled out his chequebook and wrote out a cheque for the bill, put it into an envelope, put a stamp on it and addressed it to the dentist. Then he looked up at me over his glasses and said: "It's bad enough to have your wife take on a lover without having to pay for his dental work as well." I didn't know what to say.

"Did he ever mention it again?" said the dark-haired girl.

"Yes. A month later he was reading the newspaper in the evening, and he looked up and said: "I think it's time you came to a decision about that English boy." Since then he hasn't said a word.

"What did you do?"

"I phoned Brian and told him it was better we not see

... SCHNICK-SCHNACK

each other again."

The blonde woman stared at the reflections in the water of the pool for a moment, and then said:

"Tell me Amanda, you're English, you know English people, ja?"

"Well yes, I suppose so."

"Then tell me, vot class is Brian?"

"What do you mean?"

"Vere he come from in England?"

"In England nowadays they call it lower middle class, but his father was a workman so he's working class, no doubt about it."

"What, I go schnick-schnack with man from working class and you no say nothing about it to me? I thought you were my friend."

"Well things have changed a bit in England you know, it's considered quite normal to sleep with someone from the working class nowadays. Of course, one would draw the line at marrying them."

"Ach, he seemed so delicate and refined and he was really worker all the time, mein Gott …"

A silence settled down between the two friends as they let the sun penetrate their bodies. Then the dark girl said: "What did you see in him anyway? I must say I never found him all that interesting."

FICTIONS AND FACTIONS

The blonde woman smiled in reminiscence. "Is because it vas not easy for him. He lose confidence, lose excitement too sometimes, so you have to do all sorts of things to keep him interested. Very nice, take long time. Raffi, he always ready, day or night, sun or storm. Schnick-schnack in the morning, schnick-schnack in the evening, schnick-schnack after lunch. He is great big fucking bore is Raffi, but is good man. And at least he's not working-class. Look you, Amanda, I want you to make to me promise. You see me interested in man this summer, you tell me what class before it is too late, okay?"

"Okay, I'll be happy to be your social indicator."

The two women lay back in companionable silence and let the sun do its rejuvenating work. At the far end of the pool their men sat in the shade, playing cards. Their newly-burning skins were gently caressed by a slight breeze as the summer season began in Ibiza.

THE MONK'S BODY

I came down to the island with Johnny Durphy in order to keep him company while he moved his personal effects out of his house. I happened to own a large old car at the time and he had suggested that it would be nice if we could go down together and bring the stuff back in it. Common friends had told me that his wife had run off with his best friend about eight months before, and that the two lovers were now expecting a baby. I didn't ask him any questions and he didn't volunteer all that much information, but I assumed that the trip down meant that he was leaving the house to her.

The house in Ibiza was quite one of the most beautiful houses I have ever seen anywhere. It was situated halfway down a hill in the middle of a well-tended garden, a rather simple white house built along a terrace in the style of the local fincas. On a lower terrace was a swimming pool and a kind of guest house suite with a simple kitchen and a studio that Johnny said he had planned to use as a music room. He had designed and mostly built the house with his own hands about fifteen years before and was obviously completely in love with the place.

He spent his evenings drinking too much vino rosado and talking about how it was necessary to make a clean break with the past, to leave one's own story and detach oneself from all material possessions and encumbrances. In the morning, however, he would trim the vines on the terrace and retie the stems to the terrace-beams in order to make them grow in a different pattern. Then he would inspect the fruit trees to see how they were doing, being particularly concerned with the fate of the avocado trees he had planted the previous year. Only one of them had survived and it was looking pretty peaked.

FICTIONS AND FACTIONS

He'd talk on and on for hours about the various kinds of trees he had planted and nurtured, then he'd suddenly stop, take a deep breath, and say: "Actually, I don't give a shit," and stomp off to the kitchen to pour himself another vino rosado.

On the morning of the day before we left I was introduced to an attractive blonde lady in the square at Santa Eulalia. I invited her to have a coffee at the cafe terrace nearby but she declined, saying that she had to go and open her office. Since she was dragging a heavy shopping bag, I offered to carry it to her office, which was a few streets away.

As she opened her door the phone began ringing, a potential client from England was enquiring about a house she had already shown him to know if she thought the garage would be big enough to take the Mercedes he had just ordered. As she fielded this problem, she opened a bottle of apple juice with one hand and gave me a glass to fill for myself, then she tucked the receiver into her shoulder and took down notes with her other hand, reassuring her clients that everything would work out and that they need not fret. After they hung up, she said: "They all think I'm their mother. Mutti Gudrun, psychoanalyst and real estate agent. It's amazing."

"Not so amazing" I said. "You're the only native they can talk to. You're their anchor."

"Ja, but what a time waster. I have work to do."

"You could always add on a shrinking fee, like a cover charge in a restaurant."

Just then, a Dutch couple appeared in the doorway, along with a Spaniard in workman's clothes. The Spaniard was from the Post Office, he had come to collect the illegally installed telephone answering machine. Gudrun looked down her nose

... THE MONK'S BODY

at him in her best German patrician style and gave him hell in colloquial Spanish for not bringing the legal machine she had ordered from the Post Office three months before. He left with his tail between his legs. She then turned to the Dutch couple and invited them to sit down and make themselves at home in perfect Dutch while she prepared the contract for them to sign. I caught her eye and got up to leave. She signalled that I should wait around and come back after, so I went outside.

I couldn't have left, even if I had wanted to, so fascinated was I by Gudrun's rhythm and speed of thinking. I had never seen anyone as mobile, so completely adept at moulding herself into the trace of other people's ideas and wishes. The Dutch couple needed to be consoled for the loss of money and congratulated for their courage in signing a lease, so she praised and caressed them with the same words over and over again, like a litany. But it was done without cynicism, she simply knew instinctively what their state was and the right words came out of her accordingly, without any conscious effort on her part.

I had never seen anyone with such suppleness and flexibility of spirit, and I listened to her, overhearing her swimming about in people's minds in five different languages with the freedom of a fish, and I was besotted.

When we talked in her office after the Dutch couple had left, Gudrun told me she had come to Ibiza from Germany and had stayed on the island as a tour guide. She had worked in tourism for a number of years and had then set up her own partnership as a real estate broker. As we talked, I suddenly realised that I was holding her hand across the desk and touching her at every opportunity, and that she was doing the same with me. Just as our minds were frolicking in each other's wake, our bodies were simply following suit. And what was strange about it was that it wasn't consciously sexual at all, it

FICTIONS AND FACTIONS

was rather like children whose familiarity with each others' bodies is so complete that they draw energy from each other through their touch. It was a kind of pre-sexual contact which could develop into desire but which was already beyond it.

I must confess that when I realised what was going on, my first instinct was to become male, to reduce this contact by sexualizing it. I invited her to lunch, she said no she never took lunch, she preferred to go home and take the midday sun. I asked her if she were free for dinner and she accepted, saying it would be lovely to see her old friend Johnny again and that we could all meet at eight-thirty at Sandy's Bar.

When I got back to the house, Johnny was emerging from the previous evening's alcoholic vapours. I made him a cup of coffee and told him I had met a beautiful friend of his called Gudrun and that we'd made a date to have dinner with him that evening and that we'd be meeting at Sandy's.

"I don't think that's very considerate of you" he said quietly.

"What do you mean?" I said.

"I didn't come here to socialize."

"What are you talking about?"

"If you don't know what I'm talking about, there's nothing on God's earth that'll make you realise."

I was absolutely furious. "What are you giving me this shit for anyway?" I said. "I meet a pretty girl, invite her for dinner. It seems normal that we'd all go out to dinner together considering she's a friend of yours, but if you don't feel like coming, far be it from me to force you."

... THE MONK'S BODY

He sipped his coffee, then looked up at me cynically.

"She won't sleep with you," he said, "not in a thousand years."

As we climbed into the car to go to Sandy's that evening, Johnny cast an eye over my overcoat, business suit and tie, and said: "Dressed fit to kill, aren't you?" When we walked into Sandy's Bar, I saw that my clothes were far too formal for the laid-back style of the Ibicenco expatriates. Johnny, with his clapped-out Gucci loafers and worn Armani jacket hit exactly the right note of careless elegance.

The habitués of Sandy's gathered round Johnny like moths around a flame: "Johnny baby! How're you doing?" and Johnny fielded them all with consummate ease, asking about people's boats and stonewalling any more personal questions with considerable aplomb. I realised only then that Johnny was one of the most prominent cuckolds on the island, since the spouse of his wife's boy friend was also at the bar with us, chattering away brightly. I could see now why he was less than delighted at the prospect of coming back to Sandy's. Nevertheless he carried it all off very well, circulating from person to person at the bar, saying hello to all his old friends. He had after all lived off and on for fifteen years in the expatriate microcosm of the island and had had time to build up quite a network of friends and acquaintances, most of whom seemed to be in the bar that evening.

I didn't know anyone there, so I was kind of out of it. I ended up talking to a rather intense Puerto Rican girl who told me that after years of spiritual exercises she was now able to read a book without opening the pages. She would just put her hand on the spine and she simply knew. I pointed out that the next rung on the ladder of awareness would be just to look at the outside of the book without going through the

FICTIONS AND FACTIONS

timewasting process of physically touching it. "Yeah," she said, "that's true. I'll work on it."

When Gudrun walked in nobody looked up except for me. I guess they were all used to her beauty, I wasn't. She had on the same clothes she had been wearing that morning, a multi-coloured sweater and tight brown corduroy jeans with a thin belt wrapped twice around her slim waist. The electric blue of her eyes framed by the pale shoulder-length hair seemed to project a beam right across the café. I came up to her, kissed her on both cheeks in greeting, and went off to get her a drink at the bar. Johnny greeted her like a long-lost friend, embracing her and kissing her full on the lips. I came back with her white wine and we chatted a while before Johnny was once again taken over by all the old sweats.

Gudrun and I moved to the niche underneath the staircase where we sat down and began talking together. The same thing happened as had happened that morning: I was completely mesmerized. We sat there talking about I don't know what with my hand holding hers and my knee touching her thigh next to me. I had the impression that her blue eyes could see right through me, right through the parts of me I didn't like or was ashamed of, and yet still liking what she saw. And I suddenly thought: "If I could only see myself now as she sees me, I wouldn't have a problem in the world."

What was extraordinary was this capacity for undivided attention: I had the feeling that I occupied her totally and absolutely. This of course was untrue, and I had seen for myself how untrue this was that very morning when I had watched her dealing with five different people in four different languages, each one of them convinced that he or she was the only one that counted. But this is something I only realised much later, upon reflexion. For the moment, I was well and truly besotted.

... THE MONK'S BODY

After a while Johnny came back from doing the rounds and we began to discuss what restaurant we would be going to. There ensued a long discussion between them about which establishments were patronizable and which were beyond the pale because they had gone off so badly. It was a conversation that only an Ibiza expat could be party to, so that I was effectively shut out of the discussion. I remember thinking how strange it was that everybody who lives on an island always ends up thinking of it as the centre of the world.

It was ultimately decided that we'd go to Marianne's across the street, mainly because she had been in Sandy's earlier and therefore knew that Johnny was on the island. If Johnny left without going to her restaurant at least once it would mortally offend her status as one of Johnny's old friends. So we trooped across the road and went into her restaurant. Marianne came to greet us, extending her cheek to be kissed in a birdlike gesture, holding the rest of her body well back as if afraid we might make a grab at her stern. She sat us down at a corner table with me next to Gudrun and Johnny opposite her. We ordered our food and a bottle of white wine, and the converstaion began to centre around people and events on the island that I had no knowlege of, so that for the most part I was unable to contribute to the conversation. When the talk would take a more general turn I would venture some remark, and the remark would be taken up by Johnny, turned around and examined, and then somehow it would be found wanting and discarded. The talk went on more and more animatedly between Gudrun and Johnny and I fell more and more into silence, feeling vaguely resentful without quite knowing why. When the time came to pay the bill, I put my hand into my pocket only to remember that Johnny had borrowed half the money I had on me just before setting out for dinner and that I therefore no longer had enough money on me to pay the bill for all three of us. He acknowledged Gudrun's thank you very

FICTIONS AND FACTIONS

graciously as he paid the bill with my money.

It was decided to go along to La Villa, a new bar that had recently been purchased by a famous racing car driver. It was a pleasant place, all white, in a building set slightly back from the street, and there were the usual Ibiza bench-like seats organised in nooks around the walls of the bar with mattresses cut to size on them all to make it comfortable. We sat down three abreast and ordered our finos, the two men on either side of Gudrun. The same kind of half-tacky half-gossipy talking went on as before. Johnny and she would gossip about various people they both knew and who were right in front of us at the bar just out of earshot. Whenever the racing car driver, who was sitting at the end of the bar, went away to one of the Formula One circuits, his wife's lover, who was sitting to our own left, would climb in the toilet window, which had been left open on purpose, in order to see the racing driver's wife. The husband didn't know anything about what was going on, but since the house was conveniently situated at the top of a hill, all the the neighbours had an unencumbered view.

The desultory talking went on as before, with Gudrun and Johnny hitting it off together and me remaining rather silent by their side. Occasionally Gudrun would turn to me to say something but Johnny would always focus the attention back upon himself by means of some transparently generalized philosophical type of remark that indirectly referred to his own suffering and situation. This manipulation was clearly designed to elicit a motherly response from Gudrun, and it was carried off quite brilliantly because there was no obvious demand being made, it just sort of happened that way. And it also just so happened that he had one hand on her thigh and the other locked in her left hand as this went on, making it impossible for her to turn towards me so that he was mobilizing her both as a friend and as a woman.

... THE MONK'S BODY

Gudrun accepted this quite happily and her considerable power of concentration was now quite focused on him. Johnny then began to let the male part of his little web take the upper hand. He began praising her beauty in the form of a dialogue with me, using me to echo what he wanted to say to Gudrun, and I happened to remark that her hair was almost albino. "Almost albino" he repeated, laughing derisively, "Honestly, what a thing to say!" and I was reduced to impotent silence once again, because nothing in the world was more beautiful to me in that moment than Gudrun's almost albino hair, and he had once more completely twisted and turned round the intention I was trying to express.

Suddenly I was projected back in time to the period when I was around Johnny, about twenty years before. We had shared the same apartment in New York City when he was studying music at Juilliard and I was in Divinity School. We shared the apartment for about six months and it was at that time that the friendship had grown up between us. Our lifestyles were very different: I was an early riser and I became used to making coffee for Johnny and whatever ever-changing girl would emerge from his bedroom in the mornings. There was only one of all the girls that I myself was interested in. She was an acquaintance of Johnny's and mine and he knew that I wanted her. I invited her to dinner one evening and since Johnny happened to be in the apartment, he came along as well. By the end of the meal she was talking only with him and when she came back with both of us for a drink he seduced her right in front of me. When they came out of the bedroom the next morning I made coffee for both of them, and I never said a word about it to him or to anyone else but I found myself another apartment and within two weeks I had moved out.

I maintained my friendship with Johnny over the years and in fact had completely forgotten the incident until tonight.

FICTIONS AND FACTIONS

And as I sat there next to Johnny and Gudrun I was overcome by a wave of irrational anger. "My God" I thought, "the bastard's going to do it again!" And so I sat there seething and listening to Johnny burbling on, watching pattern. His speciality was to get himself involved in some impossible intellectual proposition, bog himself down in his own fabrication, and then smile with delightfully modest self-deprecation, saying "I'm not very clear, am I?" so that Gudrun would reassure him.

"Not only are you not clear" I broke in, "but you're full of shit."

Gudrun and Johnny both turned toward me with the same look of amazed disapproval at this unprovoked attack. Johnny calmed the situation down with his usual polish, saying that perhaps I hadn't understood the full implications of what he had been trying to express, then he and Gudrun turned their backs on me once again and went back to their dialogue.

At that point I realised I had to get out of there for a while. I stood up and put my coat on, saying: "My eyes are hurting from the smoke in here."

"What are you going to do?" said Gudrun.

"I'm going outside for a minute to bay at the moon" I said, and left.

The moon outside was in a half-crescent. I looked up at it, then cast my eyes about to see if there was anyone in the street: there was no one to be seen. I glanced at my watch; it was now two-thirty, then I walked down into a sidestreet, just in case a car might come around the corner of the street I was in. "What a strange world" I thought to myself, "that you should have to hide yourself in order to pray." I shut my eyes and the sharp night air cooled my eyelids as I gathered my

... THE MONK'S BODY

thoughts together to see over and beyond the moon.

"Oh Lord," I said in my mind's eye, "you've got to help me now. I pulled out of the sexual rat-race twenty years ago because of this guy, so look, please don't let me get back into it now. I'll make love to this woman if it's your will that I do so or I'll not make love to her if such is your will. Protect me from envy, don't let me become jealous, don't let me lose sight of my great good fortune, the gift you bestowed on me of becoming aware of Yourself, and the possibility of discerning your trace in the hearts of others. You've given me neither beauty, nor riches nor power, because you know how fragile I am, that I not be distracted from the adoration of Yourself. The beauty of this woman and that of every man, woman and child is but the trace of your breath upon our mirror. But please Lord, if this ridiculous self-imposed chastity of mine is wrong, make it known to me, don't let me become an evil-minded censor, because how can one possibly know divine love if one has not known human passion?"

I opened my eyes, breathed deeply and looked around. The sky was still and clear, the stars shining, the windows in the street all dark, the sleeping people behind all gathering their strength to face the morrow. I wandered around the deserted streets of Santa Eulalia for about ten minutes. In the main street a drunk came staggering up to me asking me if I knew a bar that was still open. "They're all closed at this time" I said.

When I got back to La Villa the curtains had been drawn and the door shut but not locked. I went inside: there were only about a dozen hardcore barflies left. Johnny and Gudrun were deep in intense conversation. They looked up as I came back in and sat down next to them, then resumed their dialogue. "We're still good friends" Johnny was saying, "and we want to keep it that way. I've just come back to collect a few things that I need, that's all."

FICTIONS AND FACTIONS

"You know, I lived for seven years with a German boy called Hans, I think you knew him," said Gudrun. "We weren't getting along very well, so he left me and went back to Germany. The next summer I was in the office one day when a friend dropped in and said he had seen Hans and his parents in one of the hotels. So that day after work I went over to the hotel to say hello to them. I went up to their room and knocked on their door, and when the door opened I saw that the whole room behind them was full of packing cases. I looked in the packing cases and there was everything that I owned. They had all three gone to the house, used his key to get in and had simply stripped it bare. They had taken away everything that was his and everything that was mine."

"And what did you do?" I asked.

"Nothing, I did nothing, I said nothing, what's the point? I still see him sometimes, we're still friends."

I noticed that Johnny was listening to her with great attention. It was now just past three o'clock in the morning and only two or three of the old stalwarts remained in the bar. The manager turned out a few lights as a delicate suggestion that we might all leave. We all put on our coats and went outside. Johnny had his arm around Gudrun's shoulders and Gudrun had her arm around his waist as the three of us went down the steps. In the street, Gudrun slipped her free arm though mine in order to join me to them as we walked towards her car. In front of her car Johnny suggested that we all go back to his house for a nightcap. But unlike the young lady twenty years before, Gudrun was too old a hand for that, she too was a survivor of the war between the sexes. "No, I've got work to do tomorrow morning," she said. "At least I won't have to bring them coffee in bed" I thought.

Johnny and Gudrun kissed each other goodnight on the

... THE MONK'S BODY

mouth, Ibiza-style. When my turn came I avoided her mouth because for me kissing a woman on the mouth is the beginning of making love and not just a friendly gesture. She got into her car, waved goodbye and started off as Johnny and I walked across the square to where we had left our own car. Gudrun's car drove around the square and came down behind us, then stopped about fifty yards further down the road. While Johnny climbed into our car, I walked down the street to see what she was doing. She had stopped her car outside the Post Office in order to put her mail in the letterbox. She came back to her car where I was waiting and we kissed goodnight again, this time Ibiza-style. My hand rested lightly on the small of her back inside her overcoat and I could feel the whiplash strength of her slim body. Her lips were very soft. "I'll come by and say goodbye to you tomorrow morning" I said. "Yes, do that if you feel like it," she said.

The next morning while Johnny was still sleeping, I drove the car to Gudrun's office. She was on the phone when I came in. "How nice of you to have come" she said brightly after hanging up. "How are you feeling this morning?" I said that I felt all right. "I had a terrible hangover" she said, "and when I got to the office there were two clients waiting for me." We talked desultorily for about five minutes, then she said "You'll have to excuse me now, I've got some phone calls to make." So I stood up and she accompanied me to the door, stretching out her cheek to be kissed with the same birdlike gesture of remoteness as the lady in the restaurant the night before. As I drove away I realised that I was no more and no less to her than any one of the thousand-odd clients and tourists she came across every season.

When I got back to the house, Johnny had already prepared the things we were taking away. There was hardly anything there: just two guitars, a few records, and a pile of papers. When I asked to borrow a book, he said "No, I'd prefer

FICTIONS AND FACTIONS

that nothing else be taken." As he shut up the house before we drove down to the ferry, he said: "I just didn't want him to read my letters. She can have everything else."

After we unloaded the car into the small apartment he had been renting in Madrid, he shook my hand saying: "Thanks, I couldn't have done it without you." The walls of his apartment were bare and it was furnished with a mattress on the floor. There were dirty dishes in the sink, a carton of stale milk and a piece of dried-up chorizo in the fridge from the week before.

"I don't see him lasting very long as a batchelor" I thought.

About a year and a half later I was sweeping in the refectory when a letter was brought in for me. I took it and tore it open and saw that inside there was a printed card. Up in the corner was written:

>Can Paradiso,
>Santa Eulalia,
>Ibiza, Baleares, Spain

And in the centre:

"Gudrun von Harmsdorff and John C. Durphy are pleased to inform you of their marriage, which was celebrated in Bremershaven, Germany, on August the 31st."

I turned the card over and looked for a moment at my own name and address on the front:

>Brother Ambrose of the Holy Shroud,
>Monastery of the Sacred Heart,
>viale Dolorosa
>Toledo, Spain.

I slipped the card into the sleeve of my habit, picked up the broom, and went on sweeping the refectory.

SCHWEINEREI

One evening at dusk, I came across my teacher by the side of the swimming pool at the hotel in Atlanterra where the group was staying in the summer of 83. He was looking out over the nearly deserted swimming pool at some children sitting on the edge of the pool and stepping onto a a large inner tube floating in the water. They were pushing the inner tube back and forth and having a great time laughing and shouting at each other.

My teacher had in fact been quite sick that summer, so I came up to him to see if he was okay : he frowned and went on looking out over the pool in silence.

"Is everything all right, sir?" I asked.

"Look at that" he replied.

"What?" I replied.

"Look at those children."

We watched about a dozen children playing and shouting for about three minutes in silence. I had no idea what he wanted me to see, but he was looking very stern indeed, so I realised something bad must be going on.

"What's wrong, sir?" I asked.

"The children" he replied.

"What about them?" I asked.

"They are making noise" he replied.

FICTIONS AND FACTIONS

We then went on watching them in silence as they played and called to each other in German by the pool-side. They were not exactly silent but by no stretch of the imagination could they be considered to be really disturbing anyone. I pointed out to my teacher that they were not children from the group, because all of our people's children were in the dining-room with their parents.

"Whose children are they?" asked the teacher.

"They probably belong to the German and Swiss tourists who are also clients at the hotel."

"Schweinerei" said the teacher.

By this time two or three other friends had joined us by the side of the darkening pool. We were all listening to our teacher more or less muttering to himself, and we were all equally mystified.

"Why are you saying they are Schweinerei?" I asked

"Because they let their children make a disturbance and bother everyone. Such people can only be called Schweinerei. "Well" he said in a slightly phony German accent, "I think we're going to have to do something about this situation : Augy, go and get me the manager."

First my heart sank, then I went to get the Swiss manager of the hotel and sent him to my teacher by the poolside. Then I passed through the dining-room to tell my family to hold my place at the table. When I came out to join the others at the side of the pool, my teacher was in full swing with the manager, explaining in a kind of parody of precise German anger how it was outrageous that children should be allowed to disturb the peace of honest God-fearing adults in this way, that there was

... SCHWEINEREI

a manifest disturbance taking place and that it was the manager's duty to put it right.

The manager obviously thought that my teacher was completely out of his mind, but since my teacher was head honcho of three hundred clients in his hotel, as a good professional, he clicked his heels and told my teacher that he would see to the situation. He then disappeared towards the cocktail lounge, and, as the little knot of friends stood in silence with my teacher at the edge of the pool, the parents came out of the hotel and gradually all of the little children were picked up one by one, until in about ten minutes the pool, now so dark that you could hardly see to the other side, was entirely deserted.

Someone bought my teacher some food, which he sat down and ate, still looking at the deserted pool, with the rest of us in attendance. He then got up and went off to bed, leaving us all looking at the empty pool, and then looking at each other, wondering what the hell had happened.

The answer only occurred to me many months later, after I had connected this incident with the way my teacher had behaved many years before when he had visited us in Italy and had inspected each well-head on the property where we were living to make sure they were all properly covered and protected against the possibility of children falling in. He had tested every hinge on every screen and opening.

In fact, there was no supervision at that swimming pool—it was getting dark, the lights had been turned off, the kids were in the water and their parents were all at the bar or in the hotel dining-room without really knowing where their children were. The simple reality of that situation was that those children were in potential danger. No one had noticed.

FICTIONS AND FACTIONS

It is worthwhile looking at the way this situation was resolved from more than just one point of view : what would you think of this incident if you were:

1) the manager,

2) one of the children playing in the water,

3) one of the bystanders, or

4) one of the parents?

When action is required, this is what a teacher must provide, at any cost.

True elegance is to make one's positive actions invisible.

PSYCHIATRIC DIWAN

Note: A number of our friends work in various métiers connected with applied psychology. They have nearly all told their colleagues back home that they have come to this meeting to attend a professional congress or symposium. The following is a modest attempt to produce a document that can be shown to such colleagues without entailing professional dishonour.

Hippolyte Maindron, rapporteur.

SUMMARY REPORT OF THE FIFTH ANNUAL SYMPOSIUM ON THE AFFECTVE STRUCTURAL ANALYSIS OF PHENOMOLOGICAL PATTERNS IN HUMAN INTEGRATION MECHANISMS

Following previous symposia in Arcos and Chiclana, Spain, Buenos Aires, Argentina, and Mortain, France, the Fifth International Symposium of the ASAPPHIM association was convened in Istanbul, Turkey from August 3-17, 1982.

In the welcoming address it was pointed out that the choice of venue was the outcome of a process that had been initiated sixteen years previously in the same place, when the research objectives at present being pursued were first defined in their present form. Many of the ideas which would have appeared outlandish at the time were now a perfectly acceptable part of the contemporary intellectual landscape, but in accordance with the true spirit of scientific enquiry, it would ill-behoove us to be triumphant at the fact that our "suspect" ideas should have so quickly filtered down into the world at large, since so much work remained to be done.

FICTIONS AND FACTIONS

The symposium then proceeded to elect the officers of the conference and the mandate of the Founding Chairman was unanimously renewed, both for the symposium's plenary sessions and for the consolidated curriculum committee that he has so expertly presided over for the past twenty years.

The following agenda was adopted:

1) Welcoming address.

2) Reply by the host country representative.

3) Short address on organisational matters by the representative of the United Kingdom.

4) Coffee break.

5) General discussion of the overall problematique with particular reference to the introduction of updated value systems.

6) Presentation of individual and national research projects.

7) Keynote address by the Founding Chairman and Chairman of the Consolidated Curriculum Committee.

8) Establishment of basic guidelines for the coordination of research activities on a transnational and interregional basis.

9) Definition of potential problem areas affecting the distribution and implementation of research funds in the present-day inflationary and/or recessionary economic climate.

10) Committee meetings and reports by each committee to the plenary session.

11) Date and venue of the next Symposium.

12) Any other business.

During the two days devoted to sub-committee meetings, the credentials committee decided that, except in certain specific circumstances, members were to represent themselves only in their personal and individual capacity, and not as de facto representatives of their local chapters. The financial committee undertook a preliminary examination of the previous year's balance sheet and made a pressing appeal for an extension of available research funds in order to maintain the present level of activity and to be able to undertake new initiatives as the ongoing situation required. The all-British organising committee convened informally a number of times and the Symposium voted a unanimous motion of thanks and expressed gratitude for their sterling efforts before they took the first available flight home. It was perhaps because of this somewhat precipitous departure that the financial committee neglected to pay for the Founding Chairman's hotel accommodation, thus forcing him to take his leave discreetly in the dead of night. It is hoped, particularly by those who were left behind and who had to foot the bill, that such embarrassing occurrences will be able to be avoided in the future.

The subcommittee on traditional musical influences was one of the most active in the Symposium. Not only did they make a considerable effort to harmonize their guidelines during daytime sessions, they also regaled the Symposium with a number of highly informative evening presentations. The head of the German delegation revealed himself to be an authority on the *oeuvre* of Carlos Gardel et al., and we were able to

FICTIONS AND FACTIONS

appreciate the full extent of the Saracen influence on this Toulouse-born specialist. A most lucid account of the little-known chupeta syndrome was presented with great enthusiasm by the Brazilian delegation, and a most exhaustive account of a contemporary Turkish formulation was provided throughout evening sessions by a notable member of the *Organ Zombi* dervish order. Nevertheless it would have been invidious to single out any contributions over the rest, the standard of research having been uniformly high and the fact that both successful and unsuccessful experiments have been fully reported shows that the scientific and methodological parameters adopted are of universal application.

The Symposium wished to make its appreciation and gratitude known to the many local specialists who were kind enough to present a Turkish-based approach to our subject. The informal account of the lute syndrome, presented in traditional *hutnani* form, was greatly appreciated by a core group of aficionados, and the searching analysis of the song of the reed-flute, so central to our research concept both in the West and in the East, was a most moving experience.

A series of short national presentations on ongoing research activities in member countries were presented to the plenary session. The head of the French delegation was pursuing an independant line of enquiry and felt it was too soon to communicate preliminary research results. The French delegation therefore limited itself to the creative criticism of other countries' research parameters.

The German delegation gave an account of the new decentralized management and evaluation structures they have adopted, along with an indicative analysis of their forward planning system, and representatives of the Argentinian, Brazilian and Mexican delegations gave a particularly impressive account of the increased research activity that has taken place in their regions over the past year. Countries such as Colombia and Peru were represented among us for the first time and the Symposium members expressed their warm appreciation of the efforts being made.

The Italian delegation made a noteworthy contribution to a little-known aspect of our subject: the "stomach" orientation and culinary dimension to the integration problematique, and the results of their efforts were generally considered to have been most convincing. In some countries a tendency towards divergency in research objectives between local chapters had led to the implementation of an improved system of communication updates which was helping to overcome temporary disharmonies of approach. It was decided that the present phase of expansion would necessarily entail the implementation of new management control systems in order to keep fully abreast of ever-changing research and development situations, and it was unanimously considered that the needs of national delegations have all manifested that combination of discipline and initiative that characterize a truly valid systems research approach.

The keynote address by the Founding Chairman was unanimously regarded by members as an undoubted addition to their knowledge of and thinking on the subject at hand. The form of presentation was quite novel for a scientific paper, since it combined both verbal and non-verbal communication techniques. But there was no doubt in anyone's mind that the physical demonstration of the unity principle underpinning the human integration problematique, along with the new stage of research potential expressed by the "I will take you home" concept, as manifested in the Founding Chairman's most elegant analysis: all of these elements combined to formulate a renewed covenant for all of us engaged in this ongoing research.

FICTIONS AND FACTIONS

There was no doubt that the head of the Brazilian delegation expressed the Symposium's universal attitude when he mooted a resounding vote of confidence in the forward plan presented by our Founding Chairman.

The two-day research trip to Konya in order to gather material on integration mechanisms under field conditions was judged a resounding success by Symposium members. Some even went so far as to state that this was the most significant contribution to their knowledge of the subject experienced so far. Others again felt that it was the keynote address of the Founding Chairman that had thrown the greatest amount of light on the subject. Yet again, still others felt that such considerations were basically irrelevant insofar as these contributions all interacted with each in order to form an overall pattern of knowledge which would of neccessity be personal to each delegate.

Before disbanding, the Symposium voted to leave the question of the date and venue of the next Symposium to the Founding Chairman, who would liaise with the consolidated curriculum committee in accordance with usual democratic practice.

The foregoing summary report is inevitably limited and partial, but if any member of ASAPPHIM wishes to point out salient items that may have inadvertently been left out, he or she is free to send all relevant suggestions to the Founding Chairman who will deal with each case according to merit.

A LOOK

When we sat down to dinner I had no inkling.

I took up my usual place among the twelve, fairly far down the table, not quite at the end. The boss was speaking as usual, and if the truth be told, I was listening with only half an ear. The food was particularly good that evening, and I must confess that I've always been partial to a good meal, and my attention was more on my food than him.

Not that I was bored with what he was saying, it's just that after a few years there are bound to be repetitions, so I sat there enjoying my meal, filtering out the obligatory ethical material, keeping my ear cocked for hard information whenever it would choose to come. So it's hardly surprising that when it did in fact come, it came as a surprise.

In fact I had my mouth full when I realised that everybody's attention was riveted on the boss. Everyone had stopped stock still, and I had my mouth full of bread and I didn't dare chew it up, which was highly embarrassing. It was only after the others began talking among themselves again that I became aware that our boss had announced his own death.

And then, after a moment, when everybody had begun to speak again I began to chew the food in my mouth as surreptitiously as I could, and, as I swallowed it with some relief at not having been discovered, I felt his eyes upon me. I looked up, and he was looking straight into my eyes for the first time.

Maybe I should explain that his behaviour was highly austere with me, that he would kiss others and pat them on the

FICTIONS AND FACTIONS

shoulder, but that I don't remember him ever having touched me. In fact, I went through a whole period resenting this and wondering why, before I simply accepted it without trying to understand. Similarly, he never looked me straight in the eye; he would only communicate with me through ostensibly talking to someone else, and I would overhear his words and realise that they were destined for me. He communicated to me thus for many years without anybody else ever realizing that something was being passed to me through them.

After all, I was probably the most obscure individual of the lot of us. Others came from more prominent families, others were charged with tasks, others were engaged in training activities, and I was simply left alone. And this too was something I took a long time to accept, for I was somebody who had always been enormously ambitious. I wanted love, I wanted admiration, I wanted fame, and if these were not to be available, I wanted at least to be feared. But in this too I had been disappointed by our boss, and I had come to accept my own obscurity and lack of status in our little unit, and this simply because, like the others, I knew that he knew best and that my only choice was to follow him blind, with blind faith, and to love this man as much as I could even if what love I could muster was only a pale parody of the ocean of love he had for us. Because we were to him as he was to the source, and he was our necessary relay, since if we had been connected directly to the source, we would have been blown into madness.

So that when he looked into my eyes for the first time and talked of his imminent betrayal, I knew at once with absolute certainty what I was to do. You see, it was a question of polarity, the 'yes' and the 'no' that are both inherent to the human condition. His job was to incarnate the 'yes', the possibility, and he needed a man whom he could trust absolutely to incarnate the 'no', the denial.

... A LOOK

And as he looked into my eyes and spoke of betrayal, I realised that this man was to be me and that I had no choice in the matter. The sacrifice of my body wasn't so important, that didn't really worry me, what was harder to sacrifice was my hard-earned reputation for holiness. With a start I realised how my erstwhile ambition, envy, desire for prominence and relative obscurity in the group were going to be used, and furthermore even satisfied, for there would hardly be a single man walking the earth who would not one day know my name. As the technical perfection of the situation appeared to my mind's eye, I gave thanks once again to the Almighty for not only enabling me to serve, but for giving me the joy of finding out what it was that I had been born to do.

After a few more minutes, I slipped away unnoticed from the table in order to begin my mission of infamy, and thus make known to all, within the space of a single night, the function of I, Judas the scholar, son of Iscariot, obedient pupil of my teacher Jesus Christ and servant of God.

FICTIONS AND FACTIONS

HOW TO BETRAY YOUR TEACHER

There had been rumours.

Our teacher had been seen behaving quite strangely of late. He had begun to drink, which was something we had never seen him do. When I say "we" I mean the older generation of disciples, the small handful of old sweats who were more or less in at the beginning, at the time when there were only about thirty of us hanging around the Coupole sharing our dreams with anyone who would buy us a drink.

When he turned up he put an end to that, quick as lightening. There is a major job to be done on your own minds, he said, and I am here to help you. Help you, he said, not do it in your place.

Most of us said "What the hell? Why not?" and enrolled.

On the day of my own enrollment, he did one thing which I never forgot: he ordered a large coffee with milk in the café where we were sitting and I told him that I had seen what other people were doing and that I wanted in, even if I wasn't really very informed about higher esoterics and so forth. Then he started talking a smokescreen at me all about "pure esotericism" and suchlike, and it occurred to me that I had better watch my step and keep off subjects like that if I didn't want to look like a fool. Then, as he went on talking, he pointed out that what was really at issue here was not exactly freedom of choice but rather freedom from choice.

He had lit up a very expensive Havana cigar, and the coffee was sitting in front of him, untouched. As he spoke the words "freedom from choice" to me, he took the huge cigar on

… HOW TO BETRAY YOUR TEACHER

which he had only puffed about three times, out of his mouth, and dunked it out in his full cup of coffee.

We went on talking for another fifteen minutes, during which time his cigar and coffee remained untouched throughout. He insisted on paying for both of our coffees and left his hundred-dollar cigar on the table when he went. I was impressed.

I was later to realise how important the words "freedom from choice" were to be in my own life and in the lives of others, and every time I have ever heard those words and every time there is any dicussion about "freedom of choice" my mind flicks back to that incident and I see all over again the cigar of my teacher dunking itself out in a cupful of milky coffee.

Of course since that day so many years ago, I have done some of my own reading of the canonical literature, and I have come across a number of descriptions of what is called a "marker" in the tradition we follow. It is an instance or action which the teacher uses to shock or impress you into remembering a certain thing or a certain behaviour, if you like a sort of mnemonic trigger. Anyway, the cigar incident was mine.

One thing that can be said about our teacher is that he was incredibly adept at producing events and instances of this type. All of his pupils have dozens of these stories to tell.

Once in Spain he had come staggering in, blind drunk, and had fallen down just in front of me. When I caught him in order to stand him up I could feel that his body was perfectly balanced, like a karateka. Even when he leaned against me I could tell that he was perfectly coordinated, whereas absolutely everybody else around us was convinced that he was totally out of control.

FICTIONS AND FACTIONS

This made me think a great deal about what was going on. If he was indeed play-acting, and I became convinced in that moment that he was, there had to be a reason.

At one time he had gathered a group of power-hungry second-raters around him, indirectly encouraging them to commit some fairly hairy excesses, both economic and sexual. I was invited to be party to some of the meetings of these senior groupies who called themselves the nobs: so far as I could see the subject that most fascinated them was themselves and how wonderful they all were. They were going to start a business together where unspecified products would change hands at great profit to themselves and all the friends, and they used to spend hours on the telephone making international calls on company money just in order to gossip.

They were all living proof that ceaseless affirmation can create its own dynamic and energy. Since they were all convinced that whatever they were doing was a channel for a higher form of energy, everybody believed them just as they believed themselves.

As a binding agent, gossip can have its good side as well as bad. One of the things about gossip is that it is a form of communication, even if the aim is less than noble, and all communication has a place in human affairs, no learning is really possible without it. In fact, without trying to make too much of a point of it, the human being is itself one of the most amazing communication tools ever invented, no computer can even come near it.

This is why, when echoes of what one might call serious ethical distortions on the part of our teacher first came to our ears, some of us listened to it all carefully and others chose to ignore it, just as when the nobs went bankrupt, some people lost their life savings and some didn't. The main thrust of the

... HOW TO BETRAY YOUR TEACHER

gossip was that Teach had now taken up almost publicly with the wife of one of the members of the group, who appeared to be his accomplice in the use his wife was being put to.

In fact, I trusted my teacher, even if I knew that he was a person who was capable of almost anything, both seemingly good and seemingly evil, but I always thought the good prevailed because that's what he worked towards. My impression was based on experience, not theory, because about four years before he had made a somewhat unconvincing play for my wife, sending someone to fetch her during one of the trips in Turkey, and saying to her: "Okay, the time has come" from underneath the covers when she walked in the door.

"Is that an order?" said my wife, sitting down beside him on the bed.

"No, it's a request" said our teacher, laughing.

My wife leaned toward him and said "I don't believe you" because, as she said when she told me about the incident a couple of hours later, "I could see that he really didn't look in the least bit excited."

She talked with him for a little while, and then embraced him like a sister. "I want to be useful to you" she said.

"You can be useful to your husband and children, not to me" he replied.

When she came and told me what had happened, I asked her who had been sent to get her. She told me that it was our friend Claire. I then went to Claire and asked what had been going on with her and her friend just before my wife joined the party, and she told me that when he told her to go and get my wife, she had objected, saying "No, for God's sake, she's

FICTIONS AND FACTIONS

married and she has children, you can't do that." Nevertheless, she had gone to fetch her anyway, even after saying that.

Had it been an order at that point or had it been a request? It was an interesting point, because a master demands absolute obedience, but does one obey, for instance, if the master tells you to throw yourself out of the window? When you are asked to do something you find reprehensible, does the rule of obedience still apply? Of course it must be noted that sleeping with your collaborators' wives is a well-known technique used by dictators for testing and insuring the loyalty of subordinates: Trujillo and Peron both practised it.

I knew that the top henchmen were in the habit of sending out underlings to bring back the best-looking and most consumable girls to the local boss, and I regarded this as being much more corrupt still than the fact that the girls slept or didn't sleep with the nob, because to me turning your collaborators into pimps was destructive to their inner life. The women had a choice, and if they wanted to play it this way, more fool them, but there was something about reducing your servants to pimphood that I really didn't like.

Did Claire have the option of refusing or not? Etiquette holds that you do not refuse a direct order from your teacher, but you can refuse a request. The challenge my wife had put to her teacher was an extremely subtle one, because if he had said it was an order, he would have had to live with the consequences insofar as he would have shut off her own option to choose. He would undoubtably have had to deliver as well; no mean feat if you're not really interested to begin with. His pharmacy would have to have been well provided with Amazonian aphrodisiacs to get him over that one.

To a certain extent I had to come to terms about what I was willing to accept from my teacher, and what I really thought

... HOW TO BETRAY YOUR TEACHER

of him. It's all very well telling yourself that you're on earth to serve a teaching, but what happens when your teacher begins helping himself to food that's been prepared for you? Share or not share?

Up to a point, the situation I was in was not all that different from the people who had been watching aghast when I had picked Teach up off the floor in Spain. They were all disciples and they all had to answer for themselves the question about whether this man was a drunkard or not, and if so, could they accept such a man as their teacher?

By what criterion were we going to judge his capacity to teach? Social acceptability? What we think is ethical and what we think is not? What we have been brought up to believe in or what is beyond the pale? Also what was the price we were willing to pay? Were we willing to be the laughing-stock of the friends and neighbours, when the man's own brother was sending us a hatchet man to tell us that he had developed bats in his belfry?

Most people's reasoning, I am glad to say, was fairly clear and simple. They simply decided that even if they didn't like or were worried about what was going on, they had no choice in the matter. Here was a teacher with whom they had worked to good result, they were in it for themselves, not for society at large, and they considered that if this man had something they needed they would have to stay on until such a time as that something was passed on. Once again, freedom from choice, back to the cigar.

I thought over what my teacher had done with my wife for about a month before deciding that I had to go and talk to him about it. I went to see him in England and flew into London, asking for an appointment with the elderly lady he would stay with whenever he came up to London. "Why don't you come

FICTIONS AND FACTIONS

along for tea on Thursday" she said. When I arrived there she made us comfortable in the deep armchairs of her living-room, before discreetly withdrawing to let us talk.

My wife had been sworn to silence, so when I told him I knew that he had made an unprovoked proposal to her during our time in Turkey this past summer, and that I had come to see him because I wanted to ask him why he had done so, he still had his teacup in his hand. He became very still for a moment and didn't move a muscle, and rightly or wrongly, I had the distinct impression that he was scared of me. I must confess that I did not find this unpleasant, but it was not a determining factor, so I waited in silence for his answer.

He put down the teacup and said "There are times in a teaching when it becomes necessary to do something extreme. You do this for the person and not for yourself."

"I accept that" I said, and our talking became more banal. After a little while I took my leave, went straight out to the airport and boarded the next plane home.

When I talked over the incident with my wife later that day we both realised that our two meetings with the teacher had caused a change in our relationship with him. Both of us had lost the child-like idealism we had entertained, and we now saw our teacher as a human being rather than as an abstraction under the label of "Master." We were both in our forties, both of us had been involved in the teaching for about twenty years, and it was about time for us to stop being esoteric groupies. I accepted that he shock the idealism of my wife because it was a technical requirement that this be done, but he had also shocked mine, thus giving me the chance to communicate in no uncertain terms that there were approaches I would not put up with.

... HOW TO BETRAY YOUR TEACHER

Question: did he know at the time he was doing this how it would affect me as well? Answer: maybe, maybe not. Teachers teach, it's what they are for. The question of what is in their minds may or may not be relevant to us as pupils. There is a difference between useful curiosity and irrelevant nosiness.

The fact that I had established a man-to-man relationship with him for the first time meant that I would never be able to go back to being a baby with him. I would no longer consider him as the all-approving father I didn't have: I was after all the son of a teacher myself, who in his own field was the equal of the spiritual teacher I had adopted, and maybe the time had come for me to stand on my own two feet.

A unilateral declaration of independence such as this is of course one of the biggest traps life can hold out to us, and I am afraid that I fell into it with a bang. I began hanging out with the above-mentioned mistress of my teacher: by this time she had broken off with the husband the teacher had organised for her to marry five years before—actually, that's another uncanny story. My wife and I had driven back from the wedding which had been presided over by the teacher in his five-star general disguise and all the nobs in their gladrags, and she had suddenly turned to me and asked: "How long do you think it will last?"

"Five years," I replied.

Five years later, just after the tumultuous affair with her teacher had come to an end (basically because teacher's wife threw him out of the house and the mistress's head on a platter was the price to be paid to beg his way back into the wife's good graces), her husband put an end to their marriage as well; the worm had finally turned. She was now a free agent, living alone with her child and I was just casually hanging around.

FICTIONS AND FACTIONS

I don't remember how I organised things, it must have been complicated because my two children were still young at the time, but the dedicated adulterer always finds a way. I made sure that my own wife and children were away on vacation and that her own child was visiting his father.

We were having dinner at her place when I pulled out my ace in the hole: I had been diagnosed with a cancer in the throat, and the doctors had given me a year to live. Need I add that the the first part of the story was true, but the second part wasn't—the doctors really told me that I had an 90% chance of survival, which of course turned out to be true since I'm here to write the story.

She was a nice woman, and very kind. Swallowing it hook, line and sinker, she walked over to me with tears running down her face and put her arms around me.

We spent the night in her bed, and it was wonderful.

During the pauses in our lovemaking we would talk, and here I must confess to doing my detective work between the sheets, I wanted to find out about the relationship between her and my teacher and so I pumped her relentlessly on the subject. She was completely open and guileless with me, telling me how difficult it had been sometimes to imagine the heart of the teacher during an exercise when her mind tended to focus on other parts of his body. He had told her specifically not to become involved with any of his pupils after leaving him, and in sleeping with me she was clearly disobedient, which made her feel bad.

There was an incident I really wanted to find out about, which was the famous incident of the teacher's death and resurrection, and which I had heard in garbled versions from various sources, because each of the nobs told the story with

... HOW TO BETRAY YOUR TEACHER

themselves as main player.

Briefly, what the teacher had done was to become ill. He had cleared his wife and children out of the house and had then called on a number of the top dogs to come and either take care of him, or as it was rumoured, to hold his hand as he was about to die. This in itself created unbelievable ripples because there were those who were convened and those who weren't. ("Why haven't I been invited, I who am such a faithful servant, etc. How can he do this to me?")

The lady I was with was also convened to this event, and was given the special task of ministering to his private needs while her husband guarded the door from unwelcome visitors. After a few days he finally gathered everyone around his bed, and explained in a quavering voice that he felt that his time had come, and that he had decided to place the teaching in the hands of a successor, since he clearly was not going to be long for this world. And the person he was going to choose as his successor—and here, all of the nobs waited on what he was going to say with bated breath, because each of them without exception hoped to be the one who was anointed—and the young lady saw to her amazement that her teacher was pointing his finger straight at her.

She had just been chosen as the next teacher of the age.

"And do you know," she said to me wide-eyed with her head resting on my chest: "everybody was really nice to me for the next few days. They would bring me breakfast in bed, and the German nob even proposed that we do a fifty-fifty split on the money he was making from the group there."

"What happened then?" I asked. She rolled over onto my belly and looked at me straight in the eye: "Later, sweetheart," she said, "you've got to sing for your supper first."

FICTIONS AND FACTIONS

She went on with the story over breakfast in the morning, and it was a very sorry and silly ending to the vast buildup and organised suspense of the anointment. His wife came back home, took one look at what was going on and turfed everybody out, nobs or no nobs. It was decided that the teacher had been suffering from delerium tremens and he was carted off to a clinic to dry out. The mistress's own husband finally put his foot down to his teacher and said it was about time the whole thing came to an end, and the teacher's wife told her that if she ever set foot in her house again she would kill her. All the heads of groups stopped being nice to her and bringing her breakfast in the morning, and the whole episode was wiped from everyone's memory, since it didn't correspond to the heroic vision people were supposed to have of the work that was being done.

Within three or four months it became clear that she and her husband could not go on together, and they separated.

On the morning after, my wife and kids were coming home from vacation and her child was coming home from staying with his father, so that I had to take my leave, which I did. I tried to see her again, but she was never free, so I finally realised she did not want to see me any more, and didn't insist. We spent only that night together.

Other things came along to claim our lives. I was told that she had married again, this time to someone that had not been chosen for her, a Corsican policeman so the story had it, which presumably meant that she would be well under control for any shenanigans in the future, Corsicans not generally being very sympathetic to extra-curricular activities from their womenfolk.

I myself went into hospital and began the series of treatments that would turn my hair white at the age of forty-

... HOW TO BETRAY YOUR TEACHER

five. I survived, as did we all. Most of the nobs quit their jobs with our teacher when their money was cut off and set up as independant gurus on their own, the others are still around in varying degrees of decrepitude. Most stories never end, do they, you just turn into biomass and life goes on in one way or another.

My own punishment for going after my teacher's mistress in that way was to have been successful in my quest. One is indeed rewarded in proportion to one's intention, and the reward I received was a fitting one. You see, the woman I made love to had a way of gifting herself to a man which was something I had never known before and was never to know once more. Why is it certain men or women are gifted for love, and others not? Why does one body during the act of love mean something to you and another's not? I had thought I was gifted, and was not.

Was it because she thought I was about to die? Can one learn to make love to another as if there were no tomorrow, or is it inborn? Was it because she had been so well taught by our common teacher? Was it because she had a gift for men? Was it simply because she liked men (not as frequent a phenomenon in women as one might think) and was not afraid to show it? What was it about this woman that made her so special to me, that made me feel something with her that I had never felt before in my life, and that I was never to feel again?

The doors of paradise had opened before me, I was given a brief glimpse of what life might be behind the gate, and the doors had closed again. I was well and truly trapped. Moreover, the trap had been entirely of my own making, there was no one to blame but myself. There was a quality in the love she had so briefly given me that was unique to her, and this uniqueness would be neither repeated nor extrapolated.

FICTIONS AND FACTIONS

It had happened, it was over, and it would not come again. I could watch the ambrosia being passed down the table with the absolute certainty that when the time came for the cup to get back to me, it would be empty.

"What is this teaching that produces so many divorces and breaks up families?" said the teacher's wife to me one day when she was really pissed off at her husband. At that time I was quite unable to answer, but now I think I am beginning to be able to work something out.

To start with, it is quite untrue that more marriages break up in the teaching than elsewhere, it's just that the breakups are more visible because so many couples think that the tensions inherent in a marriage can be papered over by the common pursuit of a metaphysical objective. They have to be dealt with on their own terms, like everything else. I'm told that this year in Paris there is a 50% statistical probability of marriages ending in divorce: if that's the case we are clearly doing better than average.

But there is another point here which has to do with the nature of most people's reality.

The reality of most people is not pretty; it tends to be a mixture of desire, conditioning and experience. This means that when they set their minds on a higher objective, for instance that of moving closer to the Higher Intelligence, they will use the instruments they dream with as much as the instruments they live with. Very often, these dreams have become so much part of their own reality that people are willing to kill in order to preserve them; and if one explodes one of these dreams, such as chastity, the reaction can be quite violent.

This of course does not mean that sexual manipulation of various kinds either dominates the world or dominates the

... HOW TO BETRAY YOUR TEACHER

teaching, but it is something that we all come up against and eventually have to deal with in one way or another.

Some deal with it by indulgence, some by avoidance and most are balanced somewhere in between. But the balance is a moving and shifting one, because it is humanly impossible to avoid some form of love or other throughout a twenty-four hour day.

The forms that love takes are so multiple and varied that an encyclopaedia could not exhaust them all. Nevertheless most people really do prefer to dream love rather than realize it. At the time of the events I have related above, about eighty percent of the friends were convinced that there was no sexual contact at all between our teacher and any of his pupils because it disturbed them to imagine their teacher doing that sort of thing. A certain proportion of others wanted very much to do that sort of thing themselves and were hungrily seeking implicit permission to do so. What this says about the pupils is far more significant than what it says about the teacher, because a teacher has no choice in the matter: he or she must teach from the level of the pupil and not from above. To each according to his understanding.

To people on the outside of the teaching such behaviour will only confirm their conviction that all teaching functions are taken on just as an excuse for getting it in. The fact that this may be true in a majority of cases does not mean there is no exception to the rule.

What is sure is that without dreams, particularly the dreams of perfection that we have for ourselves, there would be no teaching at all, it would not be able to exist. If people had not idealized our teacher in some way, they would not have projected a possible development onto themselves, and would

FICTIONS AND FACTIONS

not today be locked into the process of self-realization that has actually been happening.

The job of a teacher is to become both the master of dreams and the master of reality. A certain mastery of time, in the sense of when something is possible and when it is not, is also required. But if we are talking about reality and not just fiction, a teaching has got to take place at that level as well.

WYSWYG

I think I am right in assuming
that there are no hidden messages here
what you see is what you get
the idea of being plotted against
is quite simply absurd

the real state of myself and mankind
is quite nothing more or less than advanced paranoia
there is no doubt in my mind
that the world revolves around my beautiful self
it's not my fault that you're too dense to know

It was good old Heathcote that put it best
no I am not paranoid his man said
everybody **is** looking at me
and the scary thing about life on this planet
is that once this thought crosses your mind

it becomes absolutely true

This is why the only protection we have
is to dream and project ourselves into wild situations
the hairier the better   after the hundredth murder
the desire for revenge may have spent itself
if not   just dream again

Or else   take a step back and watch
something may be going on you don't yet know about
either something that you haven't come across
or you would prefer never to have known it
no knowledge is ever entirely useless

FICTIONS AND FACTIONS

How does one learn to look at a mirror
with love   how does one learn not to
there are times to do and times not to
help   I'm hemmed into my circle of nothingness
remember when you opened your door to the plague?

Back to the intention   no other way to steer
no other compass   but remember
compasses have to be reset every twenty-four hours
otherwise a deviation sets in
the best technique for doing this is prayer

Because then you're back to being a speck in the ocean
which is an accurate definition of where you are
however prominent   we are one of many
our heartburn issues just a mote of dust
and yet I am important and so are you

However hard one may try   one is not anyone else
and to add a whopping cliché
no one else is me
and the horror of such a statement
camouflages the possibility of its boundless glory

We help no one or anything
by being less than what we are
we were designed to shine not shrink
there are no hidden messages here
what you see is what you get

MY WORD

I gave my word and I can't go back on it
otherwise my whole life is forfeit
I am so angry that I wake up in the night
with my teeth clamped into the throat of another

But I am an educated man
I have learned the language of hypocrisy
and I smile back and say
I'll have to agree to disagree on that one I'm afraid

I wandered in here and now there's no way out
suicide is not an option
because it'll just be the same on the other side
my only hope is to finally mutate

Is there any way to kill lovingly
this is what I dream of every night
real or imaginary slights what's the difference
when the world daily tramples me flat

And like a cartoon figure wake up every day
and shake off the horror I absorb
slip my teeth back into my maw
clean the blood from my aching claws

and hope and pray
in the day to come
not to destroy in a minute
what took so long to build.

FICTIONS AND FACTIONS

DIRTY OLD MAN

I have never known the freedom of the hawk
who floats then dives upon its prey
I am a small man chasing after small women
a man permeated with simple notions
and simple ambitions

What on earth are you talking about
don't you think the time has come to stop the whining
where are the noble ideas you used to utter
how can you have degenerated into such babble
who do you think you're talking to

I talk to please myself if you can call it pleasure
it's more like an endless stream of bile
chomping and swallowing and washing it all down
people talking throughout and I have to answer questions
I can't take myself seriously yet other people do

I have little love for myself but react to the love of others
maybe what they see is fantasy but what if it were true
what if I could not only write but be beyond what I am
I know I don't deserve you   love   but you're keeping me alive
hold me tight good woman and breathe yourself into me

Thank you   you've given me substance I did not have
when I'm on top the saliva accumulates and then I have to spit
sweet little girl you're so silly to have an old man as a lover
just let me have my arm back will you   my rheumatism again
be it only for a moment I will be young once more

THE LEDGER

The clichés of black and whiteness drive me crazy
there is no reason for anyone to remain stuck
there are other families   other places   other races
if you don't like the one you were born into
there's absolutely no reason why you shouldn't change

None of us were born to live their lives in prison
if that is where we are   we accepted that it be so
the nature of our bars is in fact our own business
they didn't just happen   we helped in their construction
how long will we go on blaming those who put us there

It's not the money it's not even the pleasure that its for
it's something else   perhaps a form of weird logic
that tells us that what we are looking at isn't quite enough
that there's got to be something more than dancing
maybe fucking   but who with   otherwise what's the point

We are exchangers and fabricators   fabricators and exchangers
if all we're making is ourselves it really isn't enough
exchange is part of where it is   let me whisper into your ear
I never told you how much I loved you   now it is too late
is there a ledger somewhere with kisses in default

Beige and brown and in the pink   it's the music that's the key
our children's music came from a handful of slaves
an artist must have been despised and poor
if something's to be made from it   it's got to smell of death
because life's in the rhythm of the heartbeat   not elsewhere

Body to body we make the music of the spheres
burnished gold on white   white on burnished gold
my ledger just a notepad with what I should have said
my song a white man's blues arising from disaster
when I breathe into you there is no colour there

WEAVING ON THE WAY

MY TEACHER

It happened so long ago   what was I then
a sort of callow youth   but I had enthusiasm
and I was indeed capable of working for nothing

I was painting the walls in a shop
that had been bought by friends   just helping out
their friends were a little bit weird

they would make all sorts of mysterious allusions
to mysterious hidden teachings and suchlike
the implication   as always in such cases   being
that only they were bright enough to know

Anyway it was no skin off my nose
I was a young actor about to be discovered
this stuff was just a way of passing time

In fact time passed quite congenially
the people were okay   neither better nor worse
than most of the other people I knew

There was this character who would turn up
making an appearance from time to time
he looked like an oriental and behaved
very much like a cultured Englishman

A plummy accent and an ease of socializing
that bordered on the arrogant without plunging in
just like all the ones I went to public school with
of course I disliked him on sight

With many of my schoolfriends I felt
there was no human being just a mask for appearance
it would take me thirty years to see how true this could be

FICTIONS AND FACTIONS

of the man I chose to be my teacher or who chose me

What Shah said to me the last time I saw him
was "we have no friends"and also
"I don't necessarily like them all, you know
keeping up with the Joneses and all that
but I'm useful to them"

And then later on to me by the car   smiling ear to ear
"a visit from a friend is always a pleasure"
what the hell's he smiling about   I thought

I had just told him I'd do no more translations
when I disagreed both with their content and intention
I asked permission to use his stories as reference points
in my own fictions and factions

"use whatever you like" he said

When he asked for first refusal on my book
I smelt a rat   when he began to flatter me
the stench became enormous   make no mistake
if the brothers wanted to seduce you   you were gone

I never saw or spoke to Shah again

But drove straight to the home of his brother
and gave a clear report on what I had said and why
he looked at me with a poker face
"time for bed" he said and showed me to the guest room

the fun and games were done with
the work was to begin over
I had stood up to one of the greatest teachers in the world
and would eventually stand up to another

now it was time to sleep   tomorrow was another day

SUFIC LITERATURE AND ACTION

The relationship between the literature of Idries Shah and that of his elder brother, Omar Ali-Shah, needs some small amount of explanation, which I will attempt to do within the inevitable limitations of my own perspective and knowledge.

Both take their source in the very wide river of the Sufi Tradition and its many written incarnations. The "classic" Sufi teacher-poets like Rumi, Jami, Saadi or Al-Ghazali worked in Muslim societies which afforded a much greater protection to a free-thinking and free-speaking philosophy than that of the Christian societies of the time, where such-thinking people were in continual danger from the Inquisition et al.

This has meant historically that the Sufi Tradition went underground in the West for several centuries when all religious thought had to be filtered through the Holy See. This process is clearly described in books like Idries Shah's *The Sufis* and Ernest Scott's *The People of the Secret*.

What this did in the West was to leave a somewhat ambiguous historical heritage, insofar as sufism became associated in people's minds with Islam on the one hand, and with respectable or unrespectable counter-culture activities such as the Troubadours, the Carbonari or the Knights Templar, or magical/alchemical groupings on the other.

In modern times, the huge rediscovery of traditional teachings and philosophies seems to have taken place more or less in parallel to the First World War, when Gurdjieff first appeared in Russia and Turkey, when modern anthropological enquiry started to deal with so-called "backward" or economically marginal societies, and the first travellers came back to the West from Tibet, Japan and China bearing tales of

FICTIONS AND FACTIONS

"Eastern Wisdom". At the same time you have the beginnings of modern art where vision is depicted rather than appearance.

This background is necessary in order to understand the problems of the Shah brothers when faced with putting the Sufi Tradition across to the West in the early sixties, when they both revealed themselves publicly as teachers.

On the one hand, Sufi studies had become the province of a handful of orientalist academics, whose knowledge was limited to book-knowledge and whose work was mostly unreadable except to fellow academics, and on the other hand it was under the control of religious authorities in the Middle East who considered the Sufi Tradition to be, as the religious advisor to the then King of Morocco once put to me: "the refined perfume of Islam".

This view, although perfectly true as far as it goes, reduces sufism to a sort of a footnote to the real business of a religion which, by implication, should busy itself organising a society's formal worship and social jurisprudence. What this in fact has meant is that, before even beginning, you had to learn Arabic, (badly, because it's a very difficult language to learn as an adult) and the advantage here is that you are in a lifelong position of inferiority to the native speakers who are running the show. Converts are welcome so long as they remain under your thumb.

In other words, access to this way of thinking either existed in a university classroom where you would discuss Rumi's versification techniques for hours without considering what his words meant to you as a human being, or else you had to convert to Islam and abandon your identity as a westerner, causing havoc among your friends and family, who would henceforth consider you a fanatic.

It is obvious today, even if 30-35% of the earth's population

... SUFIC LITERATURE AND ACTION

is Muslim, that a universal way of thinking, which sufism purports itself to be, cannot limit itself to access by a minority, whether or not this minority is of an academic or religious nature.

The two brothers first appeared publicly in London and Paris in 1962 and began their teaching with a group of vaguely dissident Gurdjieffians, (dissident in the sense that they worked with Vera Milanova and not with Jeanne de Salzmann), although this may ascribe more thinking and intention than is justified to the bunch of dilettante Parisian expatriates that we were at the time. Jane Leconte remarked to me that when Shah and Omar first met together with the Paris mob at Bill and Mary Ellen's flat in rue Campagne Première, Shah, who was acting as spokesman for both, said on that first day: "My brother and I will teach differently, and you will not understand why."

As well as talking to us in Paris, through John Bennett and the Hoares, the two brothers encountered a number of people who had been connected to the Indonesian teacher Pak Subuh. I myself joined up in 1964, and was privileged to be able to work with both teachers until 1977, which was when the two brothers announced the separation of their teaching activities.

Idries Shah gathered around him a number of people, mostly intellectuals, and projected his message to the public at large through a learned society called the Institute for Cultural Research, whose members participated in many university seminars and conferences dealing with general cultural issues and sufic activity and literature, and through the Octagon Press which published a number of important classical Sufi texts as well as some of Shah's own remarkable literature. Also, when Shah's popularity as a fashionable writer peaked, his editions were never remaindered by the major publishers, since Octagon has ensured that his writing was constantly in print for his own and now for the next generation.

FICTIONS AND FACTIONS

Omar Ali-Shah was involved with a highly controversial critical response to the 1967 publication of his translation of *The Rubaiyyat of Omar Khayaam*, in which, with the support of Robert Graves, he conclusively established the sufic origin of Khayaam's thinking, only to be attacked by a large number of Fitzgerald-worshippers and persicologists who accused him of dishonesty and textual manipulation in the press. Refusing to even answer such charges, he then withdrew from published literature entirely and devoted himself to forming small study groups in Europe and the Americas, where he has since worked with pupils whose response to the Sufi Tradition is more heartfelt than intellectual.

I myself was witness to a new member who asked Omar Ali-Shah, known as Agha to his students, about himself and his brother; he wanted to know what the difference between the two was: "Shah teaches the intellectuals" said Agha smiling at him, "I teach the dumbos."

Now, after thirty-five years, the "informed" public response to Sufi material has evolved considerably. The remarkable body of work produced by Idries Shah has laid down a basis of historical knowledge and intuitively entertaining stories, which has brought the Sufi Tradition into the unconscious and conscious mainstream of upmarket western intellectual activity.

If you told people in the early sixties that modern civilization came to us through the medieval Arab schools of Toledo and the translators of Cluny, most of them simply thought you were crazy. Today the Muslim and sufic input to modern thinking is a matter of general recognition, even among non-specialists, and this new awareness of sufism as a mainstream and not just a "new age" activity is to a great extent due to the activities of Shah and various other people linked to him.

The activity of both brothers can be considered as a

... SUFIC LITERATURE AND ACTION

continuation of the work undertaken by their father Ikbal Ali Shah, who published around thirty books in his lifetime explaining oriental thinking and civilizations to the West.

Omar Ali-Shah's return to book covers after more than twenty years of silence took place when I compiled the talks he had been giving to groups over the years into books, all of which were originally spoken off the cuff, usually without notes.

With Agha signing, at my request, each page to ensure conformity to his thinking, I transcribed, organised and edited his tape recordings into five books: *The Course of the Seeker*, *Sufism as Therapy* and *The Rules or Secrets of the Naqshbandi Order* published by Tractus, and *Sufism for Today* and *The Sufi Tradition in the West* by Alif. His translation of *The Rose Garden* (*Gulistan*) by Saadi was published by Tractus in 1997. The response to these books has been gratifying; translations of all these books have come out in Brazil, Argentina, Germany and Spain.

Omar Ali-Shah's books can be considered complementary to Idries Shah's books, just as his way of teaching is complementary without being a 'coat-tail'. They are somewhat more technical in tone than Shah's work, which is directed towards people 'off the street' who have a feel for but not necessarily any knowledge of the Sufi Tradition at all. Ali-Shah's work presupposes some knowledge, if only because he is talking to people who are there in order to listen to him, i.e., who have 'paid for their ticket,' as it were. Thus, when you read Ali-Shah you become *de facto* his pupil, which suits some people and not others.

The subtlety of Idries Shah's achievement is that he has created a body of work that does just about everything literature can do: there is beauty, philosophy, poetry, jokes, tall stories and fascinating adventure tales throughout his work: the only problem here being that the Sufi Tradition, as such, is not about literature; it is about changing people, or to put it more accurately,

FICTIONS AND FACTIONS

giving people the mental and spiritual instruments they can use to change themselves. The Sufi Tradition does not normally consider that a spiritual transmutation can take place by reading alone; it has to be reading plus appropriate personal contact.

Omar Ali-Shah addresses himself directly to this concern without any kind of 'entertainment' detour at all. This may sound austere, but it isn't. His works are actually fairly funny and fun to read, even if entertainment is not their objective. Our ten years' experience of getting feedback from a general public that reads Shah and Ali-Shah in public libraries, shows a clear indication that these books can be dealt with and assimilated by people who are not concerned by so-called 'intellectual' preoccupations or even sufic ideas, and who may not be in the habit of reading at all. Being clear and understandable is of paramount importance, because, as Omar Ali-Shah so pithily puts it: "No real tradition can be reserved for a few Einsteins".

In a time when religious fundamentalism is on the upswing, the Sufi Tradition provides a coherent body of thought which combines absolute faith with absolute freedom of thought. That these two ideas should appear antinomic is in itself a sad comment on contemporary religious attitudes which have been terminally infected by materialism and politics. With the ex-proponents of social utopias hunkering behind university portals in order to hand out edicts of what is politically correct or not, and the representatives of churches who should know better forbidding condoms and attacking women who dare have an abortion, it is important that people realise that an inner space of reconciliation exists which is free of such terrorism.

In such a context, the Sufi Tradition is not a marginal activity: it is mainline. The same is true of its literature.

1996

INTRODUCTION TO OMAR ALI-SHAH'S
THE SUFI TRADITION IN THE WEST

If some unsuspecting neophyte, as yet unfamiliar with Omar Ali-Shah's work, happens to pick up this book in the hope of finding an elegantly argued historical narrative of the Sufi Tradition's activities in the western world, he or she is doomed to disappointment. Such accounts do exist (the best of them being Idries Shah's *The Sufis*) but what this book of informal talks sets out to do is of a different nature.

All of the talks here were delivered over the past few years to Omar Ali-Shah's friends and pupils in different parts of the world, so that a certain underlying relationship with or sympathy to the ideas is presupposed, and it is only fair to say that this may not be the case for the casual reader. In this book Omar Ali-Shah is talking to people who basically share his general philosophical option, who are sympathetic to the aims of personal transformation at the basis of this option, and who look to him for guidance.

It is important for someone not yet involved with Sufi thinking to realise this from the outset, lest they be shocked by the lack of so-called "intellectual coherence" in this series of statements. In fact a coherence is there, but perhaps not in the synthesizing spirit or intellectual justification of professional philosophizing as expected in the West. Certain basic ideas such as a belief in an all-knowing God and a belief in a possible spiritual transformation of man are regarded as given, which effectively puts a wedge between this work and academic studies of the subject. It is nevertheless an intuitively coherent body of thought, but like all intuition-based thinking, the "personal matching" is provided by the awareness of the listener or reader rather than the speaker or writer.

FICTIONS AND FACTIONS

In certain circles this will be considered a drawback because such thinking is almost impossible to summarize or label, and it is difficult to package it to sell. It is also interesting to note what an incredibly deep resentment can be provoked by the Sufi Tradition's inability to fit itself into contemporary pigeon-holes. But it is an ancient way of thought that has never stopped, and which has successfully hidden behind many different types of religious and other institutions, some of which still believe they own it. But does a parent own its child? We take care of them for a while and then have to leave them to find their own way. If we are not able to do this we stop being a parent and become a proprietor.

The Sufi Tradition is only one of the many tools which exist to enable mankind to effect a qualitative change within itself. Let there be no mistake, this change does happen, but it happens in a way which is unacceptable to the majority of people, at least at the present time, because their personality becomes less important to themselves. It happens individually, not collectively, even though collective techniques may be used to put across the message, and it tends to make people more invisible than they were before, rather than more visible. People who have changed in the inner sense will not spend their time looking for prime time exposure; they will spend their time being rather than attempting to be.

In fact, the Sufi lives in a world of significant equivalences and relevant analogies, a world in which the objective is to change one's awareness in such a way that one can become more sensitive to the continual series of messages that what one assumes to be the Higher Entity is pouring down on us. We don't really consider that our job is to acquire an encyclopaedic knowledge of something, but rather to learn the accurate recognition of the real and implicit dimension of all things that swim into our ken. This in itself is a tall order, and it

... INTRODUCTION TO
THE SUFI TRADITION IN THE WEST

requires considerable modesty, effort and common sense to do it without faking it in any way.

Otherwise of course one can "appear to do it", which is what most people do, in which case one gets many worldly rewards because it always looks good. It looks good on stage, it looks good on television, it looks good at dinner parties and on the backs of books: the problem is that it is in fact an imitation, and there is always a part of oneself, no matter whoever one is, that ardently desires absolute truth.

We say that whatever one has been or done, access to such a truth does exist, and techniques are available in the twentieth century and in the western world that can help one work one's own way toward such a thing. More than this one cannot say, because although all sorts of interesting things go on by the wayside, they apply only to the person they actually happened to, and getting too involved in recording peripheral matters can deflect one from one's fundamental target, which is a higher form of consciousness for oneself.

We believe that this higher consciousness exists, and that working for it is indeed what we are for. Otherwise, why bother? The fact that the results of such an exercise will be felt in the form of an extension rather than in the form of an omniscient awareness should not discourage one from the attempt.

The first nine talks in this book *(The Sufi Tradition in the West)* are a kind of basic study programme that Omar Ali-Shah lays out for his people in the form of an informal syllabus. The next fifteen talks are mostly concerned with the application and consequences of such study once one has made the considerable commitment required to engage oneself on this way of thought and action.

FICTIONS AND FACTIONS

Yet another possible reading of this work is as an enumeration of some of the incompatibilities that exist between what one might call "twentieth century attitudes" and a longer view of mankind.

When we look at an archeological dig or a soil profile we can see that the very thick layer of matter immediately below the present-day surface corresponds to a relatively short period over time. It can be made up of last year's leaves etc. As you go back further in the time represented by the soil profile, the layers become thinner and thinner, in other words less and less visible, even though these layers are representing longer and longer periods of historical or physical time. This tends to be the way we look at ourselves historically: we are preoccupied with the present surface and immediate past to the detriment of the rest.

What this means here is that a person can use this book as a time lens to view one's present-day life and situation from afar off. Someone who is not specifically interested in the Sufi Tradition can therefore still profit from a book such as this because it expresses a vastly ancient way of thought in a familiar and simple twentieth-century vocabulary and context. And the point of view on our sacred cows and institutions from "back there" is tough and unsentimental, even if it is fundamentally informed by love.

1994

THIRTY YEARS ON

History is what some people have thought to be significant.
Idries Shah

It is more or less impossible to draw an objective portrait of any particular group of people, even if they shared a common general intention, because their viewpoints, even within this intention, were all very different. Nevertheless we were all linked to each other by being pupils of the Sayed Omar Ali-Shah, Naqshbandi, and in telling their story I am probably telling my own story more than anyone else's. But my view is that of a pupil trying to bear witness, and who was almost never alone in the experiences undergone. I tell it as I saw it and nothing is invented.

Our story as disciples begins around 1960, with a number of people in London and Paris who had first been in contact with Ouspensky's teaching goups and later in contact with Ouspensky's own mentor, Gurdjieff.

Some description of the study context in London and Paris before the arrival of the Shah brothers is necessary. Traditional studies were generally known as the *Grand Oeuvre* or *Work* before the arrival of the Shah brothers who were to initiate the practical implementation of Sufi studies in the West. Without wishing to fight old battles anew (I myself was not around at this time), it can be said that Gurdjieff's death in 1949 left a fairly messy heritage with many different people trying to carry on the work he had begun with students in the West.

Jeanne de Salzmann, one of his early disciples, eventually imposed a measure of "order" on the various activities and succeeded in institutionalizing a so-called "Gurdjieffian" teaching. Her authority was accepted by many of Gurdjieff's

FICTIONS AND FACTIONS

followers but by no means all of them; she was able to set up an organised hierarchy under her own leadership which has been dynastically prolonged by her son Michel.

By the beginning of the sixties there were quite a few people who had known Gurdjieff and Ouspensky personally and who nevertheless were unwilling to accept de Salzmann's claims to teaching competence, who had refused to go along with this "succession" in the fifties, and who were on the lookout for a properly mandated exemplar of the ancient teaching, because even if they only had counterfeit gold in their hands, they realised that the true gold had to exist somewhere in human form.

During this period in Paris, a woman called Vera Milanova Page, who had been the widow of the famous French poet René Daumal, who was the wife of the British landscape architect Russel Page, had refused to submit to the rule of her contemporary Jeanne de Salzmann, and had organised a small group of students based on Gurdjieffian ideas. She had been close to Gurdjieff herself and her teaching was strongly influenced by him, although in contrast to others, she declared herself to be a "preparer" and not a fully-fledged teacher. There were other informal groups in London organised around ex-disciples of Gurdjieff, which meant there was a sort of unofficial ongoing Gurdjieffian activity supported by older members who had known him personally and who knew what life with him had been like.

Vera Page came down with cancer in 1961 and died the following year. The future of the study group in Paris became a matter of great concern, all the more so since some of the younger people began manifesting a desire to take over and 'get things moving', something that the older members were wise enough not to desire. They had already seen a takeover of their teacher's work by one of their own contemporaries, and did not want it to see it happen again.

It was at about this time that Reginald Hoare read a travel article about Afghanistan in *Blackwood's Magazine*: in this article there was a description of a Sufi exercise that was known only to the top ten ranked Gurdjieffians of the period. Reggie Hoare thought that behind the pseudonym of the author there had to be someone who knew a great deal about the teaching and where it came from, and he wrote a letter to the author care of the magazine's editor in order to make contact with him.

It was Idries Shah who replied to Hoare's letter as author of the article, which he was later himself to describe as "trawling". Reggie met him, became convinced of his validity as a mentor of what at the time was being called the Greater Work, and began to introduce him to various Gurdjieffians in London and Paris, and through John Bennett, to others who had been connected to the Indonesian teacher Pak Subuh. Shah agreed to teach some of these people and rejected others.

Although Russel Page was under considerable pressure to take on the leadership of the Paris group himself, to his great credit he asked Shah to take on this drifting group whose leader had just died, and Shah accepted. The first meeting between Idries Shah and the Paris group took place in the spring of 1962. Omar Ali-Shah or "Agha" as we came to call him, was still travelling at this time: he appeared on the scene in October. My wife Catherine remembers being disappointed when Shah first said his brother was going to come and live among us in Paris, she asked Shah why we had to make do with his brother: "My brother and I are the same thing" replied Shah.

Shah's instructions were to write a personal letter stating why one was in the group and what one expected from it, to cease reading the canonical literature by Gurdjieff and

FICTIONS AND FACTIONS

Ouspensky, and to stop the practice of the *mouvements* (an example of these stylized and robotic movements can be seen at the end of the film *Meetings with Remarkable Men*, where they represent evolved consciousness: the people on screen are mostly adepts from that time).

In 1962 and 1963, activities were mostly centred in England, generally around the Coombe Springs centre which was made available to Shah by John Bennett. There were three-day meetings, basically parties, which served to get people familiarized with each other (note: A good deal of lying has found its way into print in recent years about Coombe Springs, Bennett and Shah; more on this in a later chapter). This pattern of casual weekend gatherings was to continue at Shah's place at Langton for many years. Teaching took place in this informal context: there were never classrooms or workshops.

The first Thursday night exercises in Paris began with listening to the *Om Mane Padme Om* mantra, followed by tapes of Shah reading Sufi texts and stories. The Lataif came later. It was in England that Shah announced that his brother would come and live with us in Paris. We were less than impressed, we wanted the real teacher, not a stand-in.

The publication of *The Teachers of Gurdjieff* by Rafael Lefort in 1966 completed the breakup with the Salzmann succession, because this book, which even today makes many Gurdjieffians froth at the mouth, gives a clear account of the origin of Gurdjieff's own learning process (which he always swathed in poetic vagueness) and the implicit limitations to his personality and teaching. For the first time someone who seemed to know what he was talking about pointed out that Gurdjieff had never completed the course he had engaged himself on, that he had claimed mastership in the West without having been properly mandated to do so and that as a result his teaching suffered from his own serious personality limitations. He was not an impostor, but his strong personality combined with his own personal limitations hobbled his teaching, since he had not arrived at a sufficient level of awareness to incarnate all its dimensions, particularly the ethical and religious aspects. He was a remarkable man who did not seem to love God.

In all of the reports on Gurdjieff's actions and behaviour, whether sympathetic or unsympathetic, one gets the impression of a man in a hurry whose impatience could lead him into brutality. According to Mme de Hartmann's book, he once said life itself was too slow a process to create teaching situations and such situations had to be contrived in order to be able to do the job. This is perhaps where his system failed: wanting to work too quickly, he was capable of breaking his students. The point here is that if one trusts the capacity of a student to learn, one must also trust his or her rhythm of assimilation, in other words as a teacher you have to key into the teaching function of life itself. A true teacher in the Tradition has a precise awareness of the function of time; taking on the development of another human being requires an absolute knowledge of when action or inaction is needed.

The one idea which was and still is unbearable to Gurdjieff's followers is that he was one of many people who passed through the hands of the *Kwajagan* or Central Asian school of Naqshbandi Sufis. They feel he must be entirely self-originated, which is impossible. Lefort's book attracted criticism for being cast in fable form, and it was also pointed out that Gurdjieff's teachers would no longer have been alive to talk about it in the sixties. But insofar as there is no indication in the book about the events recounted having happened in the sixties, the argument doesn't really hold water: how can you criticize a book both for being a fable and for being inaccurate on dates?

FICTIONS AND FACTIONS

Agha came to live with us in Paris in 1963 and 1964. Many non-esoteric activities were launched at this time: a space was rented and sales of various objects, mostly junk, were organised to raise a little money. It was necessary at this time to decompress from the personal power orientation of the Gurdjieffians. People talked a lot together, hierarchical barriers were broken down, and one sees now that Agha was weaning people from an overtly "esoteric" thinking pattern that had become obsessional; we needed to talk and interact with each other more simply. After the Thursday exercise we would all go bowling with Agha, playful as children. People would meet on Sundays to play croquet or Monopoly.

The friends were asked to bring along their esoteric literature for inspection, and most of it ended up being sold off to second-hand booksellers. Once again, this operation must be seen in context. To my knowledge Agha has never censored anybody's reading matter since, and would not particularly think of doing so.

Right from the beginning Agha was always saying that he was a "traditionalist". Fine, why not? We certainly didn't object. We were full of good will and had absolutely no idea what this might entail. Thirty years later, we're beginning to get some idea.

We were in the mid-sixties, but Agha always seemed to be able to come up with equivalences to the ancient teaching. In May 1968, when the streets were awash with revolting students we were spending the night in the Tradition shop to protect it rather than in the street breaking up those belonging to others. He wasn't very enthusiastic about certain cultural icons of the time such as Beckett and Bergman because he considered that they worked towards a closing-in of the mind, a sort of ersatz spirituality which, it must be said, is very much

... THIRTY YEARS ON

a hallmark of contemporary art.

The organisation of camping and other trips together is an example of an old technique which Agha recycled for modern times. Caravans and the pilgrimage to Mecca (and later to Compostella) were means of breaking down social barriers and suspending daily routines, thus providing novel common experiences and refining the contact between dervishes in the old days: it is probably fair to say that our own modest caravans and gatherings fulfill the same function.

We had an old antique store that became the Tradition shop after the group had put a considerable amount of labour into it. I came along in 1964 to help my friends the Poles with the plastering, and became besotted with a beautiful young lady called Catherine, with whom, *mirabile dictu*, I am still married today. I had no idea what was going on with the people around me, and it was Catherine who first explained to me why they were there, because there was an intensity in the relationships which was not exactly palsy-walsy. The word "sufism" came up in the conversation: "What the hell is that?" I said. But we all pitched in to scrape and paint the walls with great energy and enthusiasm, without any of us really knowing how these jobs were supposed to be done.

Personal story: the night before the opening of the boutique was a Thursday. While all the others were doing the Thursday exercise, I went on working and cleaning up the building dust and rubble because the shop was still filthy and needed to be prepared for the grand opening the next day. Instead of joining us to clear up after the exercise, most of the group went off to a restaurant nearby leaving only a few of the young ones to finish off. Agha and his wife passed by on the way to join the others, and he immediately took in the situation, rolled up his sleeves without saying anything and began right away to do the cleaning by our side.

FICTIONS AND FACTIONS

He had a highly personal style with the broom and dustpan. He would sweep all the junk and garbage into a large pile right in the middle of the shop, and then go off to look for the dustpan, tracking everything that he had swept up back over the floor. He would then find the dustpan and bring it back into the middle, whereupon he would have mislaid the broom somewhere, so that he had to put the dustpan down somewhere else and go looking for the broom. He would then carefully sweep everything back into the centre of the shop, and the whole process would begin over.

This scene played itself over and over several times: by the end we had all stopped work and were just looking at Agha with our mouths agape while he went on with this frenetic and useless activity without cracking a smile, it was like watching Buster Keaton.

Suddenly, and I still don't know why, something occurred to me. Agha was *us*. He was in fact incarnating everything I had seen going on in the shop for the past six months: Bella pouring nitric acid on the tiles in order to clean them and reacting indignantly when we screamed at her after it had dripped on us from above; Jean-Pierre doing such a brilliant job of stripping away the plaster that he ended up in the building next door, etc., etc.

I was working as an actor at this time, but it was strange and impressive to see that he was playing us without guying us, without the implicit superiority of the comic actor. Not once did he grin to show it was all a game. There was no reassurance, he was serious, totally identified with the work he was doing, and completely inefficient. What I realised in that moment, and which changed my life for good, was that he was not only showing us where we were, but that he was doing it from where we were at the time, in other words not downwards from above our station, but from straight on, at the exact level of awareness we were in.

... THIRTY YEARS ON

Now we all have things in our life which we did wrong and things we did right: my own "quiet pride" is that with not much to go on and not knowing anything much about the Tradition, I recognised my teacher. One could of course tell this story from another perspective: maybe it was my teacher who did me the honour of letting himself be recognised by me.

Today I know that I had in fact received a certain training without realising it. It was only after my father died in 1988 that I understood that his example of practical maieutics in the printmaking workshop he ran throughout his life had provided me with the means to evaluate what a teaching master in fact does. I trusted Idries Shah and Omar Ali-Shah because my father had shown me that you communicate knowledge from necessity, not from desire: they were the only people I ever knew who matched my father's purity of intention.

It is very difficult to put across our lack of awareness at that time. We had no idea of a master's status and Agha never talked to us about how we should treat him or make use of him: he simply waited for the penny to drop. We'd all go off to the bowling alley after the Thursday meeting, we'd slap him on the shoulder and tell him dumb or dirty jokes: it never occurred to us to invite him for dinner, in the restaurant he paid his own way.

For several months he stayed in the home of two of our friends before a small studio apartment was found for him in the fifteenth arrondissement. The place belonged to a friend in the group, and it was basically a large single loft-type room with a high ceiling and an inside balcony which acted as the sleeping area. A curtain was discreetly drawn across the balcony sleeping area to separate it from the downstairs living space, and we always stayed downstairs without going up the staircase to the balcony because it would have been indiscreet to go into Agha's personal space. One day the owner went up

FICTIONS AND FACTIONS

the steps just to check that everything was all right. He came back down with a strange expression on his face, and said to another friend: "Hey, didn't you say that you were going to put the bed in?"

"No," said the friend, "I thought you were going to do it."

For the past three weeks, Agha had been sleeping on a sheet spread out on the floor. He never said a word to anybody, and never complained. He just waited it out, that's all.

One of Agha's favourite hobbies was automobile mechanics. Agha used to like tinkering with an old car which he had installed in the garage of one of the friends on the outskirts of Paris. He would turn up on most Saturday afternoons to tinker with the engine or the bodywork of his Jaguar, sometimes taking tea with the friends, sometimes continuing to work alone and sometimes not turning up at all. At the insistence of his wife, who wanted to be able to plan weekends ahead for her two young children, this friend finally worked up enough courage to timidly ask Agha if he wouldn't mind phoning beforehand to say when he was coming. "Of course" said Agha with a smile, "I quite understand," and he never set foot in their house again.

Catherine says that when the first camping caravan to Morocco was organised in the summer of 1964, at all stops throughout the trip everybody remained sitting at cafe terraces between Paris and Tangiers, obediently waiting for Agha to give instructions. No-one ever felt that it might be up to them to take an initiative, so they all waited very patiently. Since he never said a word, everybody sat there looking at each other for two weeks in Tangiers before starting on the trip back home.

Even though our attitude towards Agha could veer

... THIRTY YEARS ON

between infantile dependence and brash over-familiarity, he took it all with kindness, carefully hiding any impatience he may have felt. Trial and error, not to mention stretching and lamination. A major trap is to think you can be pals with the teacher, but we didn't know that then.

To be fair, not everyone was like this. The above-mentioned Bella had understood what the scale of a master was, but since she was considered one of the "crazies" of the group, we weren't going to be convinced. Her childhood playground had been the camp at Auschwitz, and she was to die very young of bone cancer: maybe it was this experience of living at so much greater a level of intensity that gave her a greater awareness of reality.

1965 was the year of the trip to Turkey and Konya, it was the first and last trip that both Shah and Agha did together. It also functioned as Agha and Anna's honeymoon: to our surprise, he had appeared one day at the shop with Anna on his arm saying: "I would like you to meet my wife." Although he was living among us, we knew absolutely nothing about his private life. I myself was now covering as a salesman at the shop when not dubbing films and acting in the theatre. Little by little it turned into my main job: I'd gotten myself into a serial which was never to end.

The first Paris tekkia was installed above the shop in the Passage St-André-des-Arts (it's a tearoom today). After the inauguration, Agha and his new wife Anna moved back to Britain.

On the group trip to Granada in 1967, at a campsite just out of town, an English enthusiast was searching everywhere for a Sufi teacher with his disciples whom he had been told were staying at a camping ground somewhere in Granada. When asked, the proprietor of the site replied that there was

FICTIONS AND FACTIONS

nobody of that description here, just families with their children. Agha walked his baby in a perambulator and put up a lean-to tent next to his microbus in order to shade little Amina during her siesta: once again, it didn't occur to us that we should help him, in fact I remember him shinnying up a tree to attach a tent cord for me. He spent some time underneath my ancient car to repair it: it seemed quite normal that he should wait on me.

The Englishman spent a week looking for us high and low and finally caught up with us the day before we left.

It would be impossible to exaggerate the euphoria we were in at this time. We had the run of the candy store: a two-headed master in the form of Agha and Shah, both of them extraordinary in their combination of caustic humour and underlying tenderness, the English and French groups were one, a couple of shy Spaniards had attached themselves to us, South America or the United States had not yet joined the caravan, and we thought in all sincerity that the whole deal had been quite obviously designed for us alone, that the work was already done and that all we had to do to gather its fruits was to hold out our arms.

In 1967 *The Rubaiyyat of Omar Khayaam* was published by Cassell's in a new translation by Robert Graves and Omar Ali-Shah. Robert Graves was then the most famous English-language poet alive and Agha's association with him gave him probably the highest press and public profile he will ever have.

It must be said here that the translation was just about entirely Agha's: Graves's contribution to the text (he didn't know Persian) was probably no more than a dozen minor revisions. If one compares the text with Graves's own work, whether poetry or translation, the style is clearly different. In fact he implicitly recognized this when he wrote in the preface

... THIRTY YEARS ON

that the invitation to be co-author of this translation "was the greatest poetic compliment I had ever been paid."

Nowadays, when the sufic influence is completely recognised throughout Arab and Persian literature and culture, it is difficult to imagine the bomb-like effect of this translation and the amount of anger it provoked. The Fitzgerald version of the *Rubaiyyat*, although completely contradicting the intention of the original Persian text, had become sacrosanct: generations of British children had been brought up on it, and who cared anyway if Fitzgerald could hardly read Persian and had turned it into an anti-religious tract? Who cared if the concept of "wine" in Sufi lore signified the drunken state one enters into when one begins to know God? Who cared whether the Fitzgerald version, although elegantly versified, was a crass parody of the original? These were two weirdo Afghan brothers who didn't have a University or a bunch of endlessly footnoted conference contributions to back them up and, as the polemic developed, the reaction of the literary establishment became increasingly hysterical, concerning itself as usual with track records rather than with what you're saying. Since nobody wanted to discuss the real issue, which was whether Khayaam had been a Sufi or not, the polemic soon focused on secondary issues having to do with the Persian manuscript the translation had been made from. The Shah brothers were accused of being confidence men or worse.

This polemic was actually nurtured by the brothers themselves, with friends being encouraged to write letters to the editors of all the papers (either for or against, the opinion didn't matter) and with replies to the replies to the replies in all the letter columns. Because the biggest insult of all was that Idries Shah's books were becoming bestsellers at this time, and Tom Maschler at Jonathan Cape wanted to catch the wave by turning him into a popular guru like the Maharishi. The British

FICTIONS AND FACTIONS

orientalists who controlled the educational and university institutions were green with envy, their books sold in the hundreds, not thousands, and they took a very dim view of this upstart taking over their turf.

Endless bickering took place about the authenticity of the translation manuscript and Agha was challenged to produce the original Persian text: in the end he decided not to play this second-rate game and he never did produce the manuscript, preferring to pull out of the match if it was going to played with people with this kind of intention.

Omar Ali-Shah has been as good as his word, he only came back into print twenty-five years later when I started editing and compiling books from his talks to students. Idries Shah found his way back into the good graces of academia through the manifest quality of his writing and research, and also by a very simple expedient: he began to publish their work.

Of course it is perfectly true that academics have always had a problem with the two brothers (although there are more and more exceptions to this rule): they sense an absolute refusal to jump through the academic hoops of specialist publications, lectureships and final acceptance by their elders and betters. At the same time there is distrust from the pious Muslim end of the spectrum, who consider it very doubtful indeed that two Muslims should be teaching sufism without first insisting that their students convert to Islam. The basic question here is one of method: are learning Arabic and converting to another religion, with its inevitable reverberations on the immediate surroundings and family of the student, really indispensable to Sufi apprenticeship? Does everyone have the time to spend years learning another language? Is sufism reserved for an intellectual or other elite?

... THIRTY YEARS ON

The basic response is that political or religious pressure groups of any kind are irrelevant to our purpose and we cannot be submitted to them. We obey the law of the land and also claim absolute freedom to think and speak as we please, because any research laboratory must have the freedom to make mistakes. Once again, if Islam covers 35% of the world population, is it really conceivable that a universal way of thinking should be limited to two-fifths of the planet?

Back to the group in Paris: at the Easter meeting in 1968 Agha produced the first of a number of shock waves when he asked us to stand up and be counted if we were engaged in the Sufi work, which would henceforth no longer be known as the "Work", as with the Gurdjieffians, but as the "Tradition".

He had never asked us for any overt demonstration of this kind: we were all dignified and well-behaved people; some of us even thought ourselves to be intellectuals. We were men of the world, not militants.

He then told us that he was going to have to stop taking care of us. I never believed him for a moment: such an idea was inconceivable. Maybe he was talking to only some of us: maybe it's really what he wanted to do; this incident has always remained an enigma to me. I can't explain it and I'd better not try.

My own interpretation of what was going on throughout this time is that the incidents of this period represent a kind of litmus test, i.e., an evaluation by the two brothers about how the Tradition would be able to "take" in the West, because there had been no laboratory in the West since Gurdjieff's approximation in the thirties. In any case from that time on, the two brothers followed different roads, or "agreed to disagree" as Agha put it to us.

FICTIONS AND FACTIONS

Agha himself has written: "As far as agreeing to disagree with I. Shah, it was a simple matter but a fundamental one: he is the theorist concerned with projecting the Tradition in (such) a way that it would be 'acceptable' to academics and other professional philosophers and intellectuals."

In this letter Agha goes on to say: "I am not a theorist. I know what I am trained to teach and communicate and carry out, and I do it in the most efficient way. I do not seek 'approval' from western thinkers. I do not want honorary degrees and academic applause. My first responsibility is to those who put their trust in me, and if I have to use a shocking, even strange, activity in order to communicate knowledge or energy, I will do it, even if it may cause people to be scandalized." (Letter of October 10, 1986)

The first junction that took place between our new friends from South America and ourselves was during the group trip to Assisi in the summer of 1969. We thought they were very nice but found them a little over-enthusiastic in the way they expressed themselves. Bernardo went so far as to encourage them to "liberate the energy" of certain artifacts in a nearby church, in other words steal them. Agha instructed that the objects be put back where they were taken from without anyone getting caught, and the person responsible was politely thanked and sent off to work on his own in September.

The birth of our two sons meant that Catherine and I did not attend trips between 1970 and 1973. Throughout this time Agha pushed hard to start up groups in South America. Work in Mexico had begun, groups were organised on behalf of Agha in Italy and there was a strong expansion into Germany. The new groups in Mexico, Brazil and Argentina had great vitality and enthusiasm and their people were completely different in temperament from the predominantly Anglo groups in Paris

... THIRTY YEARS ON

and London. Their perception of the way one was supposed to work was also completely different.

In 1977 the axe fell: *"My brother and I have agreed to disagree on certain aspects of the projection, of the workings and the techniques employed within the Tradition."* The two channels were separating, and it was a shock whose reverberations are still felt today because the assumed enmity metastatized in the subordinates. What appeared unthinkable at the time now seems fairly logical with hindsight. What was confusing at the time, and which confuses people even today, is the fact, as Irina Hoare once put it to me, that "many people, once bitten by the Tradition, cannot ever leave it, even though they are unable to find enough trust in themselves to commit themselves entirely to a master."

In this activity there are often a lot of people waiting in the wings, convinced that they have a starring role. It is also such people who tend to find their way into print and become "experts" on the subject for the outside world, since they entertain the illusion of their own sufficiency of knowledge and feel themselves empowered to either sell or denounce the Tradition. The truly committed understand how limited their own knowledge is and what misunderstandings they can provoke. A lot of our friends had been quite happy pursuing a Gurdjieffian orientation which stressed personal power at the expense of a submission to a higher intelligence, and many did not want to see our activity changing its focus, which it did, inexorably.

When Agha began to introduce invocations, zikrs and prayers in Arabic taken from the *Koran*, the filtering process became quite radical, it really separated the men from the boys. There are in fact very few still with us from the original anglophone contingent, because many of that first generation of students had broken off from their church of origin and they

FICTIONS AND FACTIONS

were now being forced to come to terms with their lapsed faiths. Until now the Tradition activities or its previous affiliations had offered the possibility of an activity without focusing on God, because the word God is a major unmentionable with Gurdjieffians. Now there was no escape, we were cornered: either we were believers or we weren't.

There was also a more subtle pressure being applied because Agha was pushing very hard on the Spanish and South American connections, creating new groups and new responsibilities everywhere, and some of us were beginning to feel a bit left out. New members tend to take five years to know better than you, then they have to forget what they know. Many new members came into the Tradition at this time, and a building programme for the construction of tekkias or dervish meeting-places was initiated and realised over the next twenty years.

From the perspective of thirty years, one can clearly see that Agha's way of working has indeed been in a more classical mould than his brother's: group meetings, prayers in Arabic, collective exercises and activities, and the encouragement of a feeling of belonging and identification which is almost military in nature. While not participating directly in Idries Shah's teaching operation after their separation, my feeling is that it took place mostly in the form of a direct relationship between mentor and student, with books as the primary contact, and that using a group as a tool or relay mechanism was less important to him as a technique.

At Easter 1976, the Brazilian and Mexican friends joined us for the meeting at Pierrefitte. The weather was horrible, rain and sleet followed by snow and ice. The friends, who were mostly without overcoats, had arrived fresh from the South American summer and were put up on the floor of the church hall without any heating or bedding, while the members of the Paris group retired to their heated hotel rooms for the night.

Across the street from the church the large warm house of one of our friends remained empty so that Agha and Anna who were staying there would have a place to get away to. Perhaps our South American friends were able to see the delicate supper being prepared as they swigged down the duty-free tequila they had opened up as a possible remedy against the invading cold. The next morning, members of the Paris group smelt the alcohol on their breaths and found this quite shocking: these South Americans really didn't know how to behave. When word later got back to us about how our friends didn't feel us to be very hospitable, the reaction of most of us was that such people lacked proper respect towards their elders in the Tradition.

At the Easter meeting in Arcos in 1978 an incident took place which gave me much food for thought. On the last evening, among the many Spanish and Brazilian friends who were meeting Agha for the first time, a show of songs and dances was organised which ended up in a near-riot with everybody applauding and screaming: "Agha! Agha!"

With his usual calm, Agha came up on stage and proceeded to praise the selflessness of his wife in words that could have been taken from the mouth of any professional politician on the campaign trail. There was of course an immediate feedback: the whole room rocked to the cries of "Anna! Anna!" and people began to jump up on the tables and stamp their feet. The tables were on moveable struts and began to fall over, and one of the Brazilian friends was caught underneath while above her the others went on stamping: she ended up with a broken leg.

I glanced over at the object of all this adoration: Anna's

face was a study in white terror; she was poleaxed. All of the ex-Gurdjieffian Anglo friends began first to look at each other, then at the surrounding craziness: was this really what they wanted from a spiritual discipline? A few months later, they had all bowed out.

And why did Catherine and I not follow them out, even though we were by no means a fan of this kind of thing? Simply because, the next day, when I talked to the friends who had led the applause and the cheering, I realised that this "spontaneous" event had been organised by Agha himself. It had not just happened by accident; it had been carefully planned and orchestrated. My curiosity was too strong to let go at that point: I wanted to know why.

Fourteen years later I think I am now beginning to come up with at least the beginning of an answer which satisfies me, although I quite understand that it may not be satisfactory to others.

This is it: once one starts off a process of overly grandiose self-identification, a concomitant process of this grandiosity's self-destruction is set off at the same time; I would consider this a more or less inescapable law. If, as an individual, one has associated oneself too closely with this grandiosity one will feel that one's essential being is being destroyed along with this useless shell.

When a trap like this is held out to us or rather when we hold it out to ourselves, the result can be quite horrible. One can blame oneself or one can blame others. One then either swallows hard and gets on with it, or else one walks away in a huff. Some stay, others walk away.

If one accepts the existence of such a law, it can be said that it will apply at all levels and should not be considered a purely intellectual concept. It applies to every area of one's own behaviour as well as to the relationship with one's teacher. The phenomenon does not have to do with belonging to a group even if it is group interactions that make the phenomenon manifest: what is involved here is a brimming-over of emotion which pushes one towards the unfortunate idealisation of an imaginary hierarchy or the misplaced worship of one's own psychic phenomena.

In any real Tradition, one is ultimately forced to define the limits of one's own commitment to the teacher, to the Tradition and to oneself; and non-conventional or shocking behaviour by the teacher is an indispensable part of the array of techniques available: it enables the teacher to ensure that a testing process is really taking place, and that the pupil's choice is truly his own and not based on mere seduction or personality-worship. If a teacher did not test one's trust by casting doubt upon himself, he would be cheating the student by preempting his ever-present option to leave.

When viewed from outside, as in the foregoing incidents I have related, the normal cynical and/or conditioned view will be that the teacher is engaged in a process of self-interested manipulation. It is only when one has been able to experience the workings of the Sufi Tradition over a long period of time that one begins to see how the time factor meshes into individual situations and perceptions, and effects its change on the human material involved.

One of the hardest things for a westerner to do is to learn to trust his or her teacher, because the entire western intellectual tradition (with a small 't') is based on developing a skeptical and narrowly analytical view of reality. In the Sufi Tradition, we would consider such a thing to be part of the inevitable environmental or social conditioning one has been subjected to and which must be overcome.

FICTIONS AND FACTIONS

It therefore comes as no surprise that both academic orientalists and religious professionals of all confessions, whose strength is rarely humility, react by saying: "Who do these Sufis think they are, looking down on us?" In fact we are only saying that we are not the proprietors of knowledge, only its servants, and western education has got its priorities wrong because information only begins to have some value once a basis of self-knowledge has been achieved.

This begs the question: what is self-knowledge? Insofar at it applies to themselves, everyone has their own answer to that question, and everyone is probably right. Suffice it to say that in the Sufi Tradition such knowledge is regarded as being worthy of a lifetime's study and work. Belief enters into this picture, because there has to be some kind of measuring-rod that enables us at least to aspire to perfection, whether or not our destiny is to attain it. The road is a long one, very discouraging sometimes, and there has to be a project to keep us on the path.

If one looks at it in this way one can consider that a Sufi teacher and a Sufi group are simply technical instruments designed to provide a relay between an individual and a higher order of knowledge. In order to become engaged in such a process, one must assume for the time being that, at least theoretically, such a higher knowledge does in fact exist and that it can be connected to a knowledge of the personal self.

Let us be very clear about the limits of any philosophy or way of thought: the Sufi Tradition, as such, cannot create self-knowledge, cannot create belief, cannot create trust and did not and cannot create an awareness of God. Nevertheless it is a technique which can be used by any individual, whatever their background or capacity, to build upon and add to any of the above. But as Omar Ali-Shah points out time and time again: "I cannot do the work for you."

... THIRTY YEARS ON

It is obvious that some people, when they read about people breaking their legs or sleeping on the floor in the cold, will say: "What does this have to do with spiritual development? These people are savages!" The only answer I can give to such a reaction is: "Yes, but I aspire to something else. I may be a savage at the present time, but with the help of God and the Tradition, I will not always be this way."

The state we are in is the state we are in. This state may be somewhat less glorious than we think. If this is indeed true, the master's job will be to raise us up from where we are and not from where we think ourselves to be.

The duty of a Sufi teacher is to do what has to be done: he does not necessarily have time to flatter us or the inclination to explain himself. In any case, things can only be explained up to a point.

1992

FICTIONS AND FACTIONS

STATING THE OBVIOUS

(Original preface to the 1991 Tractus Books edition of
Sufism for Today by Omar Ali-Shah)

Some people might reproach this book its lack of thrills because it eschews the magic and marvels that are generally sold under the heading of "esoteric sciences". We live in a time when an artisan-like approach requiring the slow assimilation of a restricted number of techniques working in parallel is very undervalued in comparison to the zappy impacts that come at us from our audiovisually-conditioned mental environment. The magic and the marvels sell the books, and a master/disciple relationship will be presented in such lurid terms that nobody will imagine that the utterances of a master can be legitimate if they are not in broken English, if the interchange has not taken place in a mountain cave or the Gobi Desert, or if the intention is not to kick some villain's teeth in.

Everybody likes a good story, so there's no point in turning up one's nose at this: the problem only begins when the novelization and dramatization of such experiences take over to the extent that the less overt and more subtle content of this type of interchange is discounted. Nevertheless, it must be said that certain perceptions and possibilities which were previously limited to a very few people are now being scattered into the general context of society more than ever before.

When I first became interested in the Sufi Tradition, if you happened to mention to a normally educated person that a great deal of modern science and thinking came to us from the Arab world through the medieval Sufi schools of Toledo and Montpellier, and the translators from the Abbaye of Cluny who worked with them, people thought you were mad. Nowadays this is widely accepted as legitimate historical fact, which it is.

So things don't necessarily get worse: the problem is that success brings drawbacks in its wake insofar as irrelevancies become associated with the main thrust of the teaching. The fashionable "new age" type of thinking is both positive and negative in terms of the kind of awareness this book would encourage. It is positive in the sense that the inner development and/or transformation of man through his own efforts is now considered a viable possibility and potential hope for people, and it is negative in the sense that it tends to use purely emotional criteria to judge if the process is actually happening.

The Sufi Tradition has no monopoly on knowledge; but insofar as it is itself a technique, access to what knowledge it can communicate has to be funnelled through a certain discipline, a focusing of intention, and a certain amount of trust in the fact that someone else may better know what you need than you do yourself.

In the West, the whole process stands or falls by the acceptance of a teacher. In the East there is a certain pre-existing culture in this regard, but such an acceptance does tend to go against the grain of a western education in the humanities (here again, technicians and craftsmen tend to be more realistic: they know you learn a technique from someone who can practise it better than you).

It is true that a lot of cheats and thieves have worked this area in the West, but just as many psychiatrists have abused their clients, it is by no means axiomatic that they do so. As Idries Shah pointed out, the old saying that "Counterfeit gold proves the existence of real coin" still holds true.

It basically boils down to the capacity of people to

FICTIONS AND FACTIONS

discriminate: if people are not given a series of fairly simple guidelines which they can use as instruments to see their own situation and present state, they will tend to go towards a wish-fulfilling and sentimental Disneyland of the mind, in preference to an objective view of their own person and possibilities. The book that follows can fulfill such a function, assuming that a desire for what one might call uneasy knowledge does exist.

So let the reader beware: there is no instant eureka-type enlightenment to be gleaned from this book because for this to happen, the reader's own time, experience and commitment will have to be keyed in alongside the information contained in the book, and this does take time and some familiarisation. What this book can provide, however, is a clear and lucid account of how one can look at one's own present-day circumstances, life and times in order to begin to develop a personal view which is both objective and loving. Some people may feel this to be an unexciting prospect: Walt Disney is more entertaining. It depends on what one wants.

Sufism for Today should therefore not be read like a novel that hasn't done its job if it didn't keep you up all night: it is more like an engineering textbook than a romance. Read it a chapter at a time in a relaxed sort of way, rather than trying to gobble it all up at a single sitting. The book is simple, and for a good reason: the science of man has always existed and has always been open to all, irrespective of a person's education, background, or even what is habitually regarded as their intellect.

What is laid out in this book is in fact so simple that it could quite easily slip between one's fingers like water: yet it is because of this divine simplicity that the Sufi Tradition has never stopped, even if it has occasionally had to go underground for a time, like a river in midsummer. As Alfred

... STATING THE OBVIOUS

North Whitehead once said: "It takes an unusual mind to undertake the analysis of the obvious."

The words here are those of a teacher who is more like an engineer of the spirit than a saint, and who talks like a technician rather than like a priest. He talks this way because he is trying to give us the technique that he himself was trained to use: it is up to us to take it on board.

Emotion is not the point here: as the man in a *New Yorker* cartoon said to his kids in the car while he was changing the rear tyre in the rain: "No I can't switch channels, this is reality."

1991

FICTIONS AND FACTIONS

INTRODUCTION TO IKBAL ALI SHAH'S *ISLAMIC SUFISM*

Ever since *Islamic Sufism* went out of print nearly twenty years ago, aficionados have been passing dog-eared photocopies of this book to each other, carefully preserving their copy because they have seen that when they let go of their own, the book somehow sinks into their circle of friends never to reappear. I don't know if anyone has ever tried to keep a league table of books most frequently stolen from bookshops or private library shelves, but I would wager that *Islamic Sufism* comes high on the list.

The question I will attempt to answer is—why? Why should a book written 64 years ago, seemingly as a handbook for the Sirdar's Indian pupils, have achieved a near-classic status in the West through word-of-mouth only, without the benefit of the slightest publicity or promotion? What interest does an attempt to reconcile Sufi and Hindu philosophical positions have for a contemporary European? Or, to put it more crudely, what's in it for me as a westerner?

The answer is a great deal, because the Sirdar Ikbal Ali Shah was way ahead of his time in perceiving the spiritual crisis already hitting the West in its obsessive worship of material gain, and institutionalised religion's inability to deal with the situation thus created. Much of this book feels as if it was written yesterday, for instance:

> ... *The modern Moslem fondly hopes to unlock fresh sources of energy by narrowing down his thought and emotion. Both nationalism and modern* (i.e., western-based) *atheistic socialism, at least in the present state of human adjustments, must draw upon the psychological forces of hate, suspicion*

... *ISLAMIC SUFISM* INTRODUCTION

and resentment which tend to impoverish the soul of man and close up his hidden sources of spiritual energy ... Neither the technique of medieval mysticism nor nationalism nor atheistic socialism can cure the ills of a despairing humanity. Surely the present moment is one of great crisis in the history of modern culture.

His unsentimental view of contemporary religious cliché is not based, however, on the crass skepticism of so many western intellectuals but on a realistic assessment of the true scale of effort required to implement the spiritual transformation that sufism demands. He cuts a swathe through both religious sentimentality and the modern plethora of philosophical and psychological positions to say that our development always has, and always will, depend upon what we do, for:

Conduct, which involves a decision of the ultimate fate of the agent, cannot be based on illusions. A wrong concept misleads the understanding; a wrong deed degrades the whole man, and may eventually demolish the structure of the human ego.

The illness he is diagnosing is therefore western as well as eastern, because this narrowing of focus is surely a hallmark of contemporary knowledge, where data processing and other relatively simple techniques are used to create infinitely complicated subdivisions, to be turned into various kinds of intellectual chess games by an élite. The same process takes place in religion, whose concepts are turned into yet another hunting ground for specialists, leaving the man in the street to feel that he has been cast aside by those in the know.

But like any good doctor, Ikbal Ali Shah does not limit himself to a relevant diagnosis, he also indicates positive steps that must be taken to overcome man's tendency to worship his

FICTIONS AND FACTIONS

own routines. The answer lies in individual conduct, because mankind is less in what he thinks than in what he does, and he can rebuild himself only on that basis.

> ... Mere concept affects life only partially; the deed is dynamically related to reality and issues from a generally constant attitude of the whole man towards reality ... The evidence of religious experts in all ages and countries is that there are potential types of consciousness lying close to our normal consciousness. If these types of consciousness open up possibilities of life-giving and knowledge-yielding experience, the question of the possibility of religion as a form of higher experience is perfectly legitimate and demands our serious attention.

Thus, 64 years ago this remarkable man had a completely clear view of the challenges that men would have to deal with as they now prepare themselves for the twenty-first century's information and technological explosion.

> The modern world stands in need of biological renewal. And religion, which in its higher manifestations is neither dogma, nor priesthood, nor ritual, can alone ethically prepare the modern man for the burden of the great responsibility which the advancement of modern science necessarily involves, and restore to him that attitude of faith which makes him capable of winning a personality here and retaining it hereafter.

The life eternal was available to mankind before, just as it has always been, but there is and always has been a price to be paid for the realization of one's own being (which he calls 'ego'):

> There are no pleasure-giving and pain-giving acts; there are only ego-sustaining and ego-dissolving acts. It is the deed that prepares the ego for dissolution, or disciplines it for a future career. The principle of the ego-sustaining deed is

... *ISLAMIC SUFISM* INTRODUCTION

respect for the ego in myself as well as in others. Personal immortality, then, is not ours as of right; it is to be achieved by personal effort. Man is only a candidate for it.

The challenge is mighty, and can appear daunting to some, or alternatively, ridiculously easy to those of us who think that all you have to do is follow a few rules and regulations. But the beauty of such a situation is that awareness is open to all men and women alike in precise proportion to their understanding. Its reality is situated beyond creed and doctrine, since the word *Islamic* in the Sirdar's formulation is less a doctrinal hoop to be jumped through than a simple definition of the model of consciousness that the Sufi is expected to study. As Ikbal Ali Shah puts it in his preface:

The Koran is the first and last textbook of Sufism, and the Prophet Muhammed the greatest Sufi of all times. Whosoever, therefore, does not subscribe to this idea, despite the fact that he may be following an Occult Way, is not a Sufi.

This raises a question I must answer for myself, because no one can answer it for me. Does my own adherence to the Sufi Way mean that I must deny or devalue my own story as a baptized western Christian? I think not, because if I truly accept the Prophet Muhammed as a divinely inspired messenger of God, I become a Moslem in that moment, and who has the right to say otherwise? Must I adopt an oriental robe and wear a uniform to love the Prophet for what he did? The truth here is that the inner way or *haqikat* cannot be submitted to the criterion of the *shariat*, or outer observances. Nobody but God can say who or what I am.

The less happy episodes in the history of Christianity are there to show us what can befall a religion when it abandons its

FICTIONS AND FACTIONS

inner and personal content in order to devote itself to the easier aims of social regulation and political power. Needless to say, Christianity does not have a historic monopoly on stupidity.

A word on the Sirdar as a teacher is perhaps not out of order. He was trained by his father, the Nawab Amjed Ali Shah, who had been trained by his own grandfather, Jan-Fishan Khan of Paghman. In turn he trained his own sons, Omar Ali-Shah and Idries Shah to follow his footsteps in making the Sufi Tradition available to the West. Like him, his sons devoted their lives to this end; and in the case of Omar Ali-Shah is still doing so. Their elder sister Amina Shah has been active as a storyteller and writer. Idries Shah's career as a teacher, writer and communicator of traditional Sufi lore has been a determining factor in the recent acceptance of Sufi ideas in the West, and his death in 1997 has been a major loss.

Although it is clear from this book that the Sirdar's Moslem faith was impeccably orthodox, we have no record of the Sirdar insisting that his western pupils formally convert to Islam. In fact he is even on record as being somewhat disapproving of conversion, because of the consequent upset to the person's family and social context, which thus makes it not indispensable to the Sufi apprenticeship. Nevertheless, some of his Indian pupils were asked to become Moslems, perhaps to compensate for an overly fatalistic life-attitude, but such incidents can only be judged when one has a knowledge of the people and context of a given event.

The Sufi Tradition is transmitted by the adoption of various external routines to begin with, but as the pupil matures over the years, the teaching is more and more realized by means of essences, which are expressed in the domain of intimate signals existing between the teacher and taught. The flexibility this necessitates means that the Sufi Tradition cannot ever and has never been controlled by external rules or popular acceptance. Non-Sufis feel that Sufis should look like them—i.e. wear a uniform which labels them socially. Sufis feel they should be allowed to disappear, since awareness can only truly be reported to God.

This is why intellectuals and religious authorities, who both depend on external prestige, are continuously fighting against this form of knowledge which, based as it is on revelation, can only be expressed as an improvisation and not in the form of a rigid doctrinal corpus. This fight can also take the form of imitation, such as the recent phenomenon of western intellectual orientalists forming themselves into their own quasi-dervish circles. Something may come out of it—we'll see.

I did not know the Sirdar personally, but I did indirectly come across an example of his flexibility as a teacher when my wife and I met a middle-aged architect at a dinner party, who in his younger days had been been the Sirdar's pupil near the end of his life in Tangiers. He told us an interesting story: according to him, the Sirdar, with all his worldly experience and knowledge, was not above telling a drug-consuming young hippy, which our dinner guest was at the time: "I'll give you an exercise that will give you a bigger high than the drugs you're taking, but you'll have to lay off all substances first, because they won't work together."

What is interesting here is the Sirdar's ability to speak the pupil's own language. *Speak to each according to his own understanding,* as the Prophet once said. The Sirdar was willing to represent himself as a guru if it served a purpose. The Sirdar died soon after this incident and the person involved never pursued the Sufi Tradition further, but having been weaned from substance abuse, he also never went back on drugs again, and was to live out a full and honourable life.

FICTIONS AND FACTIONS

A teaching function was thus accomplished *without the pupil himself being aware of what had happened*. The man overcame his own drug problem and the Sufi exercises were, as far as he was concerned, only something he happened to be doing at the time. When he told me the story quite casually at that dinner party many years later, he had no particular gratitude toward the Sirdar. It's a classic case of being taught something in spite of oneself.

Again, we touch here on the idea of teaching by essence—it was not necessary for our young man to recognize the Sirdar as benefactor or as a 'great Sufi', it was only necessary for him to get off the drugs. Sufism was the focus by which it could happen.

The elegance of the true teacher is to make himself visible or invisible according to requirement, and that requirement does not necessarily include public fame or even recognition from the taught. If that man went through the rest of his life considering the Sirdar to be some sort of hippy guru, so what, it's a fair bet to say that the Agha Khan or Kemal Ataturk or the King of Egypt would not have considered him in this light. Had our young hipster known that the Sirdar occupied a position of prominence in the world, he would never have accepted his direction. But there was a job to be done, and it was accomplished, and this will always be so. A teacher is for teaching is for teaching.

2000

OPEN SECRETS

Editor's Foreword to
The Rules or Secrets of the Naqshbandi Order by Omar Ali-Shah

Before launching a book like this onto the marketplace, a few words are required, not as a warning on the packet along the lines of "Esoteric literature can be damaging to your mental health" but to establish a kind of guideline for people who have not yet had the chance of familiarizing themselves with the Sufi Tradition and thinking.

The knowledge the Sufi Tradition seeks to inspire is a way of feeling and doing rather than the western idea of a body of intellectual information. This means that the person who comes along with no previous formal knowledge of the subject need not feel inferior to people like myself who have been trying to do it for more than thirty years. The reason is simple: most people grow up in the context of a biological or surrogate family, and manage willy-nilly to develop some form of personal vision as they grow into adulthood. Everyone is hence already in possession of some form of learning equipment even though from the point of view of the Sufi Tradition, this can be somewhat rusty or under-used.

The techniques of the Tradition, of which this book is but one amongst others, are thus designed to make use of and maximize on what a person already knows. The basic idea of such techniques is that they are to be used in conjunction with one's own experience and the daily context of life. This means that you key them into your everyday life, as opposed to placing them on a metaphorical "altar" for purposes of worship.

Why it is considered necessary for a teacher to supervise

FICTIONS AND FACTIONS

such an activity is that people who start off in anything they have not done before will always be somewhat disoriented. After a while they may not be quite so lost but they can still pursue one possibility or avenue of research to the detriment of another, which leads to an unbalanced apprehension of real phenomena. It is the presence of a teacher, whose job is to monitor the learner's work, that enables less time to be wasted in a possibly fruitless quest.

To a certain extent, one can consider that this apprenticeship is similar in nature to that of a manual craft. My father was a teacher of itaglio printmaking and he was sorry when, from the fifties onward, the black ink used on the plates began to be sold pre-mixed with linseed oil. In the old days, one had to grind the ink from dry cakes and mix it into the oil using a grinding-stone on a piece of plate glass. Getting a properly smooth texture of ink was not an easy thing to do, and most apprentices would have to grind the ink for a long time (a process known in French as "broyer du noir") before being allowed to even begin using it themselves on the copper or zinc plate.

When I asked him whether the ready-mixed ink was not as good as the other, he replied "Oh no, the ink itself is fine. It's the relationship with the ink that has changed for the worse."

I don't think it is stretching the imagination too far to say that this book should be considered as one might consider that dry cake of ink, a basic component to a great deal of work to come. There is no label on the side of the ink-cake telling you how to turn it into a beautiful image: the image must come from oneself. The burin won't make a line by itself, but the conscious hand can learn to use that burin. Or, as Omar Ali-Shah repeats over and over again, knowledge must be usable to exist.

... OPEN SECRETS

There can therefore be no possibility of using this book as a sort of formulaic cookbook for esoteric wisdom. Nevertheless, the possibilities of use to which this book or that ink can be put are infinite, so that there is no point in becoming discouraged. One finds one's own way.

If one treats this book with the respect and attention it deserves, it can help almost anybody, so long as they key it into their overall life context without becoming obsessive over details, because that is when a consciousness loses its flexibility. One has to bring the whole of one's own life to bear on the concepts contained in the book, and it is only from this point on that the concepts themselves will acquire some meaning. If one tries to reduce this book to a kind of "how to" manual, this type of thinking will, of itself, render it useless.

A word on the framework of thought within which this is all taking place. To quote Omar Ali-Shah in his preface to *Sufism for Today*:

> *The Sufi Tradition is not a religion, nor is it a cult. It is a philosophy of life, and its purpose is to offer to man a practical path to enable him to achieve a measure of higher consciousness, and through this elevated consciousness, to be able to understand his relationship with the Supreme Being...*
>
> *This philosophy has been handed down throughout the ages. It has retained the ancient quality and has guarded its ancient secrets so that it may be available, unchanged and untarnished, to those who seek deeper wisdom through deeper consciousness.*

This is therefore the frame within which the present book must be considered. If you believe that such a thing is possible,

FICTIONS AND FACTIONS

read on, or take this book to the check-out counter and take it home with you. If you don't believe that such a thing is possible, don't waste your time: put it back on the shelf of the bookstore and go to the movies.

The *Rules or Secrets* are instruments to this general end, no more and no less. When used for lesser ends, they will at worst turn against oneself, or at best become totally useless. The intention with which one uses these techniques will very precisely define the level at which they can work—in other words it can be all or nothing. They are in no sense threatening, but one should just remember that one is handling powerful instruments. Those of us who have some experience of the Tradition know that the acquisition of inner weight makes our mistakes heavier as well.

The rules in this form were in fact laid out many years ago, in the sixteenth century. The first eight of these rules are said to have been drafted by Sheikh Kwaja Abd al-Khaliq Ghujawani who is buried in Ghujawan on the road between Bokhara and Samarkand, and the last three by Bahaudin Naqshband, founder of the Naqshbandi Order of Dervishes, whose recently restored shrine is also near Bokhara.

As Omar Ali-Shah explains in one of the chapters, the word "secret" in the Tradition implies less something which is confidential than something which is of an intimate nature. It is therefore more useful here to consider secret as being of the nature of the intimate, something which addresses itself to the most secret part of the self. If one allows them in, this is the area where the rules can develop and flower, and it is in fact the only place where they can grow. If one tries to use them in any other way, say for impressing people with one's knowledge or for establishing domination over others, they will dissolve, or worse still, turn against one. There is nothing mysterious in this process, they should just be used in a loving way.

The various concepts expressed through these rules are almost infinite in their possible and varied applications, which is why Omar Ali-Shah does not reduce this flexibility of application by giving many precise examples. As he says, if one prescribed a recipe-like usage, such as "use alone in a crowd when you're in the subway during rush hour", one runs the risk of limiting its usage to the subway. The possible situations in which one might use this and other concepts are so varied that people trying to develop themselves by using this technique could conceivably have their horizons narrowed by too many suggested applications.

For this reason, if anybody feels that what is stated in this book appears to be vague, it is because Omar Ali-Shah is subtle enough to realise that there has to be enough room left over for the reader to be able apply his or her own options and experiences to these concepts. He is addressing himself to the feel of the rules' use, rather than to the passing personal situations and events one uses them on. Comparing notes or talking over how one applies them with someone else can be useful, but when this is done outside of a context where people have a similar intention, distortions usually develop. There is a certain narrow efficiency in dogmatism, and people can go off on this kind of tack, dragging others with them. This is one of the reasons why the supervision of a teacher is considered necessary in the Sufi Tradition, which tends to play down the importance of so-called "powerful personalities."

One of the most important things a teacher does in the Sufi Tradition is to judge when something—if anything—is required. You don't get stripes for length of service, but after a while you do get a bit more sense of how long things take, call it a feel for pattern. We are talking here of decades, not of hours

FICTIONS AND FACTIONS

and minutes. Yet some important things do happen quickly, which makes it impossible to generalize.

A few words on the way Omar Ali-Shah works with his people may be in order here, since there is much fantasizing about gurus and teachers from the mysterious East, and anyone reading this book becomes de facto his student, insofar as these talks were all delivered to his students over the past fifteen years.

He does not invade his students' lives, create dependency or use systematically shocking tactics to achieve his (and their) ends, although he is capable of doing so. All family ties and relationships are to be respected and built on, recourse to all artificial stimulants discouraged. He uses the normal time-frame within which we live, which means that progress will often take longer than one would have hoped, and a shock or a provocation will be held in reserve for exceptional cases, for instance when a pupil is falling into a rut of some years' duration. A Sufi teacher doesn't walk into a room with his 'guns blazing' unless there is some teaching point to the operation, but he still has to keep it in reserve as an option if nothing less is adequate for the situation.

The notion of time and appropriateness to the situation is paramount, as well as the 'keying in' factor. One can say that, generally speaking, people have a tendency to be impatient, and western education feeds this tendency by promoting the illusion that you 'know' a subject when you have assimilated a certain amount of basic information about it. In the *Fihi ma Fihi*, Rumi likens a man who says "I understand" to a person who has just filled a skin bottle with sea water, and who then holds it up saying: "This is the sea."

This tendency also means that people won't consider they

... OPEN SECRETS

have learnt something unless it has taken a very heightened or dramatic form. In other books Omar Ali-Shah has pointed out how people get drawn towards cathartic-type experiences where they are torn apart, the better, 'so the assumption goes, to be rebuilt again afterwards.' Certain therapists and many false teachers batten onto this kind of attraction by working in terms of conflict rather than towards harmony, and there is a certain pattern in the western world, where people have been naive about this kind of abuse, in which this kind of thing has been used as a technique.

My own short observation of Idries Shah and longer observation of Omar Ali-Shah, as teachers, leads me to think that they do arrange things, but within a certain limitation. They are highly respectful of the pupil's own rhythm of assimilation over time. Omar Ali-Shah works through small groupings of people, but there is no trace of the high-pressure and money-grubbing tactics one associates with "cult" situations. It should not be forgotten, however, that the discipline required from a teacher who really does respect the capacity and rhythm of his pupil, and who carefully works with and around it, is of an exceptional nature, because working this way requires immense patience. This patience can be learnt from a teacher, but not quickly, insofar as this discipline within an overall flexibility takes a long time to assimilate.

If one can develop something analogous to this kind of patience towards oneself, it will help one to make powerful use of this book. The key to this book's use is familiarisation: the closer one gets to these concepts, the more one can apply them to the various inner and outer circumstances in our lives. The more one does this, and the more transparent one makes oneself to these concepts, the more these developmental modules can then work through us; almost—but not quite—in spite of ourselves.

FICTIONS AND FACTIONS

In the earlier version of this book, the editing was "harder" in the sense that we tried to get as close as possible to proposing a single version of each rule. Time makes one more modest. In this greatly expanded edition of the first book I have gone back to the original transcripts and have followed the original extracts more faithfully, which means that there is a certain amount of overlap.

Some may consider this repetitious: my feeling is that it is useful to watch Omar Ali-Shah considering and reconsidering a subject at different times, as one might look at the work of a painter returning to the same scene throughout his life, throwing a slightly different light on the subject each time, because he knows that the essence of his life's work is in that place.

1998

THE LAUGHTER OF BABOONS

There have been a number of denunciations over the years of the Shah brothers, sometimes in the newspapers, and sometimes in books. The response of Agha and of Shah was always clear and simple: they never answered the various charges levelled against them because to do so would have in fact legitimized them and made them seem more credible than they actually were. It's the old story of trying to prove a negative fact, somebody publicly accuses you of being a swindler and it then becomes incumbent on you to prove you're not, and you get drawn into a real mug's game where you can only look ridiculous. Saying "No, I am not and never have been the lover of Brigitte Bardot" just makes you look dumb.

The charges against Idries Shah and Omar Ali-Shah were that they were a couple of manipulative orientals of doubtful origin. The people behind this idea usually had an axe to grind: they felt they were adequately covering the territory in 1962-65 and they did not want competitors. But first and foremost the reputation of the Shah brothers rested on the authority of books they had written, and not on their so-called charismatic personalities. Omar Ali-Shah had already published his translation of Saadi's *The Rose Garden* in French, and Idries Shah's *The Sufis*, *Tales of the Dervishes*, *Caravan of Dreams* and three volumes of *Mulla Nasrudin* stories all came out within a very short period; an unusual achievement by any standard because all of these books reflected different faces of sufism, all undeniablely true, and combining aesthetic beauty with historical weight.

Also there was the connection with Robert Graves, who threw the full weight of his prestige behind Omar Ali-Shah in his famous (and scandalous) translation of the *Rubaiyyat of Omar Khayaam*. There is no doubt that Graves was useful to both

FICTIONS AND FACTIONS

brothers: Omar Ali-Shah met his future wife when she was staying at Deya to plan a thesis on Graves, and Shah was given access to Graves's publisher, who put out the original edition of *The Sufis*, perhaps his most important historical work, and still the most clear and complete book ever written on the subject. *Between Moon and Moon*, a compilation of Robert Graves's correspondance, throws an interesting light on Idries Shah's *The Sufis*:

> *I'm not surprised at the slow start of (the sales of)* The Sufis *because you took care not to make it read like an advertisement for a new World Religion; and (it is)* scattered *rather than set out plainly.*

He then goes on to give Shah a slightly patronizing lesson in what good writing ought to be, which is fair enough in a sort of avuncular way from an older writer, but not all that relevant insofar as Shah always knew exactly what he was doing. To be fair, Graves also adds:

> The Sufis *is a marvellous book, and it will be recognized as such before long. Leave it to find its own readers, who will hear your voice spreading, not those envisaged by Doubleday.*

Nevertheless, when Graves says: *Various facts of immense interest to readers in* The Sufis *are thrown away by deliberate unemphasis*, he is making a very subtle point. The content of this book was quite sensational at the time of publication because the sufic influence underlying western culture was relatively unknown at the time: nevertheless Shah downplayed the emotion instead of pumping it up. The book was not completely original in its content, because much of the information it contained had been around for centuries, but in the way it was presented it was totally original. For one thing the book presents itself as a work of serious history, which it most certainly is, yet it begins with

... THE LAUGHTER OF BABOONS

a fable called *The Islanders*, which introduces the book almost without explanation or justification. This approach is so different from all other historians or critics of the time that it stood out like a sore thumb. Here was a writer who was not limiting himself to the external description of a real phenomenon, he was also communicating the actual feeling of sufihood like a storyteller or poet. It was a book that functioned on a number of different levels at the same time.

Here I must declare an interest: it was reading this fable in conjuction with my meeting with the author's brother Omar Ali-Shah that brought me into the Sufi Tradition in 1964. When I read this story I had a feeling of immediate recognition, in fact it was almost disappointing to read the rest of the book and find out that a way of thinking I had always thought of as my own personal view was in fact being shared by all sorts of people I had never met, possibly wouldn't be seen dead with, and that it had all been going on for centuries without me realising. It was a real blow to my ego, and it was not to be the last.

But what has been an absolute constant in the various denunciations of Idries Shah and Omar Ali-Shah is the complete inability of these people to come up with anything stupid or boastful *in their own writings*. The accusations are always that "they present themselves as" and then you look in their published work and there is nothing to support these assertions. At this point you begin to think that some of these denouncers have an axe to grind, and quite a few times there seems to be a post-Gurdjieffian smell to it: very clearly *The Teachers of Gurdjieff* is a book which stuck permanently in the Gurdjieffian craw.

Also, the wit and humour you find throughout the two brothers' books is in stark contrast to the earnestly paranoid negativity that characterises their attackers. Having witnessed

FICTIONS AND FACTIONS

certain things myself, I would like to at least provide some balance to the assaults of the attackers, at the risk of providing PR for liars. Peter Washington's *Mrs Blavatsky's Baboon* even bases the dénouement of his whole book on a supposed thievery perpetrated by Idries Shah, which I know to be untrue because I myself happened to be around Shah at the time of the "Coombe Springs affair" which is presented by Washington as Idries Shah's supreme swindle.

To be fair, one should add that Shah and Omar-Ali Shah (who is mostly relegated to the footnotes) are not the main subjects of Washington's book, which mostly centres around Blavatsky, Besant, Leadbeater and the beginnings of Krishnamurti, and some of the hairier episodes of Gurdjieff in a sort of debunking exposé of the naivete and fraud that accompanied the arrival of "oriental wisdom" in the West. For a journalist/historian this kind of thing is an easy target, it's like shooting fish in a barrel. On the fringes of esoteric groupings you always have a crust of idealistic sweethearts who love to talk about themselves, and who do so, endlessly. They become the experts. There is also a kind of "touch of the tarbrush" racism in this kind of literature: the British have always felt that orientals, like Americans, shouldn't be taken too seriously.

The problem is that you can't dismiss all of this stuff out of hand: Krishnamurti refused the supreme guruhood he was being groomed for and Gurdjieff and Ouspensky, for all their faults, were indeed the harbingers of something important. People like René Daumal or Katherine Mansfield were not complete idiots, and if they took it seriously there was probably something there, Daumal's diaries make this clear.

To get back to the famous Coombe Springs "swindle", I myself put together a short play, *Earthly Traps*, based on a story by Clifford Simak which received its one and only performance at a three-day party at Coombe Springs in the summer of 1965.

... THE LAUGHTER OF BABOONS

We performed it as theatre-in-the-round in the structure known as the Djami which had previously been used as the exercise-hall for the *Latihan* exercise when the Indonesian teacher Pak Subuh had been in residence. Quite a few people at that party were ex-pupils of Subud, and without my realizing it, my little play in that space marked the beginning of the deconsecration of what had been going on before. The building was a temporary structure made out of wood, and didn't really look as if it had been built to last. The image implicitly put forward by Elwell-Sutton of Shah tearing down a church is wildly exaggerated.

Shah's situation around that time was, in fact, very delicate. He had been given Coombe Springs to use as a teaching centre but John Bennett had not only not moved out, he had first offered him the place and had subsequently set himself up as an alternative teacher for all the pupils that Shah had turned down. Shah and his students found themselves in a kind of weird ghetto surrounded with the old ex-Subud and ex-Gurdjieffian sweats, all the more hostile because Shah had told them he would not be able to be their teacher. Bennett tells this story in his own words in his autobiography, *Witness*, which is not particularly hostile to Shah, something which the Shah-attackers all choose to ignore.

Instead of just turning the place over to him, Bennett made the mistake of taking on all of the students Shah felt he couldn't work with, and they both lived at Coombe Springs in uneasy proximity for a number of months before Bennett himself chose to move out. It doesn't take a genius to realise that it was clearly impossible for Shah to work under such conditions. It's not a question of advanced esoterics here, if Shah had been teaching engine repairs the situation would have been the same. To my knowledge, Bennett was never expelled from Coombe Springs; he moved out of his own accord, and he bears no particular grudge against Shah in his autobiography, rather the opposite, in fact.

FICTIONS AND FACTIONS

Possibly it was the intrigues of that time that made John Bennett realise that he did not in fact have a vocation as a spiritual teacher: anyone with any direct experience of this kind of situation knows that when one accepts the label of teacher one is immediately surrounded with self-serving greed. People begin to confide all sorts of personal secrets to you whether you want to know about them or not, it goes with the territory. Then they ask you to put in a good word with God about their mother-in-law who is dying of cancer. Nobody in their right mind would want this kind of thing: it's to be avoided at all costs, and those who accept such a responsibility do so because they have no choice.

Bennett was no fool, even if he is presented as a gullible idiot by these writers; he probably handed the teaching responsibility over to Shah because he simply realised that he himself was not cut out for it. He was an exeptional intellect, wrote extremely useful books such as *The Dramatic Universe* and *The Masters of Wisdom,* ran a business and set up a school for adult education at Sherbourne and he does not appear to have held it against Shah for selling Coombe Springs and moving to another location where he would be able to create his own environment without having to deal with the old associates. John Bennett also gives us a very clear account of the sufic origin of Gurdjieff's teaching on p. 135 of *Gurdjieff: Making a New World* which confirms the ideas first put forward in *The Teachers of Gurdjieff.*

Bennett's own words and actions therefore indicate that he felt that Shah was legitimate as a teacher, and the fact that he did not attack him in print is significant, even if he did fudge the question of taking on Shah's unwanted students in later editions of *Witness.* Neither he, Ted Hughes, Robert Graves, Doris Lessing, Desmond Morris or Robert Ornstein were or are sheep-like mouthpieces for the guru Shah, as has been

... THE LAUGHTER OF BABOONS

claimed, and nobody who has read a word that any of them have written would even begin to think so. All have their own stature as thinkers and writers, and if they have nourished themselves, as did I, from Shah's words and/or presence, it's because they found something there that was worthwhile.

As an analogy, when artists like Picasso, Miró or Giacometti came to work in my fathers' printmaking workshop in Paris before the war, there was a collaborative exchange of knowledge, it wasn't a kindergarden with the teacher telling you to sit up straight. It is truly amazing that people should have such a crass and sentimental view of what being a student in sufism really is like, it's not at all like going back to school. Actually, it's far more difficult, but that's another story.

In Peter Washington's hatchet job on Shah, there are a few other tidbits of British snottiness and snobbery I particularly enjoyed. One is that he and Omar were brought up in Sutton, South London, so that it is implicitly understood that all this business about receiving a Sufi education all over the globe has to be fake. Well, what isn't fake is the languages the two brothers spoke: their mother tongue was English (not surprising with a mother from Scotland) and they both spoke near-perfect Farsi, Pashtu and Arabic. Shah spoke Spanish without an accent. I worked as a linguist for twenty-five years and can certainly tell if people know a language or are faking it. In addition to the above four languages, I watched Omar Ali-Shah work in French, German and Spanish: his wife is Italian and he understands enough to correct the proofs of his Italian translations. Now I am no snob, but you don't normally acquire that kind of linguistic capacity in Sutton (although for all I know there may have been a situation such as one had in certain central European families: a football team of nannies of different nationalities working them over and speaking a different language every day).

FICTIONS AND FACTIONS

So the simplest explanation is probably nearest the truth: they travelled around the world with their father, and their education was made up of many different impacts at many different levels. The brothers are exactly what they have always said themselves to be and I see no particular reason to disbelieve them. Sometimes the simplest explanation for something is the best.

According to Washington, their father Ikbal Ali Shah "dabbled in literature, politics and business" after being "an unsuccessful medical student in Edinburgh." Once again, comments like this are the quintessence of British snobbery. His published output is over thirty books in English alone, he has also published in Arabic and Urdu, and having edited and gone over the material word by word I do know what I am talking about when I say that *Muhammed: The Prophet*, *Lights of Asia* and *Islamic Sufism*, to take only the three I published myself, are works which, although written sixty-odd years ago, are as relevant today as on the day they first came out. In spite of occasional Anglo-Indian awkwardnesses (which may be due to the editing of the time), as a writer, Ikbal's language has the sweep of a poet, where the language of his sons and daughter is far more idiomatic and more in the mould of storytelling.

In the Unesco archives in Paris I came across articles and conference contributions written by Ikbal Ali Shah when he was working with professor Gilbert Murray and the Agha Khan at the beginning of the League of Nations. He may not have been a front-liner but he most certainly was a respected intellectual of his time; the conference minutes bear witness to this. As friend, biographer and occasional advisor to King Fuad of Egypt, Kemal Ataturk and the Agha Khan, he most certainly moved in circles that were not limited to South London even if he was domiciled there. But not a single book of his is cited in Peter Washington's impressive bibliography: it's easier to

… THE LAUGHTER OF BABOONS

pretend implicitly he's some kind of meat merchant who never wrote a book (He's in trade, you know!). As they say in my home town of New York City: "Come on, gimme a break!"

This is more than snobbery, it is intellectual dishonesty, just as it is intellectually dishonest to say that Idries Shah "disappears from public view" for ten years. What exactly is meant by such a comment? Did he go into hibernation? Was he in jail? Was he selling dirty postcards? Like his father, Idries Shah wrote at least thirty books: he has to have put all this material onto paper at some point; these books, which are all in their own different ways, very good (see later), have to have been written some time. Also, like his father, Idries Shah produced a fair number of potboilers for money under pseudonyms. He had no particular regard for this output, which I gathered had been done to earn a living for his family, and I remember him handing me a copy of one of these paperbacks, saying: "Here, even if it's hardly worth the paper it's printed on".

Now is it possible to stop and think a moment about words such as these? These are not the words of a guru who is taking himself and everything he does seriously. If he is putting out a few potboilers for various paperback publishers, it is also an indication that he is not making a fortune out of his pupils or out of people like Bennett. Turning out paperback originals is bloody hard work and badly paid, or at least it was in the fifties and sixties. Peter Washington, who is a professional editor, should know this. Implying that people are dishonest without providing hard evidence of such dishonesty is the historian's equivalent of the gutter press.

It so happens that my own father was born in East London, attended Whitgift school on a scholarship, became a chemist and geologist, then chucked it all in to become a painter and engraver in Paris. The boy from Croydon (no, not Sutton, Croydon) became enthused over the possibilities of itaglio printmaking, participated in the Surrealist movement in Paris in the twenties and thirties and began a workshop in which all the greatest modern artists of his time came and learnt to make their own plates. In my father's workshop there were never more than fifty people working at one time, yet this workshop really did change the course of modern printmaking by handing the initiative back to the artists who made the images, as well as through the numerous technical innovations my father was responsible for. What I mean to say by this is that my father, with no money and with very few people in his workshop at any one time, actually changed the course of modern art and is universally recognised as having transformed the medium of printmaking.

My point here is that there is a complete misapprehension about what a teaching does and how it works. You don't need many people, they simply have to be the right ones, awareness and knowledge-communication create their own dynamic flow. The interaction between master and disciple is not a scholastic phenomenon; it is a exercise of obedience and discipline which is itself a rehearsal for the submission and obedience to God that will come at a later stage, when the pupil will have learned the language, as it were, of true worship in place of the various routines and clichés that pass for such.

Neither Omar Ali-Shah or Idries Shah ever recruited; the books are out in the marketplace and people who feel the echo try to find the source. There's no money in sufism and very little prestige. Shah was a best seller in the late sixties but now sales, although regular, are just ticking over, and without Octagon and Tractus maintaining availability some of the books would have gone out of print. Peter Washington probably made much more money denouncing us than we ever made

... THE LAUGHTER OF BABOONS

producing the original material. But then of course the gutter press is more fun to read than the *Times Literary Supplement*, so I suppose one shouldn't complain.

Of course there are a few small satisfactions, such as when Everyman Books sent us a request to use the Omar Ali-Shah version of Saadi's *The Rose Garden (Gulistan)* for an anthology of Persian poetry to be edited, yes, you've got it, by Peter Washington, who first roasts the translator as an incompetent and dishonest boob and then asks him for text for his anthology.

One can indeed hear the baboon laughing in the far-off distance.

2002

FICTIONS AND FACTIONS

INNOCUOUS IKBAL

James Moore, in an article of quite extraordinary venom entitled *Neo-Sufism: the case of Idries Shah* (obtainable on a site called *Gurdjieff Heritage*) dismisses Ikbal Ali Shah's *Islamic Sufism* as an "innocuous popularization". Once again, the problem of giving free publicity to evil and libellous bullshit arises. All of the hatchet-wielders against Idries Shah refer to an article by L. P. Elwell-Sutton in *Encounter* which came out in 1975. The only problem with this article is that it is as much an attack on Gurdjieff as it is on Shah, which involves James Moore in some interesting twists and turns.

Their basic thesis is that Shah is selling a sufism without God, an accusation which is belied on nearly every page that Idries Shah ever wrote. It is true that he modulated the language of classical religious devotion and adapted it to the rationalism and scepticism of our postwar generation. Nevertheless, everything he writes is predicated to a belief in an all-knowing God, and the concern with man's individual development has no other objective in mind than approaching this reality. Where he differs from formulations of the recent past is to consider that belief in itself is not enough to ensure salvation, something which has already been said many times by Sufis such as Al-Ghazali and Rumi.

In this, his writing is perfectly consistent with that of his father, who is an impeccable orthodox Muslim. For the moment, let us look at the innocuous Ikbal (from *Islamic Sufism*, Tractus Books p. 265):

Poverty is not-being without existence

To interpret this saying is impossible, because what is non-existent does not admit of being explained.

... INNOCUOUS IKBAL

On the surface it would seem that, according to this dictum, poverty is nothing, but such is not the case; the explanations and consensus of the Saints of God are not founded on a principle that is essentially non-existent.

The meaning here is not "the not-being of the essence", but "the not-being of that which contaminates the essence"— and all human attributes are a source of contamination: when that is removed, the result is annihilation of the attributes, which deprives the sufferer of the instrument whereby he attains or fails to attain his object—but his not-going to the essence seems to him annihilation of the essence and casts him into perdition.

I have met with some scholastic philosophers, who, failing to understand the drift of this saying, laughed at it and declared it to be nonsense—and also with certain pretenders to Sufism who made nonsense of it and were firmly convinced of its truth, although they had no grasp of the fundamental principle.

Both parties are in the wrong: one ignorantly denies the truth, and the other makes ignorance a state of perfection.

Now the expressions "not-being" and "annihilation", as they are used by Sufis, denote the disappearance of a blameworthy instrument and disapproved attribute in the course of seeking a praiseworthy attribute; they do not signify the search for non-reality by means of an instrument which exists.

Dervishhood in all its meanings is a metaphorical poverty, and amidst all its subordinate aspects there is a transcendent principle. The Divine mysteries come and go over the dervish, so that his affairs are acquired by himself, his actions attributed to himself, and his ideas attached to himself.

FICTIONS AND FACTIONS

But when his affairs are freed from the bonds of acquisition, his actions are no more attributed to himself. Then he is the Way, not the wayfarer, i.e. the dervish is a place over which something is passing, not a wayfarer following his own will. Accordingly, he neither draws anything to himself nor puts anything away from himself: all that leaves any trace upon him belongs to the essence.

I have seen false Sufis, mere tonguesters, whose imperfect apprehension of this matter seemed to deny the existence of the essence of poverty, while their lack of desire for the reality of poverty seemed to deny the attributes of its essence.

They called by the name of "poverty" and "purity" their failure to seek Truth and Reality, and it looked as though they affirmed their own fancies, but denied all else. Every one of them was in some degree veiled from poverty, because the conceit of Sufism betokens perfection of saintship, and the claim to be suspected of Sufism is the ultimate goal, i.e. this claim belongs only to the state of perfection.

Therefore the seeker has no choice but to journey in his or her path and to traverse the "stations" and to know their symbolic expressions, in order not to be a plebeian among the elect.

Those who are ignorant of general principles have no ground to stand on, whereas those who are ignorant only as regards the derivative branches are supported by the principles.

I have said all this to encourage you to undertake this spiritual journey and occupy yourself with the due fulfilment of its obligations.

The foregoing text may be considered difficult and complex by some, but insofar as he presents Sufism as a difficult undertaking requiring considerable personal effort, I don't see how in the world one can call it "innocuous". Here are a few more quotes from the Sirdar (text entitled *Sufism and the Indian Philosophies* in *Sufi Thought and Action* ed. Idries Shah, Octagon Press). I consider it one of the clearest statements ever made about western religion, what is required from the Sufi, and how one can distinguish between religion and sufihood.

> ... We have to make a clear distinction between the inner philosophy of the Sufis ... and the philosophy of religion. The difference, briefly, is this: in all forms of ordinary organisational religion there are certain beliefs and certain practices which, taken together, are taken to be sufficient to imply that the practitioner is a believer in that religion. But the members of the intitiatory schools go very much further than this. First, they say, you must know what religion really is. Then you will know whether you believe in it or not.
>
> Buddha's teaching was clearly designed to make the disciple conscious of himself first; so that subsequently he would be able to banish 'self'. It is obvious that in order to banish a thing, you must first learn to recognise it. In order to recognise it, you must develop in yourself the ability to assess it.
>
> There is no golden key to enlightenment. Both the Sufi and the Indian schools teach that man must be capable of receiving a teaching before he can be taught. There can be no attaining any enlightenment until the individual is ready for it. It is to produce these favourable conditions for understanding, that, in both the Indian and the Sufi systems, there is the institution of the human guide or teacher, whose first task is to prepare the disciple for the knowledge of himself, so that he is able to become enlightened.

FICTIONS AND FACTIONS

In the following extract, the Sirdar deals with western psychology and philosophy:

In western countries, books on oriental religion and philosophy, many of them of a more or less 'occult' nature, are appearing in increasing numbers. A second major aggregation of books is concerned with psychology.

Western man is facing the crisis of trying to replace his failing religious values with a personality which shall give meaning and purpose to his life.

Personality, that much misused word, is derived from the Latin word persona *which signifies 'A Mask'; a mask worn during a stage play with the intention of conveying to the audience something of the character portrayed by the actor. In the East personality is very far from a mask. It is the external view of what actually is inside the man. The objective of practical philosophy of the Sufi and Indian schools is an inner transformation.*

... Western philosophy, upon which depend many of the lines of thinking of the past two centuries, is built partly upon Greek and Roman philosophy. In the form in which this philosophy reached the West, the odds were heavily weighted in favour of pure speculation and juggling with words. In the process of transmission of the knowledge of the ancients to the West, a very curious thing happened. In the teachings of Pythagoras and Plato, there is indeed a concentration upon the intellect. But it is only this one portion which appears in books. Equating the teaching of the western classical world with those of the East will show that the intellectual exercises which pass for philosophy are only a part of the picture. The important part—the actual practice of self-cultivation—has been left out. It survives in the Sufi and Indian systems.

... INNOCUOUS IKBAL

The Sirdar then enumerates sufic influences on western thinking and philosophy before pointing out:

However, philosophical movements in the West which are based upon eastern models rapidly turn away from the main theme; that of self-realization. There is only one reason for this. No school of study can survive entirely by means of theory on the printed page. The continuous and repeated refreshment of Indian and Sufi teaching has come about and been maintained only because there has been a perennial succession of teachers, masters, those who knew how to carry the disciple from one stage to the next in this mission of self-realization.

... The essence of initiatory knowledge, for the Indian schools and the Sufis alike, has always been their common denominator: the search for truth through a blending of theory and practice. I have set myself the task of explaining what mediocre scholastics have made a dreary and footnote-loaded task, by means of ideas and references which are easily grasped by all. For if there is to be any reality in self-development, that reality must ultimately be a simplicity, not a multiplicity ...

Here are a few other quotes from the Sirdar (*Islamic Sufism*).

Solitariness is propinquity to Satan. (p. 30)

Evil, say the Sufis, is nothing but the circumstances by which human beings are surrounded. Man believes materialism to be real, and this belief gives rise to all the wickedness in life. In the Being of God it has no part—for it is but the imagination of the human mind: unreal, phantasmagorical. These can be entirely dismissed when man forgets his frailties and thinks of himself as the spark which must be purified, after the hideousness with which he alone has surrounded himself is forgotten, and only the return to the Infinite dwelt on. (p. 39)

FICTIONS AND FACTIONS

... All the agitation of beginners, when the Divine influence descends upon them, is due to the fact that their bodies are opposed to it; but when it becomes continual, the beginner receives it quietly. (p. 288)

... The Sheikhs agree that the power of knowledge should be greater than the power of Wajd (ecstasy), since, if Wajd be more powerful, the person affected by it is in a dangerous position, whereas one in whom knowledge preponderates is secure.

It behoves the seeker in all circumstances to be a follower of knowledge and of the religious law, for when he is overcome by Wajd he is deprived of discrimination (Khitab), and is not liable to recompense for good actions or punishment for evil, and is exempt from honour and disgrace alike—therefore he is in the predicament of madmen, not in that of the saints and favourites of God.

A person in whom knowledge (Ilm) preponderates over feeling (Hal) remains in the bosom of the Divine commands and prohibitions, and is always praised and rewarded in the palace of glory; but a person in whom feeling preponderates over knowledge is outside of the ordinances, and dwells—having lost the faculty of discrimination—in his own imperfection. (p. 297)

... The only danger to which the ego is exposed in this Divine Quest is the possible relaxation of his activity caused by his enjoyment of and absorption in the experiences that precede the final experience. (p. 101)

... If we look at the matter from the standpoint of anthropology it appears that a psychopath is an important factor in the economy of humanity's social organization. His way is not to classify facts and discover causes: he thinks in

terms of life and movement with a view to creating new patterns of behaviour for mankind. No doubt he has his pitfalls and illusions just as the scientist who relies on sense-experience has his pitfalls and illusions. A careful study of his method, however, shows that he is not less alert than the scientist in eliminating the alloy of illusion from his experience ...

... The Arab historian Ibn Khaldun, who laid the foundations of modern scientific history, was the first to make a serious approach of this side of human psychology and he reached what we now call the idea of the 'subliminal self' ... Jung, however is probably right in thinking that the essential nature of religion is beyond the province of analytic psychology ... (p. 93)

In *Turn Off Your Mind* by Gary Valentine Lachman, the same theme of debunking all that is magical and esoteric is pursued, and Idries Shah is attacked as the quintessential manipulative sixties guru, in a rehash of the Washington/Elwell-Sutton accusations. What is interesting here is that Lachman, who is a musician, should be so unaware that the learning process in sufism actually resembles learning music or another language more than anything else. You do the same scales or exercises over and over again, and at some point, which comes at a different time for everyone, you begin to be able to speak in the new language and improvise your own thinking. And of course you also make mistakes, it's obviously part of the territory.

Nevertheless the objective being pursued, even if the divine substance is difficult to define in words, is real and not a figment of the imagination. As the Sirdar points out, it is because of the central reality of the godly substance within ourselves, which is of abiding importance, that we are actually pursuing our quest to know it and reveal it. But make no

FICTIONS AND FACTIONS

mistake, even if such a substance is weak and buried in ourselves, it does exist.

Magical thinking is of a different order. *Reality is malleable, something our postmodern sensibilities feel instinctively* says Lachman, and this is where the Sufi tolerance ends, because at this point, anything goes. You're neither here nor there, and so what anyway, what's the difference? Is God a virtual entity? If there is no objective reality there can be no God. If God is just a product of human imagination, we might as well worship ourselves, which is what many do, incessantly.

> *The conception of Sufism, according to the Sirdar (Islamic Sufism p. 119) ... is part of the composition of man ... Their (Sufi) doctrine teaches them that man is composed of two substances, the Spiritual and the Material.*
>
> *It is the Material which hinders the wayfarer's march towards reality on account of its shortcomings, or what is termed Alloy. It is that Alloy which has to be removed so the Purified Sufi may be absorbed into the absolute Reality and thus be illuminated by its radiance. This is, then, the purpose of the Sufi to attain. For:*
>
> *... "Body is falsehood and Spirit the truth*
> *Thy true substance is concealed in falsehood"...* (Rumi)

It may be true that in this day and age some people feel that the life of the spirit is a sort of fantasy. Nevertheless, for the Sufi it is true, and because it is real, it must be worked on, and it is the worthwhile project for an entire life. The fact that such realities cannot be measured in terms of money, prestige or even rods, poles and perches is either significant or not significant. But who uses rods, poles and perches as an instrument of measurement today?

2002

SHAH THE WRITER

I am told that after Shah died, a number of his friends gathered at Langton to pay homage to a man who was very much loved. At this time some sheets of paper were distributed which put together various things he had written at different times about life and death and the life hereafter. One of the witnesses to this event said to me that one of his children pointed out that Shah himself disapproved of his work being cut up into palatable pieces in this way, that he had consistently refused all anthologizing of his work, that his writing was designed to be read in the precise order within each book that it had been written in, and that it was therefore inappropriate, however honest the intention or emotional the occasion, to chop up his words into bits and pieces in order to fit them into a pattern he himself had not been responsible for.

Anyone writing about Shah as a writer must keep this point in mind, otherwise one reduces Shah to the status of one's own mouthpiece. Very little serious criticism or literary analysis of his work has come out since he died, one of the reasons being that there is a lot of material in print he produced or supervised himself. The fact that he tooted his own horn tends to preclude him being taken seriously as a writer, but unlike almost everyone else in the game, he tooted on behalf of a tradition and not for himself. He felt that this way of thinking was important and that the question of introducing into the West was a matter of great urgency, because it could then and can still act as a counterweight to the materialism and power-fantasies that infect western minds.

My thesis is simple: I think there is a case to be made that the range of his thinking makes him one of the great writers of the century, even if his reputation and readership at the present time happens to be more limited to people interested in Sufi ideas than it used to be.

FICTIONS AND FACTIONS

In fact, the faithful general readership that built up around Shah is not made up of specialist scholars: they are just normally educated people who react very simply as human beings to the universality of his stories, particularly to his humour. This is the tremendous originality of his literary work: he writes about sufism, but at the same time he is writing about it he is also expressing its essence in a good-humoured way, with the laughter and humour of the tales creating a sort of distance from oneself that enables one to see one's own behaviour in a different light. Humour is tremendously important in sufism, not as the systematic jokery you see in show business, but because it is one of the best possible ways of achieving the beginning of an objective view of oneself and how one really behaves. The capacity not to take oneself too seriously does not mean being disrespectful towards oneself, it is just the beginning of being real.

To communicate the flavour of Idries Shah's writing, here are quotes from *Reflections*, made from his own stories and aphorisms. I have limited myself to very short texts for reasons of space. Although all culling from Shah does him a disservice, my intention here is to quote him extensively enough to let him make his own mark on the reader and give an idea of the range and variety of his thinking to those who don't yet know him, if possible, without reducing him to what I think is interesting:

HISTORY

History is not usually what has happened. History is what some people have thought to be significant.

WHAT I SAY

If you are uninterested in what I say, there's an end to it.

If you like what I say, please try to understand which previous influences have made you like it.

If you like some of the things I say, and dislike others, you could try to understand why.

... SHAH THE WRITER

If you dislike all I say, why not try to find out what formed your attitude?

DROWNING

To drown in treacle is just as unpleasant as to drown in mud.

People today are in danger of drowning in information; but, because they have been taught that information is useful, they are more willing to drown than they need be.

If they could handle information they would not have to drown at all.

TRUST

None should say 'I can trust' or 'I cannot trust' until he is master of the option of trusting or not trusting.

LOCAL AND REAL TRUTH

The existence of relative truth does not prove the non-existence of universal truth.

FREEDOM

'I always looked at the alternatives' said the sheep: 'I can munch or I can bite.'

COMPREHENSION

Mankind does not have a capacity of instant comprehension.

So rare is the knowledge of how to train this, that most people, and all institutions, have compromised by playing upon man's proneness to conditioning and indoctrination instead.

The end of that road is the ant-heap; or, at best, the beehive.

ORIGINAL PERFECTION

He was yellow, plump and soft, his surface broken up, the movements ungainly, full of uncertainty, covetousness and hunger.

His main desire was to attain a state in which he would

FICTIONS AND FACTIONS

want nothing, need to make no movement, present a smooth, uniform and delicately satisfying face to the world.

He did not realise that he was a chicken who wanted to be an egg.

SUBORDINATES

Almost every day I am reminded of Saadi's reflection that there is no senseless tyranny like that of subordinates.

HUMILITY

Humility cannot be taught by propaganda, although slavery can. Shouting for humility is a form of arrogance...

Real humility is not always the same as apparent humility. Remember that fighting against self-conceit is still fighting: and that it will tend to suppress it temporarily. It does not cure anything.

Remember too that humility of itself does not bring an automatic reward: it is a means to an end. It enables a person to operate in a certain manner.

UNKNOWN

There are literally thousands of wise people, unknown to the ordinary man. They teach in a manner which is not recognized as teaching by the herd. They continuously influence man.

People who respond to authority-figures and weird things are unable to make any contact with them. Other people lack information and preparation.

DEBUNKING

Once upon a time people used to become established as authority-figures and were then respected for centuries, even for thousands of years.

Then came the age of debunking, which is still with us. People started to debunk almost as soon as a reputation had been built up.

But there is another phase now: people are being debunked almost before they are famous.

THINKING THAT ONE KNOWS

People who think that they know all are often unsufferable—rather like those who imagine that they know nothing.

BEING

There is :
What one wants to know and what one wants to be.
And also:
What one can know and can be.
Deny these limitations and people will give you anything you want.

Affirm them and you have exercised true selfishness: telling the truth.

VIRTUE

If your own vice happens to be the search for virtue, recognize that it is so.

WHO CARES?

It is not only a matter of not caring who knows—it is also a matter of knowing who cares.

SUGGESTION AND ATTENTION

The effect of a suggestion tends to be in proportion to the prestige of the source of the suggestion.

Prestige is itself 'accumulated attention'. Accumulated and frozen attention.

Attention-fixing does not require the presence of the object. It may even occur, develop and become fixed through the absence of the object.

FUNCTION OF RELIGIOUS SYMBOLS

When you see a traditional religious symbol today, you are generally looking at a piece of technical apparatus (or a

FICTIONS AND FACTIONS

representation of one), whose use has been forgotten—above all by the descendants of its own original designers. This is generally due to the growth of the superstition that a thing of beauty or associative significance has to evoke sentimentality, and that function is less sublime than emotion. The reverse, in fact, is the case.

TIME

Two microbes said:
'We may not seem to be much, but you just wait a little.'

UNRELIABLE FRIENDS

You need not wonder whether you should have an unreliable person as a friend. An unreliable person is nobody's friend.

BELIEF

If you believe everything, you are not a believer in anything at all.

STIMULI

When a person has a jaded palate, as we all know, he needs more and more piquant and probably more varied taste-stimuli to activate it.

In current cultures, the result of over-stimulation of the mental palate is today obvious.

The analogy of the palate, however, is not completely exact, because the human mind has capacities of 'taste' which in contemporary societies are not satisfied at all.

The lack of this stimulus is because it is not realised that, in this area, a stimulus need not be intense in order to operate.

The result of this ignorance is that people will not give a 'gentle' stimulus a chance to operate, and reach forward to whatever seems most likely to afford them instant or deep stimuli.

Such people have almost completely put themselves outside

the range of the less-crude stimulus. It is only when they are prepared to entertain the possibility of its existence, and prepared, too, to test its working, that they can be communicated with.

We can make no progress with a demand like this: 'Give me chili-powder, but let it taste like rosewater.'

GENEROSITY AND WISDOM

How are generosity and wisdom connected?
Here is one way:
A generous person may not have wisdom: but, unlike others, he has the means to gain it.

SAYING A THING

It is not important to have said a thing first, or best—or even most interestingly. What is important is to say it on the right occasion.

DESIRE

Desire without orientation is a game. What a pity that people should turn it into hypocrisy by pretending that it is something higher. When a game is being played, there is nothing higher possible to the players at that time.

MIRACLES

What are called miracles, which people either believe in or do not, have a quite different function from what emotionalists imagine. They are useless if they only impress emotionally.

They are, in reality, either by-products and indications of some extra attainment, or exist to be recorded, inwardly, by a special organ of recognition.

MAN

There is no inconsequential man. But what he has done to himself, and what has been done to him—that can make him inconsequential.

FICTIONS AND FACTIONS

THE STAG

When the lion had eaten its fill, and the jackals had taken their share, the ants came along and finished up the meat from the bones of the haughty stag.

EVOLUTION

A man is deficient in understanding until he perceives that there is a whole cycle of evolution possible within himself; repeating endlessly, offering possibilities for personal development.

LYING

Look at the phenomenon of lying and its relationship to fools.

Fools lie to explain or conceal their foolishness. It is not a remedy, but they use it.

Liars, again, are fools because a lie may be found out, and gambling fools are not different from the ordinary kind.

The liar fools himself that he will not be found out, and the fool fools himself that his lie will cover his folly.

It is not easy to avoid being a fool. It is possible to realise that one has been one. The remedy is not lying.

Again, it is possible to realise that one has lied, and to avoid it. Foolishness and lying being so much of a continuum, being truthful can help towards being less foolish.

It is for this reason, because it is constructively useful, that traditional teachings have stressed the need to tell the truth and be as truthful as possible. Truthfulness means being efficient, effective. Lying is an attempt to make inefficiency into its opposite.

This is why all forms of self-deception are 'lying'; and the person who foolishly cannot see the truth can approach it by practice in avoiding, at least for a start, some forms of lying.

... SHAH THE WRITER

Many durable, 'moralistic' teachings are specific and effective exercises gone wrong.

LICHEN THINKING (EXTRACT)

....'Everything is accident'
'Everything is of supernatural origin'
'Some things are accident, some things supernatural'
'I do not know what to think'
'I can believe, and therefore I can believe that mere opinion is the same as knowledge'
'I have inferred some things, therefore they are true'
'I have observed some things, therefore I can observe others'
'What cannot be observed can be inferred, what cannot be inferred can be felt, what cannot be observed, inferred, or felt cannot have any relevance to anything and is therefore nonsense.'

How fortunate that humanity is different from lichen.

BANAL

Banality is like boredom: bored people are boring people, people who think things are banal are themselves banal.

Interesting people can find something interesting in all things.

SECRETS

A real secret is something which only one person knows.

ON TEACHING STORIES

... there are people who are unable to detach from ingrained beliefs about stories for long enough to profit from their other dimensions. In some cases, fortunately, it is enough to challenge the resistance merely by saying "An orange has nutrition: this does not prevent you from enjoying it." Beyond saying this, one can do little to explain precisely how teaching-stories work, or what they mean ...

(All quotes from *Reflections*; teaching story quote from *The Sufi*

FICTIONS AND FACTIONS

Mystery ed. N.P. Archer, Octagon Press)

The foregoing extracts of course don't do justice to Shah the storyteller: *The Tale of the Sands* in *Tales of the Dervishes* has already attained classic status. Nobody who reads that story ever forgets it, because of its beauty and the spiritual depth of the analogy it represents. Once again, it is pointless to try and make a list of nuggets in Shah's books, they all twinkle out differently at one according to one's own experience, age, and their very significance even changes in the light of one's own lifetime and experience, because almost all his work really is, in Geoffrey Grigson's wonderful phrase "an extension of the proverbial".

This doesn't mean he's always perfect. Perhaps because as a writer he's not all that interested in building psychologically well-rounded characters, I find his novel *Kara Kush* a little wooden, even though it's a beautifully-written suspense novel in the manner of John Buchan. The power of *Kara Kush*, based on events in the life of the freedom-fighter Massoud (and which helped to create the man's legend while he was still alive) comes from the author's powerful relationship with his beloved Afghanistan.

Basically the problem of all writers is that of form: can you mould yourself into the available models or do you have to invent your own? For me, Shah comes nearest to inventing his own form with the teaching stories, not the travel literature (*Destination Mecca*) or the magical compendiums (*The Secret Lore of Magic* and *Oriental Magic*) even if they do contain interesting material. As a writer Shah is also quite willing to make use of serviceable models. Of course I'm not helped by my own prejudices here: magic bores me stiff and the armchair travelling so beloved of the British happens to be a pet hatred of mine. But I do recognize that it is a medium through which a good deal of interesting and important information can be scattered.

... SHAH THE WRITER

Magazines like *National Geographic* add to human knowledge.

In between the lines of *Darkest England* and *The Natives are Restless* one can feel his ambivalence about Britain, even if the tone of the books is jocular and affectionate. In fact this is what annoys me about these books, it's like reading old issues of *Punch*. I think he put on rose-tinted glasses to make his books more appealing and I feel he is more himself when he is caustic; his last works bite like acid. He and his siblings grew up in a half-British, half-Afghan family, and my feeling is that they decided to join themselves to the British Establishment as a matter of policy rather than from conviction. If the Sufi Tradition was to be projected in the West it had to look respectable. This was not cynicism, it just made sense not to bite the hand that fed you.

Almost all of what Shah is writing about is applicable here and now, and yet also completely timeless. It is the very lack of emotional rubato in his writing that makes it possible to read the same book of stories over a few years later and see that what one saw the first time around has been superseded by another albeit familiar book that one didn't quite notice enough the first time. The change is not in the book, it's in oneself.

Shah himself knew exactly what he was doing in this regard, the ambiguities and shifting realities throughout his work weren't a sort of happy accident, they were all carefully calculated effects. Very few modern writers and novelists have worked towards expressing this kind of multifaceted reality: among the great moderns only Joyce comes to mind. The feeling you get from the "artistic" writers like Scott Fitzgerald, Hemingway, Carver, Bukowski or even Beckett, just to name some of my own favourites, is that they are narrowing their focus in order to arrive at one single possible interpretation of what is happening. They end in despair and no possible take-

FICTIONS AND FACTIONS

off for the reader is indicated. Most conventional literature creates prison cells for the mind, whereas Shah is continuously removing bars, because Shah sees the human being as a free agent even if he does need deconditioning.

In contrast to the cellmakers, Shah used the primary seduction of bedtime stories to make his points. The critics who have accused him of reducing sufism to children's stories do have a point, although I would consider it a quality rather than a fault. The children's story is the beginning of all literature, including theatre, movies and showbiz. It is mummy telling us a story before we go to sleep. Mankind's need to tell stories in order to make symbolic sense of the world is a primordial necessity which comes to all of us from childhood. Tapping into this undefended area of accessibility was a brilliant move in terms of communication. The same technique was used by Shah's father who set up a fiction-making workshop with Achmed Abdullah, Sax Rohmer and other writers before the war to produce children's tales, adventure stories, tacky novels and travel literature. His son Tahir now carries on the family trade with his own anthologies and travel books, and his daughter Saira Shah has become a noted journalist and documentary film-maker, so the family tradition seems set to continue.

Idries Shah made use of genre writing in a very sophisticated way. He knew exactly what literary seeds would flower early to the reader and which blooms would become perceptible at a later date. As his pupils, we were all told to read his books fairly slowly, without hurrying through them, and all of his books were to be reread every seven years. If one does this the books really do seem different; the difference of course being the effect of time on ourselves.

To me this is one of the most significant and subtle elements in his writing and, by extension, in his teaching: he knew he was laying down a syllabus for people who would never know who he was and who would therefore be insensitive to his personality or charm, and yet his work, although no longer selling with the chart-topping success of the late sixties and early seventies, is still totally relevant to people today. Vast numbers of his aficionados are not particularly interested in sufism and have no particular desire to go further in its study: they appreciate Shah for the insights he provides into life, society and themselves, and intuitively comprehend that reading Shah has a cleansing effect on the mind. The stories stay in people's memory to an astonishing extent: when two people who enjoy Shah stories meet in a public library for instance, they can spend hours telling their favourite stories and Nasrudin jokes to each other, completely oblivious to their surroundings.

The reason why such reactions are possible and even characteristic of Shah-fanciers the world over is that he really has pulled out and revealed to all (very often using pseudonyms) the components of the research he has done, because make no mistake, beyond some academic carping about the meaning of some words, nobody has invalidated the basic thesis that he and the people around him have successfully put forward over the past thirty years: (1) that Sufi thinking is not an appendage to Islam but is at its very core, just as it is at the core of all religion, and (2) that western science, philosophy and even its tradition of religious freedom came to us through the Sufi influences emanating from Andalucia, Sicily and the Middle East.

In 1960 these two ideas were totally disregarded in the West; today in 2002 it can be said that the majority of informed opinion would agree with both points. All the encyclopaedias and normal information sources contain basic information about sufism and its influence on the western world,

FICTIONS AND FACTIONS

information that was only known to a few university orientalists forty years ago. Also, at a time when retrograde and archaic forms of Islam are being increasingly used to manipulate the credulous and ignorant, it was particularly important to differentiate between sufism and Islam, and to make sure people realised that Islam was its protector, not its owner. Shah was extremely worried by the Islamic retreat into archaic and anti-western attitudes, he even said to a friend one time that if there was going to be a world war three, it would take place between the Islamic world and the West.

Neverthess Shah was not anti-Muslim as such, he just felt that Islam was moving in a dangerous direction by letting itself be taken over by tyrannical subordinates whose aims were more political than spiritual. If you try and practice the New York City/ Greenwich Village type of dissent in which I was brought up in places like Syria or Iraq, you get killed. Also, neither Shah nor Omar Ali-Shah require conversion to Islam as a prerequisite to Sufi apprenticeship, and quite predicably, this created a violent opposition which is still ongoing today, particularly among the western converts who see people like myself (a baptised Christian who considers Muhammad to have been a divine messenger) as the ultimate hypocrites. Idries Shah points out that if sufism because intrumentalised, it would have to change its name.

The other source of opposition to Idries Shah and Omar Ali-Shah comes from the Salzmann-Gurdjieffian dynasty. All of the top post-Gurdjieffians met with the two brothers in the early sixties and became convinced that the two brothers were in fact legitimate teachers. What they then did was to propose various deals to the Shahs which would enable them to retain their own influence with their followers while profiting from whatever input they could get from the brothers. The deals proposed included dividing the students between them and even financial incentives. When the Gurdjieffian hierarchy

... SHAH THE WRITER

realised that working with the brothers meant that they would themselves have to go back to being students again with no privileges, their enthusiasm waned. When *The Teachers of Gurdjieff* was published in 1966, they became mortal enemies of Shah because they thought he wrote the book. Once again, the old story of ideological battles and irreconcilable differences.

Its latest edition contains a brand new foreword by a Mr Richardson consisting of new age slop in which the Sufi Tradition is considered to be part of an available esoteric menu. Written with the unctuous superiority that you find in all hangers-on, it shows that some of the old sweats still have a lot to learn. Shah himself has written quite clearly on the menu phenomenon, saying:

> *"It is not possible to study this teaching in parts or with preconceived ideas"*; also: *"... The automatic application of study-courses which are thought to be of universal application is a degeneration of a teaching-system"*; and again: *"The second defective technique is the one which collects all the materials from several traditions and phases of teaching, primarily because they are good. This impossible effort in fact creates a scattered concentration, and the individual and the group develop what is called in psychology today, disassociation.*

Here, there is absolutely no difference between Shah and his brother Omar Ali-Shah Omar, who says:

> *One cannot take significant techniques or aspects of one philosophical teaching, which may be the Tradition or Buddhism, Taoism, to which people add some sort of spooky thing like stars, the Tarot, omens or various different superstitions: this leads to complete confusion.*

Of course today at the beginning of the twenty-first

FICTIONS AND FACTIONS

century many of these differences of opinion can seem to have a quaint feel to them, like discussing Victorian petticoats. But the coherence of a teaching has to be respected, otherwise you fall into the esoteric soup of the soup phenomenon, where the memory of something that was real once upon a time is taken as being good enough to base an activity on.

The real achievement of Ikbal, Amina, Idries and Omar together will have been to take the Sufi Tradition away from the esotericists for good and hand it over to Mr Joe Average, because the pressures of the life around us (wars, disasters, ethnic cleansing and enforced emigration on a scale we have never known) are forcing the man in the street to develop Sufi traits just for survival. In a world where half the population starves and the rest put up fences, the Sufi Tradition is no longer a luxury for a happy few: it has become more vital than that, and they were the first to realise.

To a certain extent, one can say that a good deal of the literature put out by Shah and friends under various pseudonyms was designed to act as a decoy. It occupied would-be students and opponents alike, and inflamed critics to a quite amazing degree. A lot of it was fake: Shah knew perfectly well that he was not a founding member of the Club of Rome; he was a member for a short time and was politely asked to leave because he didn't turn up to meetings; but this mythology around Shah's public personage was necessary in order to provide the dream-lie without which no truth can exist, because a student must always have a choice. Many underlings believed the myth; others backed off from this form of vanity and made their own progress. Even today, people go around showing each other bits and pieces of the pseudonymous canon in order to prove that Shah was saying something against his brother, against scholastic critics and the university, or against conventional religion. Those who show such texts to others are holding up a mirror to themselves. To me, the whole operation was a kind of Venus's fly-trap, a sort of chewing-gum that was set out in order to occupy the kind of minds that are able to obsess themselves over such matters rather than stand back and see the functional beauty and logic of a wider reality at work. The real question here is in the eye of the reader: does one want to be lifted by a poem or prefer to pore over endless footnotes?

To be lifted by a poem you need to be light and not heavy to start with, and the twenty-odd books which Shah signed with his own name provide sufficient study materials in themselves to get a great deal of the feel of sufism. If what one wants is just entertainment, there is no lack of that as well. As literature the material is sufficient unto itself, in fact there's more than enough there to satisfy the most discriminating reader. But since Shah himself is continually talking about groups and worship, can these books on their own make you into a Sufi? In other words can one change one's consciousness through literature alone?

The anwer that runs through all of Idries Shah's work is unambiguous: no, a Sufi apprenticeship cannot be accomplished alone, because a single awareness, when combined with another is not a simple addition of one plus one, it is a multiplication similar to that of the neurons in a human brain being galvanized into manifold activity by contact with other neurons, say under the impulse of an emotion, an intention, etc. The individual is essential, but it is not enough. When put in liaison with other people, the energy multiplies. In Shah's own words:

> ... *It must be further stated and understood that no effort of this sort can take place on an individual basis.*

> ... *It is not possible to study this teaching in parts or with preconceived ideas. Students should follow a course whose*

FICTIONS AND FACTIONS

totality produces the needed result. If they take isolated parts of this teaching and try to systematize them, study them with the intellect available, or study fragments of the teaching that are part of a whole program, it will inevitably put the student back into the second domain (the mechanical domain moved by intellect and emotion).

As I see it, the problem with trying to get a complete view of sufism through Shah's books alone is that they can make one a bit too pessimistic in one's view of oneself. The virtuosity with which he takes apart the various mechanisms we deploy in order to keep the truth at bay can breed a somewhat self-defeating attitude in the reader whereas, when you actually knew the man, his enthusiasm and even his unfeigned interest in you would build you up. I lived in Paris and so did not see him very often, but I do remember that gathering around Shah was like being in front of a fire in winter, a source of warmth, comfort and stimulation. Now I do know one can parody what I am saying here, because I most certainly never cuddled up to Shah, but the intelligence of certain people acts like a beacon; it helps you to direct your own thinking without doing your thinking for you.

As examples, during the course of a normal conversation he would say things like "Suicide is not an option, because you're in the same state on the other side" or "Astrology has lost its accuracy because the physical relationships between the planets have changed since the science was invented." He was a man who was generous in spirit, continuously providing you with food for thought, and such remarks were always said in the context of daily interchanges, for instance over dinner; they weren't ex-cathedra pronouncements.

What sticks in my mind about Shah now is the wit and warmth, the wit never degenerating into facetiousness and the warmth never overbearing. He was quite simply a lovely man.

... SHAH THE WRITER

He was still young at the time, only about forty, and the atmosphere during the weekends at Langton was never earnest or solemn. I remember Peter L. telling me that someone gave Shah some blank cartridges for his shotgun, so they decided to play a practical joke on two terribly serious Swedish girls who had come in from Sweden especially to visit the master and were digging in the garden with intensely religious devotion. Tassilo went sprinting into the garden towards the girls shouting "Shah's gone mad! Shah's gone mad!"; then Shah himself stepped out through the French windows, put his shotgun to his shoulder, aimed at the sprinting figure, and pulled both triggers. When the deafening report had died down, Tassilo had collapsed in a heap near the girls and was lying there motionless. As the story was later told to me, the two girls were fairly surprised.

Now here again all sorts of versions can be given of this story, according to one's own orientation. It can be seen as an an exercise in deconditioning, as a cruel practical joke by a nasty and manipulative older man, or as a couple of enthusiastic young disciples adding to the apocryphal legends that have grown up around Shah since his death. Knowing the man, and having been around the people involved at the time it happened, I consider the story to be true even if I myself was not witness to it. But it doesn't take much imagination to see how one can idealize and magnify a story like this, just as one can use it as an example to debase and trivialize Shah's teaching mission. For a teaching master, reverberation is the name of the game. Teachers use both the positive and negative reverberation of their personalities and reputation to force pupils into making fundamental decisions about themselves and their commitment.

The problem of writing about Idries Shah as a writer is that the organisation and layout of his books make something happen in the reader which simply doesn't enter into what is

FICTIONS AND FACTIONS

normally called literary criticism. In the anecdote about Shah I have just cited, I ask the reader to consider what viewpoint could be inferred from the story and point out some possible interpretations; in other words I am requiring that the reader both experience the story as a reader or as a listener, and then turn the story back and forth in his or her mind in order to be able to look at it from various different angles.

Over and above the actual meaning or moral of the story itself, this capacity of being able to reexamine what one has just read is very much part of the author's intention, in other words his stories carry their own mnemonic which implants itself in the mind of the reader, and that story will be brought out anew by the various experiences the reader goes through, sometimes even years after it was first read. The opposite can also hold true, sometimes the recognition of one's own idiocies as one reads a story implants the story forever in one's mind. This is particularly true, at least for me, of the Mulla Nasrudin corpus.

It is very difficult to go much farther than this in making generalisations about Shah's work, because more than most writers he really does appeal to a very intimate part of oneself, and this is very much related to the specifically sufic aspect of his work. Sufis believe, rightly or wrongly, that most of humanity is living in a kind of dreamworld which cuts it off from real experience and hence prevents direct contact with God. Therefore Sufi literature is almost always predicated on the need to decondition the reader as well as entertain him.

Perhaps the most perfect of all of Shah's books in this respect is *The Book of the Book*. I well remember opening the package from Octagon Press, feeling the book's weight and thickness, and licking my chops in anticipation of the feast to come. When I opened the book it contained the equivalent of one short story and the rest was blank pages. I had slavered at the weight, not the substance. But even if it didn't go on for long the story was worth every penny the book cost, because it managed to forecast and integrate every single response a reader could possibly have to the story being told, thus indicating that the joke was on human nature and not necessarily on the reader himself. It predicted, as the *Sunday Telegraph* put it "the complete range of possible responses to itself in its own narrative."

I gave the book as a present to a number of different people, and the range of responses to it were astonishing. Some of the most conventional and paranoid responses were from people such as ex-members of the Paris Surrealists whom one might have expected to be sympathetic, whereas others who were seemingly more conventional saw the point immediately. It also made me realise that most members of literary and artistic coteries are sheep pretending to be wolves.

My friends' response to this book represented a certain step forward in my own thinking, because I came to realise through these reactions that the sufic way of thought could or could not 'take' on a person no matter what their ideological values, intellectual interests or track record. My own book *Watching the Wound* uses *The Book of the Book* as a kind of model insofar as the book itself, which tells a very different sort of tale, becomes a character in itself and plays a (fairly nauseating) role in the story being related, to the point that the last text in the book requires positive action from the reader to make it out. In all modesty, *Watching the Wound* is a sort of insane clutter and it's far from having the formal perfection and refinement of Shah, but I'm just pointing out that Shah literary spin-offs already exist, and there will probably be more of them in the future.

Of course Shah already has had an effect on "mainstream" literature by enlarging the writer's palette. When I first met

FICTIONS AND FACTIONS

Doris Lessing, she had already written two books that marked our entire generation, *The Grass is Singing*, which turned out to be the white African swansong, and *The Golden Notebook* which is at the basis of most women's concerns of the century. In no way could anyone pretend that Idries Shah created Lessing as a writer, the idea is laughable, but the quality of her writing before encountering Shah and the Sufi Tradition was more in the nature of journalism than poetry, as in books like *In Pursuit of the English* (a personal favourite of mine). My feeling is that the encounter with sufism liberated her own intuition vis-à-vis her writing and opened up various other dimensions of herself to herself which she was able to add to the commonsensical and observational qualities she had from the beginning. *Shikasta* and the *Canopus in Argos* series undoubtedly bear the mark of many talks with Shah, but her writing never softened nor lost its basic scepticism; the most one can say is that sufism may have released her imagination and freed her to pursue certain avenues of thought that might not have occurred to her otherwise. Her gift is her own and all credit goes to her for producing an impressive and consistent body of work throughout her life. Shah would have at most been a facilitator for her, never a guru, and her connection to him probably cost her the Nobel prize, because the literati don't want to see a feminist icon turning her hand to writing science-fiction. In fact, the literati punished Doris Lessing's refusal to become an omnicient author, which is the basic trap for artists.

Of course my view of Shah as a writer is a personal one, I cannot and would not want to pretend otherwise. *The Sufis*, *Caravan of Dreams*, *Tales of the Dervishes*, *The Way of the Sufi* and the Nasrudin tales I brought my children up on were all books that made me, in the sense that they provided an unconscious model for my own writing. I have even found myself plagiarizing Shah without realising it, so much have his ideas and concepts embedded themselves in my unconscious. He infiltrates your mind without you realizing it. He gave me permission to use whatever stories I needed in the plays and film scripts I was writing at the time (I use *The Girl who Came Back from the Dead* in *Middleman*) but throughout my poems there are ideas and images whose source I was unaware of when I wrote them and which come from my contact with him and his brother. I'm not in the least bit ashamed, I steal from the best. My only hope is that some day in the far-distant future someone will bother to steal from me. My feeling about this is that unconscious stealing is permissible, conscious stealing is not.

Quite a few other books by Idries Shah are more technical in tone, for instance *A Perfumed Scorpion* and *Learning How to Learn*. My publishing associate who worked for many years in the Nevada Public Library system once told me that one of the library patrons with whom she had been discussing Sufi literature told her that she had been trying to read *Learning How to Learn* for weeks and that the book fascinated her, but that there was only one problem: every time she opened the book and began to read she fell asleep. She didn't know why she had this reaction, but it was so extreme that she was determined to get to the bottom of it. So she finally worked her way through the book and said she enjoyed it very much. But at the beginning the resistance had been almost biological, it was more than just boredom.

Another library patron who asked for books by Idries Shah and Omar Ali-Shah, returned the books a couple of weeks later, saying "I liked the Idries Shah, but the Omar Ali-Shah was too much like work."

In *The Rules or Secrets of the Naqshbandi Order* Omar Ali-Shah calls Sufi literature:

> *... books of behaviour which not only contain instructions about terms of reference but also give examples of certain*

FICTIONS AND FACTIONS

situations and circumstances. That is why most of these books are broken up into a series of stories. Within the context of these stories one inevitably sees that the subject or the object of an activity is using ideas from, or thinking along certain lines, in the Tradition.

… Most of these stories, which are like medieval morality tales, have a teaching or a lesson embedded in them. They usually show the search for what one might call approximate reality, in both a graphic way as well as in the form of subconscious transmission.

The "subconscious transmission" aspect of Idries Shah's literature is perceptible to all who approach his work with an open mind. It also becomes invisible to all who approach it with an axe to grind, because such people are only using a small proportion of their sensory apparatus to assimilate the material. This is not a poetic Sufi analogy, it is fact. Obsessional thinking narrows one's focus.

One of the very mysterious episodes in the Sufi teaching which the Shah brothers brought to the West, is the fact that they chose to go their own separate ways in 1977. It was personally very hard for me to accept the split, because all my friends, including my brother, were with Shah, and they all suddenly began denouncing Agha as a madman whose pupils were fanatics because, amongst other things, Agha had begun to hold exercises in which people prayed.

Like all the others at the time I lived my own experience of this. The last time I saw Shah was just about twenty-five years ago. Not to put too fine a point to it, he flattered me and then made one or two oblique references I construed as a veiled criticism of his brother. When I challenged him on this, he replied he was only speaking generally.

... SHAH THE WRITER

I then expressed my concern to him about my own brother's decision not to pursue his connection to the Tradition and taking leave of him as teacher. His answer to me was reassuring, but he understood my concern, and I felt a powerful wave of emotion from Shah who, I believe, was thinking about his own brother as I talked about mine.

It was a strange moment. He had already dispatched a hatchet man to Paris to undermine people's confidence in his brother, and many had left on the pretext that we were becoming fanatics. This idea became such a given among many of our friends that the best man at our wedding never spoke to my wife or me again, which gave me a good deal of food for thought about fanaticism. But now Shah was almost in tears at the brotherly concern I was expressing: I leave to the reader to judge whether he despised his brother or not.

I never saw Shah again. He forced me to choose and I did so. The trap was clear: a couple of oblique references to money or conventional religion to tempt me into questioning his brother and the great big piece of cheese right there in the middle: "Do give me first refusal on the book you're doing." When Shah accompanied me to the car he was smiling widely, and I remember wondering why. Now I think it was because he could not budge my loyalty to Agha. He was pleased.

Twenty-five years later, the way the two worked independently in tandem seems perfectly logical. Idries Shah concentrated on The Institute for Cultural Research and used his publishing outfit to create a climate in the West that would be sympathetic to sufism as an autonomous way of thought, and completed his large output of books, all of which are immensely valuable. The degree of acceptance of Sufi ideas has indeed changed, to a great extent due to him and those around him. But in spite of the riches and treasures in both works,

FICTIONS AND FACTIONS

the tone of his last two books *The Commanding Self* and *Knowing How to Know*, although not without humour, is noticeably bleaker and more pessimistic than in his earlier works.

It is true that Shah was ill for most of the last ten years of his life and that his life was personally difficult due to his heart condition and a necessary separation from those he loved, but I doubt that such personal questions affected his work as a writer. He was simply confronted with the objective fact that submission to God has never been easy, and that a great many of one's pupils will possibly never take the step, because it's a step that no teacher, however great, can take on your behalf.

As a teacher one does have love for one's students and one would possibly wish them better than they are. There is frustration attached to the job. Masters probably feel they have failed, because it is impossible for all pupils to develop to the level one hoped for. Their greed becomes stabilized but it never disappears. All who teach want their pupils to learn, but certain knowledges will never be force-fed, and many don't actually want to learn.

Shah disbanded his groups and suspended all collective teaching connected to him nearly ten years before he died. In the year he died, he happened to say to my friend Willy that "the job I was supposed to do was completed ten years ago". This implies that Shah groupings, some of which have continued, were not undertaken at his initiative.

His work exists, and he has ensured its perennation through a few trusted friends. His children are writers and they will play a role.

As far as Omar Ali-Shah is concerned, of course, no conclusion is possible because the story is still far from over.

2002

MAN INTO GOD

I was despised for quite some time by friends and foes alike
when told by my teacher I was incompetent I knew it was a lie
in fact informed opinion still holds that
I polluted my spirit for good with sexual fantasies

In fact there is a hidden truth   a switchover is being planned
I am working hard to organise the worship of wonderful me
before transferring it to God   it's a technically subtle challenge
if I succeed it will be the first time it has ever been done

The challenge is one of technical subtlety
because it involves blinding people before
giving them back their sight
if there was any other way I assure you I would use it

We are born with knowledge and then it is diluted
we are born with love and then we throw it away
but all of these elements never quite disappear
they are stored in the brain in wafer-thin layers

This is why no man is without hope
the greed seems like an impregnable wall
but it crumbles very quickly
when beauty brings what's buried to the fore

Look at me   I am every man that ever lived
just another ageing adept going through the motions
yet also a fearless explorer staring down the tiger

An old man shuffles up to the pearly gates
and pauses a moment as they open wide before him
and says either my people come with me or else I do not go
and the people play and joke and don't look up from their game

no one ever saw the teacher exchanging his soul for us

FICTIONS AND FACTIONS

THE KINGDOM OF GOD

It didn't start   it sort of ended somehow
it was always going to termininate in a holocaust
a kind of sacrificial pyre   all would become clear
from the fires of the inferno purged   we would step into
the kingdom of God

The inferno we live in is one we create
from our cowardice self-importance and evil intent
the worst call on God with the most insistence
we know His mercy is our only hope of knowing
the kingdom of God

Come don't be so childish the sceptic says
no it's real we reply we know what we've done
we know how we distanced ourselves from humanity
and watched ourselves standing aloof
from the kingdom of God

From the depths of our hatred of ourselves
we are as ullage disappearing into the cask
a moment always comes when we see beyond our ken
when the future is hopeless we're forced to look behind
to catch a glimpse of the kingdom of God

Because the product of human sacrifice
was just another dream   no tussle twixt good and evil
such things cannot be the outcome of conflict
it has to be what we already know
experience is the kingdom of God

The kingdom of God is when we got it right
when we did things right by our children

... THE KINGDOM OF GOD

guided them properly or forbade them with love
when we enter the beloved body of another
that too is the kingdom of God

What we aspire to is not another world
just a distillation of the one we already know
all who live know good and evil
the experience of both is what sets off the yearning
for the kingdom of God

Already in our genes and within our experience
even if we never left the confines of our village
each has a familiarity of paradise and hell
what makes us human is our knowledge of perfection
we are the kingdom of God

The option is our own   we either go on
telling ourselves how disgusting we are
and thus doing making it all come true
or with the same eyes look at what's been done right
to see the kingdom of God

The kingdom of God is what we've done well
a time   maybe just once   when I acted with honour
once upon a time I loved and was loved
even if it didn't turn out the way it ought to have
I know the kingdom of God

So what if the Lord provides scary surprises
His handiwork is something you've just got to admire
He really does do his job very well
no blasphemy intended the bastard knows what He's doing
embedding the kingdom of God in our hearts

Even when forgetful or taking His name in vain
we cannot escape   if only because we'll have to
look at perfection in the profile of its opposite

FICTIONS AND FACTIONS

as we come out of our coma we ask the question
where is the kingdom God

It's all familiar territory   the child's grin
love given or received   preferably both
the secret generosity   the gift once made
without hope of reward   all beat a path
back to the kingdom of God

which presumably is where it somehow all began

THE PROCRASTINATOR

Avoid the issue   don't read that letter
let it sit around unopened
maybe it will go away   you never know
if you're really lucky it'll get itself buried

Because I'm a coward I am drawn to confrontation
anything rather than reveal the feet of clay
first comes the endless procrastination
then try to put it all right with ten minutes of shouting

Sometimes it does work out okay
you were justified in doing nothing
when you stand aside to let life go by you
wrong actions of other people do provide a pattern

Of what not to do   am I a doer or a letter
I do confess that I am not quite sure
I push forward to hide the passive chasm within
some people never jog they sprint and then collapse

But then as you travel   the stopping and the starts
enable you to see a bit more pattern than before
it's like in writing   you either attack head-on
or else you circle round and close in on your prey

Little by little the image builds   you learn to watch
and doing learn to do or not do   with love or without
participation is really what it's all about
our keying in is what makes us men at last

we are not alone but are defined by our exchange

FICTIONS AND FACTIONS

NOTES FOR THE FUTURE

(1) A teacher in the Sufi Tradition cannot be elected, nor can the capacity to teach be passed on in the form of an estate.

(2) In 1962, when contact was made with the West, Idries Shah was thirty-eight years old, Omar Ali-Shah forty. When they met with various interested people they declared themselves openly to be trained Sufi teachers, without providing any evidence of this beyond their own family or lineage.

(3) This gave all who listened to and evaluated them the opportunity of either recognizing and accepting their teaching capacity or else refusing it. Since no formal grouping structure existed in 1962, the decision the listeners made was their own, and there was no implicit or explicit social constraint on anyone involved.

(4) A number of people, very often people with another spiritual axe to grind, decided that the two brothers had to be fakes. To a great extent, it is their words that have found their way into the media. After the controversy surrounding the publication of a new translation of Omar Khayaam in 1967, both brothers ceased to engage in any kind of public debate.

(5) At the first meeting with the potential pupils in Paris, Idries Shah said: "My brother and I will teach differently, and you will not know why."

(6) The only interaction I witnessed between the pupils of Ikbal Ali Shah and those of his sons took place very briefly in the social context of one of the three-day parties at Langton Green. Otherwise, to my knowledge, the two sons did not take

... NOTES FOR THE FUTURE

on any of the pupils of Ikbal, although Helena Edwardes, who had been with Ikbal a short time in Morocco just before he died, was to become Shah's secretary for many years.

(7) Nearly ten years before his death, Idries Shah discontinued all collective teaching activities he was involved with (one-to-one relationships are not susceptible to analysis). Institute for Cultural Research activities were wound down and it was suggested that all further work would be accomplished through contact with books.

(8) Omar Ali-Shah's books began coming out in the late eighties and nineties accompanied by an immense expansion of activities like building tekkias and the formation of new groups. In parallel, Shah's heart condition and physical diminishment imposed a slowing-down of the activity centred around him.

(9) Prayer and exercises are characteristic of Omar Ali-Shah's way of working: the group and the feeling of belonging, in other words a certain feeling of patriotism, is an important binding agent between disciples.

(10) In theory, the study of sufism, i.e. the apprenticeship to and the apprehension of the Divine Reality, should eschew all forms of emotional clutter. This view is utopian, because it is the interplay between emotion and essence that enables the non-essential to be leached away.

(11) Lies point the way towards truth because they give people the opportunity to discriminate.

(12) Institutional self-worship has been a necessary component of this leaching process. Whether it should harden into a permanent phenomenon is questionable.

FICTIONS AND FACTIONS

(13) Concepts like "the mysterious East" and "Afghanistan" were used as emotional assemblers for about thirty years, until World War III when the war between Islam and the United States was tacitly declared. In the seventies, Shah did say to some friends that if there was going to be a third world war, it would take place between Islamic fundamentalists and the West.

(14) "The West" is shorthand for those countries which submitted themselves to the so-called "Enlightenment" and based their development on material acquisition and the industrial revolution.

(15) If cultures can be defined by their dreams, the western dream is something for nothing and the eastern dream is a return to the lost paradise. Both eschew work.

(16) In France there have been, broadly speaking, two types of intellectual who have dealt with sufism: orientalist westerners who tend to analyse it as a sociological phenomenon, or else converts to Islam who wildly resent the fact that the two brothers, both Muslims, should have taught without encouraging their pupils to convert.

(17) Genealogy and groups matter less than recognition and love. Social hierarchies, whether based on money, university education or any other form of prestige, are irrelevant. Everyone has a chance.

(18) Shah writes, Agha speaks, both improvise. I never saw one or the other speak from notes. If any of Shah's pupils had taken the trouble to record and transcribe what he was saying to people, there would be little difference between him and his brother.

(19) The grafting of the Sufi Tradition onto a materialist

... NOTES FOR THE FUTURE

and largely unsympathetic West was a supreme technical feat realised by the two brothers working in tandem, who wrested the Tradition from the hands of a few specialists and made it available to the common man. The question to be answered for the future is whether enough maturity exists in the West to enable the Tradition to be re-improvised without oriental furbelows for another generation, as it has been improvised for the benefit of the West during the past forty years.

(20) Although one does not know what the future holds, one can legitimately hope that the Tradition will be able to reinvent and reformulate itself in the West without exotic trappings while maintaining the spiritual framework of the great teachers of the past.

(21) Books are important. Tekkias can be important. Nothing is important in isolation, only in interaction. The most important of all is intelligent love for others. If this love is lost or mislaid, the teacher and/or pupil ceases to function.

(22) Those who pass judgement on their brothers and sisters have destroyed the possibility of development in themselves. Luckily, this destruction is not permanent.

(23) Modesty does not come from being nice. It comes from being lucid.

(24) The beginning of lucidity is awareness of the limited nature of one's own knowledge.

(25) Tolerance is understanding, not blanket acceptance.

(26) What remains today of the teaching structures used by Jan Fishan Khan, The Nawab Amjed Ali Shah or the Sirdar Ikbal Ali Shah? Not much, because the structures weren't the point.

FICTIONS AND FACTIONS

(27) The Tradition was grafted onto me and took. I don't know why. It will be carried on by my children and friends, whether they know it or not.

Augy Hayter, Jan. 2002

ATTRIBUTIONS

p. 9 Eva Joly has withdrawn from the French magistrature, allegedly because of threats made to her family. She now works as a consultant for the Norweigan government.

p. 23 *Desperately Seeking Susan* is a film by Susan Seidelman

p. 52 *La Cantatrice Chauve* and *La Leçon* by Ionesco are still playing at the Théâtre de la Huchette in Paris.

p. 76-82 *Earthly Traps, The Karma Connection, Middleman, Sheherazade* and *Fit to be Tied* by Augy Hayter will be published by Tractus Books. *Sheherazade* can be found in *Watching the Wound* by Augy Hayter (Tractus Books) p. 157

p. 86 Shah quote from *Reflections* (Octagon Press).

p. 85-90 *L'Oreille du Logos, In Memoriam Constantin Andronikov* ed. Marc Andronikov (Editions L'Age d'Homme, Lausanne)

p. 167 quote from character in *The Speakers* by Heathcote Williams (Hutchinson/Panther/Grove Press).

p. 186 The relationship between Vera Milanova, Jeanne de Salzmann and René Daumal is evoked in René Daumal's *Correspondance Vol. I, II, III* (Editions Gallimard, Paris).

p. 187 *The Education of a Gardener* by Russel Page (Random House)

p. 189 *Notre Vie avec Monsieur Gurdjieff* de Olga de Hartmann (Editions Planète, Paris. English version by Arkana /Penguin)

p. 196 *The Rubaiyyat of Omar Khayaam* by Robert Graves and Omar Ali-Shah (Cassell's 1967 & also by Penguin Books). The text has been republished as a coffee-table book under the title *The Authentic Rubaiyyat of Omar Khayaam* translated by Omar Ali-Shah and illustrated by Eugenio Zanetti (Institute for the Diffusion of Sufi Ideas, LosAngeles, 1993)

p. 201 tape recording of talk to Paris group, Paris, October 15, 1977, transcribed as chap. 22, *Future Aspects of the Tradition*, p. 271 in *The Course of the Seeker* by Omar Ali-Shah (Tractus Books)

p. 209 Idries Shah quote from *Caravan of Dreams* (Octagon)

p. 212 *Islamic Sufism, Lights of Asia* and *Muhammed: the Prophet* by the Sirdar Ikbal Ali Shah, all published by Tractus Books.

p. 216 on conversion: see *Sufi Studies: East and West* (Octagon) and *The Diffusion of Sufi Ideas in the West* ed. Leonard Lewin (Keysign Press, partially republished as *The Elephant in the Dark*, Dutton)

FICTIONS AND FACTIONS

p. 228 Graves quotes from *Between Moon and Moon, Selected Correspondence of Robert Graves*, ed. Paul O'Prey (Moyer Bell)

p. 230 *Madame Blavatsky's Baboon* by Peter Washington (Schocken)

p. 231 Biographical material on Krishnamurti: see *Krishnamurti, The Years of Awakening* by Mary Lutyens (Shambhala). *Witness* and *Gurdjieff: Making a New World* by John G. Bennett (Turnstone Press). There are textual differences between different editions of *Witness*. In later editions, either Bennett himself or his successors fudged the episode about taking on people Shah felt he could not work with.

p. 234 Archives of the International Institute for Intellectual Development (the institutional predecessor of UNESCO) and the League of Nations archive in Geneva.

p. 238 Stanley William Hayter *About Prints* (Oxford University Press) and *New Ways of Gravure* (Watson-Guptill N.Y.) see also *The Renaissance of Gravure: the Art of S.W. Hayter* ed. P.M.S. Hacker (The Clarendon Press, Oxford)

p. 238 James Moore *Neo-Sufism: the Case of Idries Shah* (Telos Journal) and L.P. Elwell-Sutton: *Sufism and Pseudo-Sufism* (*Encounter* May 1975).

p. 245 *Turn off Your Mind* by Gary Valentine Lachman (Sidgwick & Jackson). Information on Sufi apprenticeship, see *Learning the Tradition as a Language* in *The Rules or Secrets of the Naqshbandi Order* by Omar Ali-Shah (Tractus Books) p. 334-346

p. 248-256 *Reflections* by Idries Shah (Octagon Press) The order of the extracts is the author's, not that of Idries Shah, and they are not commented on to enable the readers to make up their own minds without this author's view cluttering them.

p. 256 *The Teaching Story* by Idries Shah in *The Sufi Mystery* ed. by N.P. Archer (Octagon Press).

p. 256/257 *Destination Mecca, Oriental Magic, The Secret Lore of Magic, Tales of the Dervishes* by Idries Shah (Octagon Press) *Kara Kush* by Idries Shah (Fontana/Collins) *Darkest England* and *The Natives are Restless* by Idries Shah (Octagon Press)

p. 258 example of workshop: *Fifty Enthralling Stories of the Mysterious East* ed. The Sheik A. Abdulla (Odhams Press, London, 1937). Contributors to this collection: Sax Rohmer, Hubert S. Banner, W. Somerset Maugham, Maud Diver, Vsevolod Ivanov, Pearl S. Buck,

... ATTRIBUTIONS

H. de Vere Stacpoole, Henry Peterson, Dale Collins, Joseph Conrad, Richard Carol, Ernest Bramah, Kathlyn Rhodes, James Morier, Algernon Blackwood, Kathleen Wallace, Anthony Mills, H. Rider Haggard, Harold Lamb, Reginald Campbell, Lafcadio Hearn, Pierre Loti, Meadows Taylor, Achmed Abdullah, John Grant, J. Railton Holden, Dorothy Black, Sidney Denham, Jacland Marmur, "Afghan", Coutts Brisbane, Dewan Sharar, Glen Aldons, Sir Walter Scott, W.B. Bannerman, M.E. Rutt, Anthony Mills, Lady Dorothy Mills, Murray Sanford, John Hamilton, Vincent Cornier, Rustam Khan-Urf, W. Gifford Palgrave, Captain Marryat, Sirdar Ikbal Ali Shah.

p. 261 Rafael Lefort *The Teachers of Gurdjieff* (Malor Books) with a new foreword by Spencer Richardson.

p. 261/262 Omar Ali-Shah quote from *Overcoming Pick n' Mix* in *The Rules or Secrets of the Naqshbandi Order* (Tractus)

p 261 & p. 264 Idries Shah quotes from private tapes which Shah distributed to students in Paris in 1964. Some but not all of this material has been published in various articles or disseminated throughout various Shah books or else published as cassettes. The manuscript I have, which is a relatively accurate transcript of these tapes, is called *Sufismo en Occidente* or *Sufism in the West* and has been circulating among students for nearly forty years. Perhaps the reason why Shah never published it himself is because the material was tailored for a particular place and time (the students at the time had mostly been strongly influenced by Gurdjieff and Shah used some 'Gurdjieffian' vocabulary and attitudes to communicate to them) and he may have felt that it was not all suitable for the general public. But times change, and the interest of this material is undeniable. Another similar collection of Shah material is *Sufi Texts* (ISBN 950-0101-06-8), published anonymously, (probably with his permission—he was working with a number of South American students at the time). This material is also historically precious as well as functional.

p. 266/267 *The Book of The Book* by Idries Shah (Octagon Press) *Watching the Wound* by Augy Hayter (Tractus Books)

p. 267 Book review in the *Sunday Telegraph* 15 March 1970.

p. 269 *The Girl who Came Back from the Dead* is from *The Suhrawardi Order* in *The Way of the Sufi* by Idries Shah (Penguin & Octagon). In *The Woman I Love* and *Godbothering* by Augy Hayter (Tractus Books), *Time Enough* is derived from Attar's *The Miser and the Angel of Death* in *The Way of the Sufi*.

FICTIONS AND FACTIONS

p. 270 Omar Ali-Shah quote on Sufi literature from *The Rules or Secrets of the Naqshbandi Order* (TractusBooks).

p. 268 *Learning How to Learn*, *The Commanding Self*, and *Knowing How to Know* by Idries Shah (Octagon Press)

Dépôt légal, Imprimeur, n° 7543